# Socrates and Alcibiades

# SOCRATES AND ALCIBIADES

## PLATO'S DRAMA OF POLITICAL AMBITION AND PHILOSOPHY

ARIEL HELFER

PENN

UNIVERSITY OF PENNSYLVANIA PRESS

PHILADELPHIA

Published by
University of Pennsylvania Press
Philadelphia, Pennsylvania 19104-4112
www.upenn.edu/pennpress

Printed in the United States of America on acid-free paper
1 3 5 7 9 10 8 6 4 2

Library of Congress Cataloging-in-Publication Data
Names: Helfer, Ariel, author.
Title: Socrates and Alcibiades : Plato's drama of political ambition and philosophy / Ariel Helfer.
Description: 1st edition. | Philadelphia : University of Pennsylvania Press, [2017] | Includes bibliographical references and index.
Identifiers: LCCN 2016049601 | ISBN 978-0-8122-4913-2 (hardcover : alk. paper)
Subjects: LCSH: Plato. Alcibiades. | Alcibiades 2. | Plato. Symposium. | Alcibiades. | Socrates. | Ambition—Political aspects.
Classification: LCC B391.A53 H45 2017 | DDC 184--dc23 LC record available at https://lccn.loc.gov/2016049601

*For Mom, Pops, Max, and Joj*

CONTENTS

# INTRODUCTION

## Why Study Political Ambition?

The most interesting reasons for studying political ambition have become the hardest to see. "Ambition" nowadays tends to signify a zealous, even ruthless desire for gain or advancement, and is therefore often distrusted in the political arena. The purpose of government in the best case, after all, is not to enrich or empower the politicians who administer it, but prudently and justly to provide what is necessary for people to live out a harmonious and fulfilling coexistence. Ambition is to be tolerated in the private sphere, if at all, and "political ambition" often connotes something akin to political corruption: a willingness to misuse political power and public trust for selfish ends. We might study this sort of political ambition in order to understand better how it can be muted, or perhaps controlled, channeled, and molded into something politically constructive. Moreover, we might study it with a view to protecting the legacy of vigilance against tyranny and oppression that we inherit as citizens of liberal democracy. Such studies of political ambition would be worthwhile. They could not, however, be as philosophically far-reaching as a study that begins with the fuller and more complex, albeit less familiar, understanding of political ambition.

Indeed, if the above description appears caricaturish, it is because we sense that political ambition can also be something noble and good. We may think, for example, of those who pursue careers in politics in order to do good in their communities and in the world, to improve the lot of their fellow citizens, to be champions of justice, democracy, and freedom of thought. Someone who exhibits this type of political ambition will see in politics not a set of mundane administrative tasks but the stage upon which humanity's most admirable goals are pursued and achieved. We are thus led to distinguish between two different phenomena, each bearing the name of political ambition. One is private ambition that merely happens to find itself in the political world and hence seeks to use political power as an expedient means to private ends. But there is also ambition that is not incidentally political, but essentially and emphatically so, seeking goods that appear to be available only in and through political activity.

What are these goods that can be attained only in political activity? The very idea may seem foreign to the modern reader, but it is the focus of much of classical political philosophy. Aristotle's famous claims that "the human being is by nature a political animal," and that "the political community must be set down as [a community] of noble actions, not merely of living together," reflect a view of human nature according to which the powerfully felt need to live nobly and selflessly points to active civic engagement as its most complete fulfillment. Virtuous political ambition directed toward civic engagement and political leadership is understood, in this Aristotelian framework, to be the highest expression of the natural human attraction to a life of noble devotion. But this characterization of political ambition also points to the tension in political life that Aristotle and his Socratic predecessors presented so incisively. Political ambition, even at its most virtuous, is never simply selfless. The desire to be the nobly devoted benefactor of one's fellow citizens is bound up, perhaps inextricably, with the desire for the vividly imagined rewards of gratitude, honor, power, and fame—a fact that is all the more readily seen in contexts where Aristotle's description of human nature resonates more clearly. The democracies of ancient Greece consistently produced ambitious figures whose zeal for political honor was so great it threatened to outstrip or distort the intention to win that honor through honorable service. Thus, even ambition that is at its core civic spirited, and that is thus political in the fuller sense, can develop a dangerous edge. And yet for a time Athens found great success in nourishing this explosive, glory-seeking form of ambition by yoking it to its citizens' deep-seated sense of patriotism and civic duty. The most brilliant and talented citizens—Themistocles, Pericles, and others—were enticed to lead Athens to ever-greater glory with the promise of sharing in its eternal fame should they succeed. But there was always the risk that the statesmen whose ambition the Athenians fed would one day throw off the yoke of the city to seek fame and power on their own terms.

Thus do we learn from ancient history how the belief that the peak of human fulfillment is to be found in political rule can be a source of political volatility: not precisely because politicians who hold this belief will abuse public trust for private gain, but rather because they may seek the *political* rewards of glory and rule without insisting on making themselves worthy of them through their service to the political community. Many centuries later, the Enlightenment philosophers who were attempting to bring stability to a chaotic political world explicitly rejected the Aristotelian claim that politics grows in part out of a natural human desire to pursue the noble. As heirs of the Enlightenment, our core political and intellectual principles can be traced back to Hobbes's premise that we are by nature not political or even social animals but individualistic and selfish ones. Thence sprang the now familiar notion that the purpose of government is artificially to impose restraints, by means of weighty incentives and physical compulsion, on the "nasty and brutish" behavior to which we resort in the absence of actively enforced law. Locke, insisting that the rulers, too, must be expected to act upon the basest motives, recommended the separation of executive and legislative powers—a recommendation keenly heeded by the American founders, who famously set out to devise a system of government in which "ambition must be made to counteract ambition." The benefits of frustrating the selfish desires connected with political ambition were judged to be worth the cost of blunting its civic-spirited dimension.

Even this rough and very partial sketch of the project of Enlightenment liberalism is enough for us to recognize how successful the project has been. The politically ambitious, as we noted at the outset, are today widely suspected of seeking personal gain at the expense of the governed—an effect of the erosion of the belief that there are uniquely fulfilling goods to be pursued in a life of civic duty. In fact, the successful promotion of the private pursuit of happiness, and the corresponding devaluation of public life, not only make political ambition appear dubious but prevent its most powerful forms from ever emerging. If political ambition grows from and amplifies the belief that the most fulfilling and lasting goods must be sought and won in the political arena, we cannot expect it to have fertile soil where government is mainly understood to be a means for securing the goods and opportunities of private life.

Yet it is plain to see that some citizens and politicians still strive passionately to achieve lofty political goals. And even if these goals—peace, freedom, equality, or whatever they might be—are sometimes imagined as means or prerequisites to other, private sources of fulfillment, examples of selfless devotion to noble causes still continue to fill the human heart with admiration and to animate citizens with hopes of bettering their communities through civic engagement. We still appear to be drawn to noble devotion—the positive and constructive root of political ambition as the ancients understood it—as an end or good in itself, and hence are presented with a question that is at once historical and philosophic. Does love of the noble reflect a natural human need or desire, the most complete fulfillment of which is expressed in political life? Or is that attraction either unessential to human nature, or separable from politics? The answer to this question would help us to recognize the necessary limits of any attempt to insulate government from the passions that often come to disrupt its prudent administration. If human beings are political by nature, then the enduring appeal of virtue and noble devotion still recognizable in modern society represents a half-dormant but ubiquitous potential, perhaps even an unacknowledged thirst, for civic engagement and the accompanying public honors. If tapped, this powerful latent desire could drive many people to pursue and obtain greater fulfillment than modern society typically offers the "private citizen" and to better their communities as a result—but it could also unleash the kind of political volatility that has been so successfully subdued. However, if the Enlightenment thinkers were theoretically justified in their rejection of Aristotle, then it may be in the best interest of future generations to continue the liberal project of stamping out the love of honor and glory or removing it from public life.

We have been led to this series of questions and possible answers by an attempt to recover an understanding of political ambition that is fading from view in our political thought and to trace that disappearance back to its intellectual-historical source. Perhaps it is inevitable that, in taking such a sweeping overview of our political and philosophic history, the questions raised have stretched beyond the reach of most human inquiry, to say nothing of our present investigation. To determine whether and how the appeal of noble devotion can be and has been re-expressed, redirected, or eroded is not a task to be completed by the study of one text or one author nor a matter to be concluded in any short time. Yet we raise these questions here because their importance to the present and future of political life seems to prevent our turning away from them, and because one's study is better guided and more prudently justified when the most compelling questions to which it may pertain are held up and allowed to lend their scope and gravity to the whole investigation. To the extent that we are here animated by concern for our political well-being, we proceed under the auspices of the historical and philosophic questions we have raised concerning the human attraction to virtue and nobility. What progress can be made here will thus be dedicated, as a collection of relevant reflections, to that broader project.

The particular inquiry we are to take up is therefore not identical to those broader questions, but neither is it merely subsidiary to them. One could never hope to determine the extent to which the human attraction to virtue and nobility reflects a fundamentally political strain of human nature without first examining that attraction itself. It is with this examination that we will for the most part be concerned, an examination that may indeed be found to be no less urgent in its own right than the broader one to which we have dedicated it. The appeal of noble devotion requires particularly careful study not only because of the complexities we have already noted—for example, that it appears to be at once altruistic and egoistic—but especially because we ourselves, as students and observers, share in the complex psychological experience we are attempting to study. The appeal of noble sacrifice, unlike that of most other naturally desired goods, is deeply bound up with one's sense of right and wrong, of duty, and of spirituality. As the Greek philosophers recognized, the noble plays a central role in the opinions and beliefs that form the moral bedrock of a human life. A critical investigation of the concept and experience of the noble may therefore entail an uncomfortable exposure and analysis of one's moral beliefs. This sort of critique was at the heart of what made Socrates' philosophic project both powerful and dangerous. Fortunately, Plato's beautified presentation of Socratic philosophy makes for a gentler ride.

## Introducing Alcibiades

Finally, we can bring the foreground subject of our analysis clearly into focus: Plato's presentation of political ambition through his portrayal of Alcibiades. No historical figure better exemplifies the risks and rewards of mixing statesmanship with the fervent desire for political honor than Alcibiades. Alcibiades grew up in Athens's Golden Age, during which, under the leadership of Pericles, the Athenian empire grew to the height of its splendor. Alcibiades had all the marks of a promising statesman-to-be: good looks, charm, a sparkling pedigree, and regular, direct access to Athens's most celebrated leader.[1] Beginning with the masterfully deceitful undermining of the Peace of Nicias, Athens's military policy came to be defined by Alcibiades' daring undertakings, strategic brilliance, and diplomatic skill. The peak of his audacity was reached when he successfully persuaded the Athenian *demos* to send him in partial command of a large fleet with the purpose of extending their empire into Sicily.[2]

In a self-contradictory manner typical of Athenian democracy, the people were wary of Alcibiades' extraordinary power even as they granted and admired it.[3] The licentiousness that Alcibiades displayed in his private life and his apparent disregard for the sacred bounds of law in pursuit of personal honor and gratification led the ambivalent Athenians to suspect him of desiring to subvert their regime and establish a tyranny.[4] On the eve of Alcibiades' departure for Sicily, multiple allegations emerged of his having profaned the Eleusinian mysteries by performing mock initiations, and accusations were leveled that he was responsible for the infamous incident of the mutilation of the Herms.[5] When the Athenians recalled Alcibiades from Sicily to charge him with these grave crimes of impiety, he fled to enemy Sparta and in time helped turn the tide of the war against his native Athens.[6] Alcibiades would, before the war was over, find himself chased from Sparta to Persia and thence back to Athens (though not before playing a key role in the oligarchic coup of 411 BC) before finally fleeing once more to Persia, condemned by the Athenians for mismanaging his naval command.[7] Alcibiades' wanton and reckless behavior in private life, especially as regards religion, cost him his place atop the pantheon of Athenian statesmen and played no small part in the fall of the Athenian empire.

Alcibiades thus epitomizes the dilemma of ancient political ambition, and nowhere more so than in Thucydides' account of his speech to the Spartan assembly. For nowhere is it made so clear that Alcibiades' love of his native city (*philopolis*) came into catastrophic conflict with his need to receive the honor and glory that he believed were his due.[8] Indeed, it should be noted of both Thucydides and Plato that they promise a much fuller and more nuanced analysis of political ambition than, for example, Hobbes and Locke, since the former two seek to expose and explore the subtleties of an important set of human passions, whereas the latter two may have too much at stake in running down ambition to give the phenomenon its full due. But it is Plato, more than Thucydides, whose account of the complexities of moral and political psychology best suits our purpose. While Thucydides invites searching criticism of the impressive figures whose deeds and speeches he portrays and adorns, Plato puts the unexamined hopes and beliefs of his characters on display through his depictions of Socratic refutations and exhortations.[9] By studying Plato's Alcibiades, we hope to gain a fuller understanding of the constellation of desires that gives political ambition its force, including the desire to be devoted to a noble cause, and to determine whether, in Plato's understanding, these desires necessarily find their fullest expression in political life.

Our procedure will be to take up a close reading of each of the three scenes in the traditional Platonic corpus where Alcibiades makes a major appearance: the whole of the *Alcibiades* and *Second Alcibiades*, and the famous, drunken speech Alcibiades delivers in the *Symposium*. The *Alcibiades* is set when Alcibiades is still a youth of about nineteen, before he has even participated in Athenian politics and before he has become familiar with Socrates. The *Second Alcibiades* appears to show an Alcibiades much changed since his first meeting with Socrates, especially in his outlook on Athenian politics, despite being at most only a couple of years older. The *Symposium* is set some fifteen years later, at the peak of Alcibiades' fame and shortly before the launch of the Sicilian Expedition, which is often thought to have triggered the downfall of Athens and of Alcibiades. No character aside from Socrates receives such sustained attention in Plato's dialogues. The character of Alcibiades therefore represents a uniquely valuable opportunity in the study of Plato. We have here not the usual Platonic snapshot of an interlocutor's refutation at Socrates' hands but a triad of major encounters over the course of many years. We can thus hope to learn about not only what characterized Alcibiades' extraordinary ambition at one time or another but also how it changed, matured, and hardened, and what role Socratic philosophy may have played in that transformation. Even for Plato, this is an unusually elaborate and dynamic portrait.[10]

It is not only the fact that Plato portrays Alcibiades at several points along the course of his development that makes the Platonic Alcibiades an object of study well suited to our purposes; it is even more the character of that development as produced by the Socratic challenge Alcibiades faces. An eminent twentieth-century political philosopher described the *Alcibiades* as "a warning of Wisdom (Socrates) to Ambition (Alcibiades),"[11] a characterization Plato would have emphatically endorsed (cf. *Alcibiades* 133d–135b). The warning in question, although constantly and subtly shifting in emphasis,[12] amounts to this: that it would be ill advised for Alcibiades, despite his great eagerness, to enter politics before he has received an education from Socrates. Hence, the Platonic presentation of Socrates and Alcibiades may seem to speak even more directly to our inquiry concerning the relationship of noble devotion to political life and to human nature than expected, since the question of whether, how, and to what end political ambition might be moderated is a central theme.

Now, we must avoid the mistake of assuming that the Socratic project has the same ends as the Enlightenment project, the apparent similarity in their attempts to tame or channel political ambition notwithstanding. To point out only the most obvious difference, Socrates here aims to educate one man in private, whereas the political philosophers of the Enlightenment wrote and published treatises in an attempt to transform the entire political world in which they lived. But neither must we assume total opposition between Plato and the Enlightenment thinkers. We should not begin from the assumption, for example, that Plato simply took the potent combination of love of honor and love of the noble to be naturally or unchangeably directed toward political ends. The Platonic Socrates, at least, seems to have thought there was *something* malleable in Alcibiades' ambition. It is better, then, not to adopt as a premise that Plato would deny the possibility of achieving the goals toward which the likes of Hobbes, Locke, or Montesquieu directed their efforts. We ought instead to limit ourselves to some preliminary suggestions as to how paying close attention to Plato's presentation of Alcibiades will allow us to clarify his understanding of political ambition and how that understanding may in turn offer some insight into our broader questions.

Socrates' attempt to rein in Alcibiades' ambition, to moderate and even to redirect it (if only for a time), is particularly illuminating for two reasons. First, the Socratic procedure of refuting Alcibiades' opinions concerning what is required to rule well exposes the connections and contradictions between Alcibiades' intense desire for fame and honor, on one hand, and his attraction to justice and nobility, on the other. Thus, we get a window on the complex character or structure of intense political ambition such as only the intricate psychological portraits of the Platonic dialogue can provide. Second, Alcibiades' resistance to the idea of deferring his political debut brings out the passions in him that most forcefully drive and sustain his ambition and that are least susceptible to being tempered by prudent counsel. In analyzing the effect of Socratic education upon Alcibiades, we need to focus on the questions of whether and how his ambition changes or remains the same. Does Socrates produce a change in Alcibiades' belief that the highest fulfillment of his ambition is necessarily political? If so, what precisely changes Alcibiades' mind? Does his new self-understanding include a psychologically and politically salutary understanding of justice, noble devotion, and honor? Or must we conclude that Alcibiades clings to his original ambitions after all? In this case, does the rigidity of Alcibiades' psychology derive from familiar and ubiquitous beliefs and opinions, or does he represent a kind of unique political extreme and exception? By pursuing these questions, we hope to reveal the Platonic psychological portrait of extraordinary ambition, or of the desires, beliefs, and hopes that give it its force, and thereby to gain, most importantly, insight into those of our own moral and political motivations made terribly elusive by their very importance to us. And we can also hope thus to become better able to say how Plato's political philosophy might provide a plausible theoretical alternative to the Enlightenment accounts that purported to supersede it.[13]

## Hermeneutic Questions in Platonic Studies

Of course, the opportunity to study Plato's depiction of the notorious and fascinating Alcibiades under the influence of Socratic education has not gone unseized by scholars. But before we can even begin to assess the existing interpretations, we are confronted with a difficulty. Many scholars today deny that the *Alcibiades* and *Second Alcibiades* are genuine works of Plato and are thus led to conclude that the *Symposium* contains Alcibiades' only major Platonic appearance. These claims require that we give some attention to the history of the Platonic corpus. The traditional Platonic cannon, consisting of thirty-five dialogues and thirteen letters, is attested by Diogenes Laertius, who credits Thrasyllus (died AD 36) with the arrangement of the corpus into the (still employed) tetralogies, and the earlier Alexandrine *Grammaticus* Aristophanes of Byzantium (c. 257–c. 185 BC) with an arrangement into trilogies.[14] In the two thousand years following Aristophanes' consolidation of the forty-eight Platonic texts, never did serious questioning regarding the authorship of any of them gain lasting credibility. And yet fierce debates over authenticity raged through the nineteenth century (especially in Germany), by the end of which it was a tiny minority of the dialogues (and none of the *Letters*) that had entirely evaded accusations of spuriousness from leading scholars. Today, scholarly agreement concerning authenticity, though far from complete, is more widespread, and where the dust has settled, a number of dialogues and epistles have earned an almost universal reputation of spuriousness. What discovery could have produced this Copernican shift in the study of Platonic philosophy?

An adequate treatment of this question would require the survey of a sprawling and unwieldy collection of arguments spanning more than two hundred years. In the case of the (still hotly contested) *Alcibiades* alone, such a treatment would, and indeed has been on several occasions, the subject of an essay unto itself, not of the few pages I could devote to it here. In lieu of a fully adequate exploration of this problem, then, I shall present some reflections pertaining to my own approach to Plato, which is necessary at any rate to make my methodological premises clear. As for the specific, textual arguments regarding the authenticity of *Alcibiades* and *Second Alcibiades*, I offer whatever insights I have in footnotes to the relevant chapters.[15]

The impetus behind the original movement to reevaluate the authenticity of the Platonic corpus was directed against the extensive Neoplatonist tradition of interpretation, which had maintained its dominating influence on the understanding of Platonic philosophy ever since its full reintroduction to the West by Marsilio Ficino in the late fifteenth century.[16] With German Romanticism in the eighteenth century came calls for a wholesale revision of inherited interpretations of the canon of Western literature, art, and religious texts, freed of dogmatic commitments and dedicated to a new form of "criticism" informed by a modern, scientific understanding of history. The application of this project to Plato, which necessarily began with heavy suspicion or rejection of the influential claims and doctrines of the Neoplatonists, came around the turn of the nineteenth century with close parallels to the "higher criticism" of biblical texts, which sought to ascertain the historical origins of the New Testament.[17] The task was to dig Platonic philosophy out from under the accretion of doctrinal mysticism that had been growing over it for centuries, to rediscover the "true" Plato who was not a divine prophet but a human being whose singular artistic genius gave life and expression to the spirit of Athenian philosophy.[18]

Rediscovering the "true" Plato certainly requires knowing what works Plato wrote, but this is no simple matter of gathering together the texts attributed to him. Even ancient sources did not accept the authenticity of *every* work that had come to bear Plato's name—the *Halcyon*, *Axiochus*, and many other so-called *spuria* (*nothoi*) had already been universally rejected in antiquity, to say nothing of the fact that the *Republic* and *Phaedo* had ancient doubters[19]—and we cannot know precisely when and from whom the thirty-six-text corpus first received its stamp of approval. We might have some hope of critically distinguishing the true works of Plato from the forgeries if we felt reasonably confident in our ability to identify Platonic style, presentation, and thought. But our notions about these will inevitably be founded upon previous experience with texts we had uncritically assumed to be Platonic. We become caught in a loop, or rather, we are stuck outside of it.[20] We cannot begin to interpret Plato without knowing what he wrote, but we cannot determine what he wrote without importing an interpretation of him. It was Friedrich Schleiermacher's rigorous and sustained attention to this very problem that gave his work on Plato the power to set the course for all subsequent Platonic studies.[21] Schleiermacher claimed that a scholar with an exceptionally intimate knowledge of the Greek language, culture, and history—a knowledge rivaling Plato's own, if possible—could, by weaving back and forth between hermeneutics and criticism, that is, between interpretation of the texts and determination of their place in (or out of) the Platonic corpus, succeed in recovering the original Platonic thought or meaning (*Urbild*) that generated the dialogues.[22]

But let us leave the discussion of Schleiermacher, his numerous epigones, and his even more numerous opponents for another time and take what perspective we can from this brief treatment of the problem of authenticity. We must admit that we will never know for certain who wrote the two *Alcibiades* dialogues; the greater the certainty with which athetizers or defenders draw their conclusions, the more suspicion we ought to have that their commitments to one position or the other have distorted their view of the available evidence.[23] On one side, there is a danger that the need to reject the testimony of those who looked uncritically to "the divine Plato" will in turn make us hypercritical, seeking and finding reasons to doubt the text before giving due attention to what may have been subtle and intentionally puzzling Platonic presentations of important philosophic questions.[24] On the other side, there are the varied dangers of slipping into the belief that Plato was divine, a mistake Plato happily invites and that has never ceased to direct the understanding of his interpreters.[25] Whatever conclusions we can finally draw about Plato's presentation of Alcibiades must follow a lengthy and multifaceted study that includes (as Schleiermacher would agree) a bona fide attempt to interpret the *Alcibiades* and *Second Alcibiades* as integral pieces of that complex presentation.

To the extent that the question of authenticity is of concern to us, then, this work can stand as a contribution to the debate. For an adequate analysis of the question of authenticity would have to weigh the plausibility of a coherent interpretive account of these dialogues as works of Plato—such as is presented here—against considerations pointing to one or more of the dialogues as spurious. And, as will become abundantly clear, a thorough interpretation of these dialogues taken together is no slight task. However, insofar as we are seeking to deepen our understanding of political ambition for the reasons outlined above, our success will depend only on the extent to which we can learn from our texts whatever lessons their author(s) meant to impart. For whether or not Plato composed the two "dubious" dialogues, it is plain to see that they were composed as dramas belonging to the world of the Platonic Socrates.[26]

## Reconstructing Alcibiades' Socratic Education

If indeed the *Alcibiades* and *Second Alcibiades* are authentic works of Plato, however, then most of the interpretive studies of Plato's presentation of Alcibiades produced in the last two centuries have been based on very partial information, that is, on the *Symposium* almost exclusively—especially to the extent that the account of the *Symposium* differs from what we find in the dialogues named for Alcibiades.[27] Not surprisingly, there is a tendency in these interpretations to focus on the details of Alcibiades' unsuccessful attempts to seduce Socrates since Alcibiades himself presents this as the great secret of their relationship.[28] Alcibiades does present us with a vivid, personal, and illuminating case study in *eros* in his *Symposium* speech, which is fruitfully compared with the more or less abstract accounts that precede his arrival.[29] But lessons about Alcibiades as a paradigm of political ambition are hard to come by in the *Symposium* alone. Interpreters who have found political significance in his appearance there have generally inferred it from the dramatic context—the banquet takes place mere months before the Sicilian Expedition—and from the fact that the Athenians would later blame Socrates for Alcibiades' *hubris* and immoderation—a fact to which Plato alludes by having Alcibiades present his "praise" of Socrates as a trial, with those present serving as witnesses, on the charge of *hubris*. It has thus often been suggested that the *Symposium* speech is meant as a complex Platonic encomium of Socrates, exonerating him from the charges made famous by his accusers, from Aristophanes to Polycrates.[30]

This interpretation, however, implies that Alcibiades' praise for Socrates outweighs his criticism, whereas Alcibiades' speech as a whole reflects a great ambivalence concerning his relationship with Socrates. Thus, Michael Gagarin concludes that "the seduction episode . . . reveals the true nature of [Alcbiades'] relation with Socrates, namely that he was frustrated in his past attempt to acquire beauty, wisdom, and virtue from Socrates, and that this frustration, which he still feels, is a direct result of Socrates' *hybris*" (34–35).[31] And yet there is no suggestion as to how Socrates convinced Alcibiades that he could offer "beauty, wisdom, and virtue" to rival the luster of Athenian politics, as Alcibiades' speech suggested he did. The theme of *hubris* is intriguing: Alcibiades' accusation of Socratic *hubris* in the context of an account of their relationship suggests the possibility that Alcibiades' own hubristic political ambition may be the result of some Socratic influence (cf. *Apology of Socrates* 26a–28a). But the more one seeks some suggestion in the *Symposium* concerning the effect of Socratic education on Alcibiades' political ambition, the more one finds that dialogue insufficient to supply such suggestions on its own. Alcibiades simply does not say enough about the content of Socrates' beautiful speeches.[32]

Of course, we expect a much fuller picture of Alcibiades' Socratic education to emerge from consideration of the *Alcibiades* and *Second Alcibiades* since these performed dialogues portray private conversations between Socrates and Alcibiades in the early stages of their association. The privacy of these conversations, Socrates' disarming strangeness, and Alcibiades' youth contribute to Alcibiades being much more candid in them than he is, drunkenness notwithstanding, in the *Symposium*. In his first conversation with Socrates, for example, Alcibiades is flabbergasted by his own inability to give a clear, consistent account of either the means he will pursue to gain political success or the goals he hopes to achieve thereby. In the process of exposing these deficiencies, Socrates is able to probe and partially to reveal the opinions and hopes that give Alcibiades' ambition its exceptional intensity. These dialogues thus promise to deal with the important political themes of which scholars find hints but no sustained discussion in the *Symposium*, and thus to present the Socratic examination of political ambition we are seeking.

Yet even in the *Alcibiades*, which has attracted increasing interest of late (unlike its much maligned sequel), interpreters often overlook the political dimension. Nicholas Denyer, the most influential proponent of the dialogue's authenticity in recent years, downplays the substantive importance of the entire first half of the work, in which Socrates brings Alcibiades to a state of *aporia* concerning his beliefs about justice.[33] Denyer does not see in Socrates' refutation of Alcibiades' opinions about the just, the noble, and the good, the gripping drama of ambition and philosophy dangerously intermingling, flirting with moral and political disaster. Gary Allen Scott's interpretation in *Plato's Socrates as Educator* (2000)—more thorough and rightly paired with an account of Alcibiades' *Symposium* speech (as well as the *Lysis*)—suffers from a similar deficiency and a similar resulting lack of attention to the first half of the dialogue (86–91). Scott concludes that "Socrates undertakes his sometimes antagonistic cross-examinations" in order "to breach the identification of the interlocutor's self with his unexamined viewpoints (beliefs and opinions)" (103). But, we must ask, "viewpoints" concerning what? Scott does not make this question of theme or content central to Socratic education.[34]

The one successful attempt to examine Plato's presentation of Alcibiades as a portrait of political ambition is contained in Robert Faulkner's *The Case for Greatness: Honorable Ambition and Its Critics* (2007), which dedicates a chapter to the *Alcibiades* and *Second Alcibiades*. The book as a whole aims to restore something of the classical understanding of grand political ambition by examining ancient and modern defenses and critiques. Faulkner identifies six essential components of the Platonic Alcibiades' ambition: "a striking pride . . . an overwhelming desire for honor and power . . . [a] wish to know what he is doing, a certain justice and nobility, an equivocal political horizon, and, finally, an impulse to turn to divine help" (86). He suggests that Socrates' understanding of the combination and interplay of these characteristics allows him to employ an accordingly complex strategy for transforming and redirecting Alcibiades' political ambition so as to render him tamer, more cautious, and "more respectful of philosophy" (90). Thus, his chapter on the Platonic Alcibiades contributes to his "case for greatness" by attempting to sketch the Socratic solution to some of the gravest dangers associated with powerful ambition.

Faulkner is especially perceptive in describing the delicacy and difficulty of the Socratic task of moderating Alcibiades' ambition. Socrates must dissuade Alcibiades from pursuing the life of despotic luxury or tyranny to which he may have become attracted (106–7) but without excessive reliance on simple moralizing, given "the impolitic and imprudent excesses that can go with moral prescription, especially in so powerfully volatile a man as Alcibiades" (108). In the *Second Alcibiades*, wherein Alcibiades has turned to prayer "for divine help to avoid facing up to the bad consequences of tyrannical desire" (114), Socrates succeeds in discouraging this prayer by unfolding "four Socratic lessons taught more or less in turn," namely, "consider what you pray for, face up to harsh deeds that tyranny requires, be aware of one's ignorance as to the gods and their wishes, follow a theology that fosters reasonable justice and rational knowing" (117). Ultimately, Faulkner seems to endorse Socrates' procedure, concluding that Alcibiades, at the end of the second dialogue, "may be less preoccupied with what he thought good and more moderate in pursuing it. He has already become less preoccupied with fear of the gods, more ironic, and more ready for theological reconsiderations. A certain openness to Socratic philosophy, to inquiry as to what he is doing, moderates considerably his passion to rule the world" (126). In Faulkner's analysis, then, Alcibiades' extraordinary political ambition was made much better and more restrained by its extended encounter with Socratic philosophy.

For all the insight he gains by looking at the *Alcibiades* and *Second Alcibiades*, however, Faulkner may arrive at too optimistic a conclusion by underemphasizing the more famous Platonic presentation in the *Symposium*. Those who take the *Alcibiades* together with the *Symposium*, who therefore make *eros* a more prominent theme in their accounts of the Platonic Alcibiades and take their bearings from the historical Alcibiades' impiety and defection, are more apt to question altogether the effects of Socrates' attempt to bend Alcibiades' *eros* away from political honors.[35] Thus Waller Newell, advancing the thesis that "Plato sees tyranny as a misguided longing for erotic satisfaction that can be corrected by the education of eros toward the proper objects of its passion: civic virtue and philosophy" (2000; 1), emphasizes Alcibiades' inability to subordinate his love of the *demos* to his love of Socrates and Socratic philosophy (90). Similarly, Mark Lutz, who suggests that Socrates' education of Alcibiades is a way for him to test the Diotiman understanding of human nature by determining whether Alcibiades is "moved by an eros to know how to be noble and good" (1998; 116), calls the success of this Socratic project into question on the basis of Alcibiades' failure to follow Socrates' example (127–30, 148–49).[36]

The question of Socrates' success or failure in educating Alcibiades is more directly necessary to our examination of Alcibiades' ambition than it may seem at first. As we have noted, the intensity of Alcibiades' desire for political success and Plato's presentation of Alcibiades' political ambition in the crucible of Socratic refutation makes him an ideal subject for our recovery of the Platonic understanding of the relationship between the pursuit of the noble and political life. The success or failure of Socratic education in redirecting Alcibiades' ambition will be an important datum in this respect. However, the divergence of opinions concerning Socrates' success or failure that we have noted (e.g., of Paul Shorey, Gagarin, Faulkner, Newell, and Lutz) serves as a caution against hasty conclusions. These assessments differ primarily because they disagree concerning the most important question in Plato's presentation of Socrates and Alcibiades: that of Socrates' motivation and intention.[37]

Clearly, we cannot know whether Socrates succeeded or failed unless we know what he was trying to accomplish.

It is likely that Plato expected the majority of his readers to have something akin to these same questions in mind, since the alleged influence of Socratic education on Alcibiades was an important factor in the determination of Socrates' fate. In fact, the infamy of the association between these two men may alone account for the unparalleled attention, noted above, that Plato gives to Alcibiades.[38] Plato's choice of Alcibiades as a Socratic interlocutor was necessarily a choice to address the corruption charge of which Socrates was convicted.[39] Indeed, we have already noted in the case of the *Symposium* that interpreters often find in Alcibiades' speech a Platonic commentary on the charge of Socrates' corruption of Alcibiades. Even the most cursory attempt to read our two other dialogues with the corruption charge in mind is enough to see that it is a theme in those dialogues as well. The *Alcibiades* opens with Socrates' claim that he is able to bring Alcibiades' designs for unbounded fame and power to completion, and the *Second Alcibiades* gives the impression that Alcibiades intends to pray for tyranny. Thus, for what may seem to be circumstantial or historical reasons, our study of political ambition must proceed with or through a study of political corruption.[40] Or rather, our attempt to learn about political ambition from Plato leads us to the questions of the aims and effects of Socratic education and of the Athenians' hostility toward it. It is a mistake in reading Plato to insist rigidly that he answer the questions we bring to him. Our efforts will be better rewarded if we seek the Platonic understanding of political ambition in its proper place, as a part of the artistic and philosophic whole in which Plato chose to present it.

We need, then, to give some preliminary consideration to the question of Socratic corruption, the most consistent theme of Plato's presentation of Alcibiades. The Athenians executed Socrates on charges of impiety and corrupting the youth. As Aristophanes' *Clouds* makes clear, these accusations were connected: Socrates appeared to the Athenians to be a sophist, teaching his young associates not to believe in the traditional gods, enabling and emboldening them to make use of deception and injustice, and weakening their patriotic devotion to the city.[41] The career of Alcibiades was damning evidence indeed, from his alleged participation in the mutilation of the Herms and profanation of the Eleusinian mysteries, to his devious undermining of the Peace of Nicias, to his defection to enemy Sparta and his role in the oligarchic Athenian revolution of 411 BC. But whereas we might expect Socrates' most illustrious student and champion to provide a vigorous defense of his master against such allegations, we have already seen that many thoughtful scholars find Plato's presentation to provide surprisingly ambiguous evidence regarding Socrates' culpability. Here again, Plato defies presumption.

The centrality of the question of Socratic corruption demands that we take it up in studying the political ambition of the Platonic Alcibiades. Moreover, understanding the paradox of political ambition requires not only that we discern its contradictory elements, for example, its selfless and its selfish tendencies, but that we examine the connection between the two sides by considering how it is that noble ambition becomes corrupted. For example, Alcibiades concludes his first conversation with Socrates with ardent promises to become virtuous so as to avoid the wretchedness and harmfulness of tyranny, but in their next Platonic conversation, he agrees that a divine gift of universal tyranny would greatly delight him. We will need to consider how the changes in Alcibiades' political aspirations reflect changes in his understanding of the goods he seeks and the extent to which these changes are due to some Socratic influence. But for now, we can note that Plato, by having his portrait span multiple Socratic encounters, challenges us to determine how a single politically ambitious person can have the potential to manifest each of political ambition's varied and even contradictory features. The theme of corruption can be used to highlight the multifaceted and yet unified character of political ambition.

Plato's most illuminating implicit reference to Alcibiades concludes with a reflection along these same lines. As part of his response to Adeimantus's concern about the viciousness of philosophy in Book 6 of the *Republic*, Plato's Socrates provides an account of an attempt to educate a youth with a "philosophic nature" that reads like a partial synopsis of the *Alcibiades*. The passage then concludes:

> "Is it possible, then, that such a man will philosophize?"
>
> "Not at all."
>
> "So do you see," I said, "that we did not speak badly in saying that even the very parts of the philosophic nature, if ever it should come to have a bad rearing, are in some way the causes of its falling away from the pursuit [of philosophy], and so are the things that are called goods—wealth and all such means."
>
> "No indeed, but it was said correctly."

> "This, then, you wondrous man," I said, "is the destruction, and so great and such is the corruption, of the best nature with respect to the best pursuit, [a nature] which comes to be, at any rate, seldom, as we ourselves say. And from these men come to be the doers of the greatest evils to cities and private men, and also of the greatest goods in the case of those who should happen to be inclined this way; but a small nature in no way ever does a single great thing either to an individual or to a city." (495a1–b6)

Thus, the passage ends with an emphatic statement of the two-sidedness of "the best nature" (cf. *Laws* 908b4–d7). Alcibiades is capable of doing such great harm for the same reason that he is capable of doing such great good. Paying close attention to the subtle changes in Alcibiades' understanding that give rise to the significant change in his disposition toward tyranny will help us trace the fine line separating noble from corrupt political ambition. The most important Platonic hint contained in this and the surrounding passages, however, is that the transition from public and private benefactor to harmful evildoer is not what Socrates refers to as corruption but rather the falling away from the pursuit of philosophy. This is a crucial Platonic theme that we must keep in mind: Socrates means something different by "corruption" than the other Athenians do. We may wonder whether from Socrates' point of view, the corruption of Alcibiades lay in the fact that his ambition remained political. Our question of whether there is a type of ambition by nature that *must* remain political is thus bound up with the question of corruption in the Socratic sense.

Our attempt to learn about political ambition will therefore proceed through the careful analysis of the changes Alcibiades undergoes, for better or for worse, in the course of his association with Socrates. Plato has taken care to make the first part of this procedure particularly fruitful, since the *Alcibiades*, in presenting their very first conversation, begins with an Alcibiades still completely untouched by Socratic thought. No Platonic dialogue presents an interlocutor so completely unfamiliar with Socratic philosophy as the *Alcibiades*. Our first task, then, will be to attempt to determine what Alcibiades *had been* as an ambitious and well-born Athenian youth approaching maturity, even as we analyze what it is that he is already *becoming* as a result of Socrates' moving rhetoric and challenging refutations. Accordingly, we will be particularly well positioned to investigate the parallel questions of how Socratic education may be a corruption from the point of view of the city and how the city's education may be a corruption from the point of view of Socrates. This investigation will consequently illuminate the whole dramatic arc of Plato's presentation of Socrates and Alcibiades through to its unforgettable conclusion in the *Symposium*, an arc that constitutes Plato's most complete account of a Socratic attempt to educate and study a soul of extraordinary political ambition.

CHAPTER 1

# SOCRATES' PROMISE AND ALCIBIADES' FAILURE (*Alcibiades* 103–116)

Writing some eight centuries after Plato, Proclus claimed that the *Alcibiades* "is the beginning of all philosophy" and that the whole development of Plato's philosophy was anticipated therein "as in a seed" (6–7). These lines are often cited as emblematic of the opinion, held by many ancient interpreters, that the *Alcibiades* should be studied first among Plato's dialogues, as an introduction to his philosophy.[1] Proclus's further claim that "every human being is more or less clearly subject to the very experiences to which the son of Kleinias too was subject" (11) is more often overlooked, and yet it may be his best elaboration of why one would put the *Alcibiades* at the head of the Platonic corpus. Proclus's provocative statements taken together suggest that Alcibiades' starting point in the dialogue portraying his first conversation with Socrates, and his first encounter with philosophy and philosophic questioning, is the point from which anyone must begin the engagement with (Socratic) philosophy. The dialogue is useful and profound as much because of what we share with Alcibiades as because of the ways in which he is extraordinary. A crucial component of the study of Alcibiades' political ambition will be the attempt to understand how that ambition is an expression, however exceptional, of opinions, hopes, and desires that are familiar from our own experience. The traditional subtitle of the *Alcibiades*, "Of Human Nature," carries a similar suggestion.

This has, in a way, already been suggested in the Introduction. The study of political ambition is most far-reaching in what it tells us about the relationship between political activity and human nature—between the love of honor, rule, and the noble on one hand and the requirements of human fulfillment on the other. But, as has also been stressed above, the task of recovering Plato's teaching concerning this complex combination of themes requires that we take up each of the questions and reflections to which he points us in its proper context, understanding every argument, every question, every reaction as the expression of a particular character in a particular set of circumstances, both within the dialogue and more generally. Plato's position is easily misrepresented by the reader who forces him to answer preformulated questions by reading and quoting passages in isolation. The action of a Platonic dialogue, the rise and fall of its key themes and questions, the ebb and flow of the interlocutors' intentions and emotions, all stand out in much starker relief once we perceive the structure of the dialogue, the way in which its various parts fit together with all of their peaks and pivots.

In the interest, then, of providing some means of keeping our bearings in an often disorienting dialogue, it will be helpful briefly to lay out its structure beforehand. The *Alcibiades* can be divided into three parallel parts (103a1–113d8, 113d9–119c1, and 119c2–135e8), each containing roughly the same sequence of three subsections: Speeches, Refutations, and Exhortations.[2] Each subsection of each part can help us deepen our understanding both of Alcibiades' ambition and of Socrates' intention. The speeches indicate features of Alcibiades' character that Socrates wishes to draw out or to suppress, and suggest some reasons why Socrates may wish to do so. The refutations bring out confusions in Alcibiades' moral and political understanding and reveal the potential course of his Socratic education. The exhortations contain suggestions of what Alcibiades might become, for better or worse, and quietly but clearly elaborate crucial features of the philosophic project Socrates intends to carry out. We will take up each of the dialogue's nine sections in turn with an eye to better understanding the relationship between Alcibiades and Socrates.

However, the *Alcibiades* can also be quite clearly divided into two halves, the first half containing the first and second Speeches-Refutations-Exhortations sequences, and the second half containing the third and last. In the first half of the dialogue, Socrates delves into an exploration of Alcibiades' beliefs about the just, the noble, the good, and the advantageous by way of a sustained examination of his political aspirations. It thus provides us with a rich and perplexing account of how political ambition may rest upon unexamined and contradictory moral beliefs. Moreover, the conclusion of this portion of the dialogue, and hence the hinge between the first and second halves, is Alcibiades' rejection of Socrates' more or less implicit insistence that political ambition seeks goods that are subordinate to or contingent upon resolving the contradictions that underlie his ambition in the first place. For this reason, it will be worthwhile to pause at this central turning point of the dialogue to reflect on what we can already say about Plato's presentation of Alcibiades' political ambition. In Chapter 2, we will turn to the second half of the *Alcibiades* with a new set of questions having been raised by the conclusion of the first.

## Inflating Alcibiades' Ambition (Speeches, 103a1–106a1)

The *Alcibiades* begins with two Socratic speeches separated by a brief exchange. These speeches help us place the dialogue on the timelines of Socrates' and Alcibiades' lives and provide some important information about their relationship hitherto. In this way, the speeches serve as a useful introduction to the reader. But the speeches are of far greater interest in the context of the drama of the dialogue itself. It is by way of these speeches that Socrates introduces himself to Alcibiades, seizes his attention, and primes him for the examination to follow. They are masterpieces of Socratic rhetoric. We must therefore begin by considering the effects these speeches are meant to have on Alcibiades and the reasons for which Socrates wants to achieve those effects.

The beginning of the dialogue makes clear that Alcibiades was a youth of extraordinary beauty and charm. We learn immediately that he has been pursued for years by a "crowd" of lovers, who only recently seem to have given up the pursuit. Socrates presents himself as one such lover and yet emphasizes his strangeness by distinguishing himself from all the others in a number of ways. He was the first to become a lover of Alcibiades, and he is the only one who remains now that the others have given up—and yet, in all the years Socrates has been doggedly following Alcibiades, he has never spoken to him before now (103a1–4). All of this suggests that Socrates' attraction to Alcibiades is fundamentally different from that of a typical lover. While the others were drawn to him and attempted to seduce him during a particular phase of his physical development, Socrates has apparently been keen to observe Alcibiades' progress from childhood to early adulthood. In short, his interest is in Alcibiades' soul and not merely in his body (cf. 131c11–e5).

While that may explain the longevity of Socrates' interest, however, it does not explain his long silence. Socrates explains, "The cause of this has been no human thing, but a certain *daimonic* opposition whose power you will learn of later. But now, since it no longer opposes, I have come forward in this way, and I am hopeful that it will not oppose in the future" (103a4–b2). Of course, this explanation does nothing to make Socrates appear any less strange to Alcibiades. Rather, it gives to Socrates' strangeness a mysterious, uncanny aura. He claims to have access to a divine power and suggests that he may be able to demonstrate this power to Alcibiades. From the very beginning, then, Socrates' privileged relationship with a divine being is an essential feature of his self-presentation. Equally important, however, is his claim of pious obedience to this divinity. Socrates' association with Alcibiades has been made possible only by the retraction of the divine prohibition, which may return, for all we know, at any time.

The importance of Socrates' appearing uniquely strange and intriguing to Alcibiades is brought out by what comes next. Alcibiades has rebuffed the advances of each of his many lovers, Socrates explains, by exceeding them in pride (*phronēma*). Alcibiades' pride, says Socrates, is expressed in his claim to be in need of nothing from anyone, "for the things that belong to you are great, beginning from the body and ending in the soul, so that you need nothing" (104a1–3). This account suggests that Socrates, who presents himself as a lover, will have to convince Alcibiades that he has something of value to offer. None of the lovers who preceded Socrates were able to win Alcibiades' favor because none of them were able to offer anything he needed in exchange. By making this explicit, Socrates is already raising the question of what he could possibly have to offer. He is also raising the question—even more perplexing than the first, if we are inclined to dismiss the crudest and most obvious answer—of what it is that he could possibly want in exchange.

The rest of the speech only heightens the implausibility of Socrates' success, as Socrates proceeds to flatter Alcibiades by listing the grounds of the youth's overwhelming sense of self-sufficiency. These are, briefly, his physical beauty, the distinction of his family and the connections thereby available to him, the greatness of his city, and most of all, "the power [he] supposes belongs to [him] in [his guardian] Pericles . . . who has the power to do what he wishes, not only in this city, but in all of Greece and among many and great barbarian races" (104a4–b8). With these gifts of fortune, and especially with his access to extraordinary political power, Alcibiades is indifferent to promises of political connections and advancement that might otherwise have made a pederastic affair appealing to a handsome Athenian youth. Alcibiades recognizes, according to Socrates, that he has overcome his lovers by boasting about all of his advantages and by his lovers' being needier than he is (104c2–4). Hence, Socrates concludes his first speech by admitting that Alcibiades must wonder at his persistence—what could Socrates, who must cut a laughable figure next to Alcibiades' "many and proud" lovers, intend and hope for?

Socrates must puncture Alcibiades' sense of self-sufficiency and convince him that he is in need of something important, something Socrates can provide. In showing us this, the first speech has set the stage upon which the whole of the *Alcibiades* will take place. But even in that first speech, there is some indication of what Alcibiades lacks. That he was said to "boast" of his advantages to his lovers means that he was exaggerating them to some degree. Indeed, the power of which Alcibiades boasts is not yet his own; he depends for it on Pericles and his other relatives. That he has "many excellent friends and relatives who could serve [him] if he should need something" is, to say the least, in some tension with his claim to have "no need of any human being for anything" (104b1–2, 104a1–2). His wealth would seem to be his most palpable source of independent power, and Socrates mentions it only to say that Alcibiades seems to attribute his greatness to wealth least of all (104b8–c1). It is political power that Alcibiades covets, and despite the fact that no lover has yet had a credible claim to be able to increase his chance of obtaining it, it must be admitted that he does not yet truly possess it.[3] Socrates' gambit will rely heavily on that fact.

But there is a more important wrinkle in Socrates' flattery of Alcibiades. Socrates speaks of Alcibiades' great possessions beginning from his body and ending in his soul; but while he admits that Alcibiades' height and beauty are "clear for everyone to see," he never specifies the matching characteristics of soul to which these supposedly point. The praise and attention that Alcibiades has received on account of his beauty have contributed to the high opinion he holds of himself, but that high opinion is surely about more than his looks. Alcibiades believes himself to be an exceptional human being in part because of his exceptional beauty. But what if Socrates could show him that with respect to his soul, he is deeply lacking and that the apparent promise of his beauty is in danger of going unfulfilled? This would be harder to make clear to Alcibiades than the obstacles that stand between him and political power, but it could also be the basis of a more powerful appeal. At this point, however, we must admit that we cannot judge the relative usefulness of the two possible appeals we have identified because we still do not know what Socrates wants from Alcibiades. The first speech has done nothing to shed light on that matter.

Alcibiades' response indicates that Socrates' tactic has worked; he is curious to know what Socrates hopes for in always taking care to be around him.

He "really wonder[s] what in the world [Socrates'] business is, and would learn it with pleasure" (104d3–5). We might even wonder whether Socrates' introductory speech was necessary since Alcibiades claims to have already been intending to approach Socrates with these very matters in mind. But the speech has allowed Socrates to begin the association at the precise moment and in the precise manner of his choosing, and the combination of his flattery of Alcibiades and his claims to divine revelation were likely necessary for the sake of intensifying Alcibiades' curiosity and interest. For Socrates now goes out of his way to get Alcibiades' assurance that he will remain and listen for however long it takes him to explain his intention. Socrates is concerned that Alcibiades will leave prematurely; he may well be thinking of the painful effect of the Socratic refutations he has in mind to administer. This already suggests, then, that Socrates both hopes to teach Alcibiades something important and difficult and that he is unsure whether Alcibiades will be up to the task.

Socrates' second speech levels a strangely flattering accusation at Alcibiades: that he harbors fantastic political ambitions. This is flattering because it suggests that the fantasy Socrates describes is within the realm of possibility. It is an "accusation," as Socrates calls it, for at least two reasons. First, it exposes the disingenuous character of Alcibiades' boasting described in the first speech. Far from being without needs, Socrates suggests, Alcibiades has awfully little compared with that which he aspires to gain. Second, the claim that Alcibiades hopes to rise to unprecedented heights of political power leaves unclear what means he is willing to employ to do so and what he would wish to do with his power once he obtained it. In short, Socrates comes close to accusing Alcibiades of tyrannical *hubris*. To determine what effect this strange Socratic move is meant to have, we must examine the details of the speech more closely.

Socrates says he will accuse Alcibiades of having more on his mind than the goods enumerated in the first speech. In fact, he claims that Alcibiades is so dissatisfied with what he currently has that were a god to offer him either to live without acquiring anything more or to die at once, he would choose to die (105a1–6). This means that Alcibiades still hopes to gain that which will make the entirety of his life worthwhile, and Socrates explains what this is. He suggests that Alcibiades believes he will come before the Athenian *demos* in a few days—we learn later that Alcibiades is about twenty years old, so he is now just becoming old enough to address the assembly (123d4–6)—and proving to them that he is worthy of honor such as no one has ever been (Pericles included), he will become the most powerful person in the city, in all of Greece, and among the barbarians who share the Greek mainland (105a7–b7). But even this, says Socrates, would not be enough for Alcibiades, for if the same god were to forbid him from gaining control over Asia too, he would again choose not to live "if [he] will not fill all human beings, so to speak, with [his] name and [his] power" (105b7–c4). According to Socrates' accusation, then, Alcibiades will consider his life a failure if he proves unable to ascend to god-like fame and power, and he expects that his imminent entry into Athenian politics will make manifest his worthiness of those honors.

One might well doubt whether Alcibiades had ever put his hopes to himself in such bold terms. It is more plausible to think of Socrates' accusation as giving voice to all that is implied in Alcibiades' hopes for fame and power, hopes that are powerful but still fairly amorphous. We should keep in mind that Alcibiades has never before spoken in the assembly—given his age, we may wonder whether he has ever *been* in the assembly.[4] The dialogue will provide ample evidence that he has given surprisingly little thought to the practical requirements of a political career or to the substance of political deliberation, advising, and decision making. Indeed, a savvier political man might simply have laughed at the fantastical extremes of the aspirations Socrates describes, and even the young Alcibiades must recognize that this vision of the future strains credulity. But his relative unfamiliarity with the limits of political reality make the boundaries of his ambition fluid, and Socrates here succeeds in capturing his imagination by inflating Alcibiades' sense that he is naturally worthy of tremendous honor. What Socrates thus reveals, as opposed to what he builds up or implants, is the sense Alcibiades has developed as a result of his beauty, family, city, connection to Pericles, and relative wealth that he is destined for greatness and that anything less would be a heartbreaking disappointment. Socrates says that Alcibiades hopes to "prove to the city that [he is] worth everything to her, and that, immediately after having proved this, there will be nothing [he does] not have the power to do" (105d7–e2). The goal here described is political power understood as the power to do whatever one wishes—the same power attributed to Pericles in the first speech. Socrates now makes it clear that Alcibiades wants for himself the power to which he currently has access only through Pericles. Indeed, he wants a power still greater than that: Socrates cites as Alcibiades' models Cyrus and Xerxes, despotic Persian kings revered by their people as direct descendants of the gods (cf. 120e–121c).

If Socrates' speech were to contain nothing more than these accusations, he could be accused of employing some quite reckless rhetoric. He has conjured an image of Alcibiades rising to despotic rule over all of humanity without for a moment pausing to raise the question of what constraints must be placed on the pursuit of such fame and power or of whether fame and power in fact constitute the great goods of which Alcibiades believes he is worthy. That image is not, however, the sum total of Socrates' speech. The speech also contains the astounding claim that Alcibiades will be unable to see his designs through to their conclusion—and therefore that he will be unable to make his life worth living—without Socrates (105d2–4).[5] Socrates' hope, he says, is parallel to Alcibiades' hope: just as Alcibiades hopes to gain great power by proving to the Athenians that he is worth everything to them, Socrates hopes to gain great power over Alcibiades by proving that he is worth everything to him and that no one but he (together with the god) can provide the power Alcibiades desires (105e2–5). This, then, is how Socrates intends to overcome the "man who does not succumb to lovers" (104e4–5). He is calling Alcibiades' bluff: Alcibiades is not perfectly self-sufficient, as he boasts to his lovers, but still entirely lacks that which he desires most intensely. Socrates must now prove to Alcibiades that all the gifts of fortune he enjoys are not enough for him to satisfy that intense desire and that he still needs something more, something only Socrates can provide.

At this point, then, it is difficult to avoid the suggestion that Socrates intends to help Alcibiades become a tyrant—if, that is, a god, and specifically "the god" who is presumably identical to Socrates' "*daimonic* opposition," would ever endorse such a project. But the dialogue will show that this is not what Socrates has in mind, leaving us in the dark as concerns our question about his god. Instead, he will try to execute an elaborate bait and switch. He will attempt to redirect Alcibiades' ambition, his exceptionally intense desire to seek his own greatest good, by making him see that he has not adequately reflected upon what the greatest good truly is. The importance of Alcibiades' ambition for Socrates, therefore, is not simply that it provides an opportunity to grab his attention. A powerful desire to seek one's own good is a trait shared by the tyrant and the philosopher. If Socrates inflames a kind of tyrannical desire in Alcibiades, it is only in order to show him that that desire is misdirected. Thus, Socrates began his second speech by saying, "If, Alcibiades, I had seen you content with the things I just went through [beauty, family, etc.], supposing that you ought to spend your life in the midst of them, I would have abandoned my love long ago" (104e6–8). What has drawn Socrates to Alcibiades is the deep restlessness of his desire for what is best, as this desire may enable him to endure the pain of Socratic refutation and of rigorous self-examination.[6] Thus, Socrates concludes his speech by telling Alcibiades, "When you were younger, before you were full of such great hope, as it seems to me, the god would not allow conversing, lest I converse in vain" (105e6–8). The greatness of Alcibiades' hope, it seems, will determine Socrates' success or failure.

And yet we still cannot say *why* Socrates wants to educate Alcibiades, and so we cannot yet say what would constitute Socratic failure or success. Likewise, it is not yet possible to say anything more about why Socrates continues to insist that what he has to offer Alcibiades is contingent on the acquiescence of a god: at most, we can say that Socrates acknowledges at the outset that there is an element of his project with Alcibiades that is out of his control. Let the following observation, therefore, suffice for the time being. Socrates has depicted Alcibiades as hoping to become a god or at least godlike. If such a hope, or something like it, is indeed an important element of Alcibiades' political ambition, then Socrates' claim to have access to his own *daimonic* power may resonate very deeply with Alcibiades. This Socratic introduction has both raised the question of how gods might look upon the *hubris* of the highest ambitions of mortals and presented Socrates himself as a peculiar kind of expert in the matter of divine prohibition. But there is also a more straightforward point here, which elaborates upon an earlier suggestion: the claim that Alcibiades is not yet able to achieve political success is weaker than the claim that he is confused about how to secure the good of his soul. Socrates' inflation of Alcibiades' political ambition has been calculated to draw out a desire that transcends the merely political.

The opening section of the *Alcibiades* provides the most explicit description of Alcibiades' political ambition in Plato. Indeed, it offers more than we are yet in a position to appreciate fully. Still, it is worth marking out at this early stage what appear to be the key features of this description. According to Socrates' "accusation," at least, Alcibiades is motivated by the desire for fame and for power—or perhaps these are two desires, one to fill "all human beings" with his "name" and another to fill them with his "power." We are not yet in a position to determine the relationship in Alcibiades' psyche between these two objects of his desire, though it seems clear enough that the desire for power is associated with a vision of total freedom from constraint. We may be fairly sure that Alcibiades himself has not yet thought through how far one must be willing to go if one is serious about the pursuit of perfect freedom. Socrates has only begun to bring those considerations to mind by suggesting that the true peaks of political achievement lie beyond not only Pericles, but even Cyrus and Xerxes, and by having his hypothetical, antagonistic deity blockade Alcibiades' path to those peaks with his restrictive ultimata.

What is special about Alcibiades is precisely that he believes he is so special. His whole life, the praise of his peers and of his elders has brought him to believe he bears the marks and the promise of greatness—not the least of which is his physical beauty—which has in turn nourished in him a supreme confidence and even a penchant for boasting. The Athenians have thereby cultivated in this aristocratic youth an unwavering and uncompromising belief that he is destined to obtain what is greatest, most honored, and most worthy of attainment for a human being. But that belief has only now begun to take on its mature shape since Alcibiades is only now nearing, and therefore beginning to perceive more clearly, the political arena in which the praise and honor of the Athenians is to be won. It is specifically at this moment that Socrates has approached Alcibiades.

## The Need for Justice in Making War and Peace (Refutations, 106a2–112d10)

Alcibiades does not admit to the truth of Socrates' accusation, but he is intrigued enough by the promise Socrates appears to have made to be willing to submit to Socratic questioning, whatever that entails (106a2–b8). Hence, Socrates has succeeded in winning an opportunity to demonstrate his worth to Alcibiades. He must prove that the fulfillment of Alcibiades' desires will require something Socrates can provide but which Alcibiades himself does not yet possess. At least for the first half of the *Alcibiades*, Socrates will argue that this crucial possession, the missing link to Alcibiades' success and the only worthwhile offering any lover has ever held out to him, is knowledge of justice. To persuade Alcibiades of this, however, will require his agreement to two questionable claims: that knowledge of justice is required for political success and that Alcibiades does not know what justice is. Socrates' winding but methodical advance through the refutations of this section will be for the sake of cornering Alcibiades into agreement on those points.

In preparation for the refutation proper, Socrates must carefully elicit Alcibiades' agreement to a number of important premises. The first such premise concerns the importance of expertise for Alcibiades' political success. Alcibiades agrees immediately that the counsel he intends to offer the assembly, which will prove his great worth, will be about something he knows better than the Athenians (106c4–d1). Socrates then takes care to secure Alcibiades' agreement to a second premise, this one about the *origin* of the knowledge that will inform his good counsel. Alcibiades agrees that all of his knowledge has either been learned from others or discovered independently and therefore consists entirely of things he once did not believe he knew (106d4–e3). Socrates will later rely on this agreement to argue that Alcibiades cannot have knowledge of justice. But this shaky premise leaves no room for the possibility of innate knowledge, knowledge acquired naturally in the course of human development, or divinely revealed knowledge—each of which is often thought to be a source of knowledge of justice.[7]

Next, Socrates needs to establish that Alcibiades' counsel to the Athenians must be just counsel if it is to be good counsel. Strictly speaking, this too is preliminary to the refutation proper—the object of which will be to persuade Alcibiades that he lacks knowledge of the just—but it is essential to its ultimate effectiveness. If Socrates were to show Alcibiades that he is ignorant about justice without first arguing that knowledge of justice is necessary for the fulfillment of his political ambitions, he would have failed to make good on his promise of proving indispensable to that fulfillment. This premise, however, will prove rather difficult to establish—not so much because Alcibiades does not believe in the importance of justice for good political counsel as because of the shallowness of his political thinking hitherto. The very fact that Alcibiades believes he has the expertise needed to lead Athens indicates the extent to which he believes, consciously or not, that his soul will keep the promise that his physical beauty appears to hold out. That is, he does not hope or assume that he will rise to prominence because of his physical charms and social standing alone (as we see repeatedly throughout the first half of the dialogue). Rather, he believes that he truly is or will be the best leader Athens can have, that he will be truly worthy of the honor the Athenians will give him. Yet this very belief is an indication of how unready he is both for the management of political affairs and for the politics of democratic statesmanship. His lack of attention to the most basic requirements of political life makes him slow to discern the important possibility toward which Socrates is trying to direct his attention, the possibility that justice is an indispensable component of good political policy.

First, Socrates must get Alcibiades to name the matter in which he intends to counsel the assembly on the basis of his superior knowledge. Alcibiades is easily able to disqualify Socrates' many suggestions: letters, lyre playing, wrestling, house building, divination, health, and shipbuilding (107a1–c12). The first three, though subjects in which Alcibiades has been educated, are matters for private education, not public deliberation. Already, then, we can see a problem for Alcibiades: political affairs are not among the subjects in which he has been educated. But then, is he any different in this regard from the other Athenian politicians? Has Alcibiades had anything but a typical Athenian education? And if not, where do capable politicians receive the education required to manage public business? The puzzle is intensified by Socrates' other examples, which *are* matters the assembly deliberates but in which, Alcibiades admits, his counsel would be inferior to that of an expert regardless of his beauty, family, or wealth. What then are the political matters about which the great Athenian statesmen have been expert counselors, and where did they obtain the relevant knowledge?

Alcibiades here completely overlooks what may be the most important possibility. Perhaps good counsel founded upon knowledge is not the most important qualification for political success. Perhaps Alcibiades' beauty, family, and wealth are much greater political assets than he appears to realize. What prevents him from getting the best of the diviner in the assembly?[8] Might not his charm and his renown carry him very far in such a competition?[9] Alcibiades betrays a striking naïveté in his ignorance of the power of political rhetoric.[10] As much as his attraction to Socrates' dazzling portrait of him as ruler over all mankind may suggest a troubling tyrannical streak in Alcibiades, it now becomes clear that he has no intention of deceiving the Athenians for personal gain—or, for that matter, of deceiving them for their own sake. On the contrary, he insists that his worthiness is based on the good he can do for the Athenians, which he is sure they will judge correctly when he brings himself before the assembly. A somewhat complex picture of Alcibiades' ambition thus begins to emerge: he will receive the greatest honors and acquire the greatest power imaginable, but he will do it by serving those he rules.

Finally, Alcibiades answers Socrates' question: he will advise the Athenians on matters of war and peace (107d3–4). Now, Alcibiades has no more expertise in these matters than he does in shipbuilding (an art that is, incidentally, important for military operations). It thus becomes clear that his lack of knowledge concerning the other matters enumerated by Socrates could not have been the only, nor even the primary, reason for which he denied having any interest in advising the Athenians about them. Advising about house building, divination, health, or shipbuilding lacks the glory of military leadership. War holds a place of unmatched gravity, dignity, and nobility among human affairs. Alcibiades senses that it is in war that he can most brilliantly and most fully display to the Athenians how much he is deserving of their honor. Socrates does not raise the sensible objection that Alcibiades is just as unqualified to be a military adviser as he is to advise about any other public matter since this would be counterproductive to Socrates' goal. Whatever deficiency he reveals in Alcibiades, Socrates must be able credibly to claim that only he can help overcome it—and Socrates could not, presumably, credibly claim to be the only one who could teach Alcibiades the art of generalship. However, Alcibiades' expressed desire to advise in matters of war and peace in fact suits Socrates' purpose well because it points to Alcibiades' concern for the noble or beautiful and thus potentially to justice. Socrates' immediate task is to help Alcibiades give clear expression to the place of justice—which has until now been only a nebulous part of his complex and unexamined ambition—in his pursuit of the noble or beautiful goal of military and political leadership. It is in examining the concern for justice in particular that the problem of concern for the noble or beautiful in general is illuminated most fully.

Eliciting a clear expression from Alcibiades of his concern for justice on the basis of his desire to be a general will require an exercise in Socratic dialectic. Alcibiades endorses the trivial premises that he will advise Athens to make war and peace with whomever, at whatever time, and for however long it is "better" to do so (107d5–e4). Socrates then pushes him to clarify the meaning of this "better" by first getting him to consider what "better" means in two other contexts: wrestling on one hand, and lyre playing, singing, and dancing on the other (107e5–108d8). The better in wrestling, says Socrates, is the more gymnastic; so to what "better" does the singer look in accompanying his song with lyre playing and dancing? Alcibiades is unable to say, even with the Socratic hint that he must consider the art (*technē*) by which these things are done correctly (*orthōs*). It is only when Socrates has him consider that the goddesses to whom the art belongs are the "Muses" that Alcibiades realizes the art is "music" and that what is correctly done according to it is the "musical." Socrates then continues: the more gymnastic and the more musical are the better in wrestling and singing, respectively; so what is the better in war and peace? Again, Alcibiades is repeatedly unable to give a reply—a shameful failure, as he admits, since these are the matters in which he hopes to advise the assembly (108d9–109a8). Finally, Socrates gets Alcibiades to see that the key consideration is of the just and the unjust by having him consider that wars are always fought over claims of having been deceived, coerced, or robbed; this finally leads to the conclusion that the "better" in war and peace is the more just (109a9–c12).

Thus concludes Alcibiades' brief introduction to Socratic dialectics. It must be said that his performance is less than impressive. Should he not, given his wish to become an Athenian general, have had some thought about the end toward which cities aim in waging war? We can try to exonerate Alcibiades on a number of grounds. He has never experienced Socratic dialectical questioning before, and so he is surely somewhat disoriented by the unexpected twists and turns the conversation takes in straying from its previously narrow focus on his future political career. Moreover, the question of the better in war and peace is admittedly complicated, especially insofar as it is morally thorny. This is particularly relevant given that Socrates' opening speeches may still be echoing in Alcibiades' ears, the tone and even the content of which would seem to suggest that the end to which Alcibiades will look in conducting war will be his own glory. If such thoughts are among the first to come to Alcibiades' mind, thanks partly to the mood set by Socrates' introduction, a combination of confusion and shame may contribute to his inability to supply Socrates with an answer. The image of Alcibiades fulfilling his ambition by becoming ruler over all humanity, in the context of the present discussion, will trigger more powerfully than it did at first a backlash of moral guilt or doubt: can it be true, he may ask himself, is it *permissible* that I shall be engaging the Athenians in life-and-death struggles for the sake of my own glory? Finally, it may be worth noting that Alcibiades is in each case very quick to note his own inability to answer and even to acknowledge the shamefulness of that inability in the most important instance. He is astute and courageous in recognizing his own ignorance, which may be a desirable trait in a Socratic pupil.[11]

Still, we must not minimize the extent to which this exchange will appear incongruous to the reader who is expecting to see Socrates converse with one of the shrewdest, most gifted, most impressive politicians Athens ever knew. We can only conclude that the fumbling young man we see here is not yet the clever and capable (albeit immoderate and even reckless) statesman he will eventually become.[12] This conclusion in turn prompts the suggestion that Alcibiades' transformation into the figure we know from Thucydides and elsewhere owes something to the Socratic education that begins in the *Alcibiades*. Could it be that Socrates does ultimately remedy the lack that separates this young Alcibiades from political success, as he appears to have promised he can? The passage we have just been considering may serve as an important example of a kind of Socratic training: Socrates has begun to teach Alcibiades how to categorize human affairs according to the good at which they aim. But it is not yet clear how or whether such an exercise might help improve Alcibiades' understanding of what is needed for political success.

An adequate answer to the question of Socrates' ultimate effect on Alcibiades requires a consideration of more than is given in this dialogue. But we can begin to shed some light on these matters by considering more carefully the examples Socrates employs throughout this discussion of the "better." By using them as analogies, Socrates prompts us to consider the wrestling teacher and the musician as metaphors for the adviser to the Athenian assembly on matters of war and peace. The wrestling teacher demands perfect obedience from his pupil. The training will be difficult, even painful; lapses in dedication, focus, or mental toughness will be met with stern punishment; sometimes, the pupil will benefit from fighting against, losing to, and thus learning from a superior opponent. The general and the wrestling teacher both wish to train the best possible fighters—but can the former, especially in a democracy, reasonably expect to employ the same tactics as the latter without incurring the distrust, even the hatred of the *demos*? Perhaps some knowledge akin to the musician's is required as a supplement. The musical education, as opposed to the gymnastic, revolves around the pleasure human beings take in the perception of beauty. The musician, therefore, has an appreciation of beauty and, above all, an ability to produce it so as to evoke a range of emotional responses in the audience. In this same passage, Socrates suggests that Alcibiades, though not a doctor, would advise that the better with respect to food is "the healthier" (108e5–9)—and yet, as the *Gorgias* teaches us, the chef who argues that the better in food is the more pleasant has a certain advantage over the doctor.[13] Here, then, is an important political lesson Alcibiades may be yet to learn: that the democratic statesman, in addition to being a sound judge of the better and worse for the *polis*, must also be able to appeal rhetorically to the people's admiration of the beautiful or noble (*to kalon*).[14]

This lesson is never learned more fully, however, than when it is founded upon an understanding of one's own concern for the noble, and Socrates now begins to lead Alcibiades toward such an understanding by examining his concern for justice. Alcibiades has agreed that the "better" in matters of war and peace is the more just, albeit with a hint of ambivalence: when Socrates asks, "Against which people will you advise the Athenians to make war, those committing injustice, or those doing the just things?" Alcibiades responds,

"This is a terrible[15] thing you're asking; for even if someone should have in mind that it's necessary to make war against those doing the just things, he surely wouldn't admit it" (109b9–c3). Moreover, while he agrees that his own speeches concerning justice must look to the standards of the lawful and the noble, his final response to Socrates' summary statement that the "better" in all aspects of military decision making is the more just is a lukewarm "it appears so, at least" (109c4–12). Alcibiades is not completely convinced that the better decision in matters of war and peace is always to pursue the more just course of action.

It should be stressed, however, that Alcibiades shows no sign of doubting that when it comes to advising the assembly, he must counsel only what is just, even if he should secretly suppose that waging an unjust war might be better. This marks the first appearance of the central contradiction of the dialogue's first half. Alcibiades believes he must counsel what is more just and that he must counsel what is better, but he is not certain that these are always compatible. Should he come to have the tremendous power that Socrates has suggested may one day be his, how will he decide the fate of a just people if its good should come into conflict with his or the Athenians' own? He is here rather emphatic in agreeing that war against the just, that is, unjust war, will be unlawful (109c4–5). Alcibiades thus displays his belief (inchoate as it may be) that justice is sanctioned by a code of law that stands above the laws created by the lawgivers in the cities—that is, that there is such a thing as natural right—even as he evinces some doubt as to whether it is always possible or advantageous to obey that higher law.[16] At this point, his aversion to open consideration of the advantages of transgressing so awesome a legal prohibition outweighs any impious curiosity. But Alcibiades' hesitation here will help us understand his reaction to the coming refutations.

With the key premises now in place—that all knowledge is either learned or discovered following a recognition of ignorance and that Alcibiades will advise the Athenians in matters of war and peace with an eye to the more just—Socrates is ready to administer the refutation. His goal is to convince Alcibiades that he lacks the knowledge of justice he will need in order to advise the Athenians correctly and thus to achieve political success. Socrates begins by pressing Alcibiades to say who taught him to distinguish the more and less just; Alcibiades' response is to suggest he had no such teacher but sought and discovered the knowledge on his own (109d1–e6). As Socrates reminds him, however, Alcibiades has agreed that he could only have sought to know something of which he supposed himself to be ignorant, and he proves unable to name a time in his life when he did not suppose he had knowledge of the just things and the unjust things (109e7–110d2). Socrates makes this clear by reminding Alcibiades of how, as a child, he would loudly accuse his playmates of injustice in their games. Moreover, Alcibiades now forcefully reaffirms his past judgments: his understanding of the just and unjust has not apparently changed since his childhood.[17] It is the same understanding by which he now identifies deception, coercion, and theft as instances of injustice (109b1–6). We thus acquire an important insight into the foundation of Alcibiades' conception of justice: it is a conception that springs in part from the basic ability to recognize infringements upon one's own good, in combination with some knowledge of the rules or laws that forbid such infringement.[18] If Alcibiades is not exceptional in this regard, but rather a paradigmatic case of the concern for justice, then it seems that human awareness or knowledge of justice has a combination of natural and conventional sources. Perhaps by gaining clarity on the distinction between these sources—and thereby, on the way in which that distinction naturally comes to be blurred in the course of ordinary moral education—one could move toward a more precise understanding of some of the more puzzling paradoxes surrounding the unity and coherence of the idea of justice.[19]

Alcibiades would appear to be refuted. He cannot name a time at which he supposed himself ignorant about justice, and so he cannot claim to know it from having sought it. But he is still, quite understandably, unwilling to accept the bizarre conclusion that he does not know what justice is. He therefore reverts to the possibility that he gained his knowledge of justice from teachers and names as his teachers "the many" (110d5–e1). Against Socrates' objection that the many are not "serious teachers"—they would not even be able to teach such a paltry thing as draughts playing—Alcibiades argues that they, after all, taught him to speak Greek, which is no paltry thing (110e2–111a4). Socrates must now undertake a second refutation. He must demonstrate to Alcibiades that the many, despite their ability to teach Greek, cannot impart knowledge of justice. His strategy in this refutation rests on two considerations: that good teachers know whereof they teach and that wherever there is knowledge, there is agreement concerning what is known (111a11–b10). Socrates argues that the agreement among the many about the meanings of Greek words is indication of their shared knowledge and thus of their competence as teachers. Alcibiades admits, however, that it is precisely over justice that the greatest disagreements arise: how can the many be said to share knowledge of the very thing that drives them to make war upon and kill one another? The many, then, cannot be invoked as adequate teachers of justice. Once again, Alcibiades finds himself refuted (111b11–112d10).

The refutation is sufficient to persuade Alcibiades that the many cannot be trusted to have taught him about justice well or correctly. But Socrates never denies that the many were in fact his teachers, those who provided him with whatever conception of justice he possesses. Alcibiades may have hit upon an important point by suggesting that he learned to recognize justice in something like the way he learned to speak Greek. For does not Alcibiades' knowledge of the words *justice* and *injustice*—and his confidence in his ability correctly to identify instances of these—give him some claim to know what justice and injustice are? Consider Socrates' own example: that the many are knowers of Greek can be seen from the fact that they agree as to what sort of thing *stone* or *wood* is and do not mistakenly reach for one when they desire the other (111b11–c4). Knowledge of any language requires and draws upon, if it cannot quite be reduced to, the ability to recognize the natural similarities and distinctions among beings or the categories into which the language groups them. To know a word and to be able to use it correctly, then, would seem to be to have knowledge of the underlying category represented by the word. Admittedly, this type of knowledge does not rise to the standard of *science* (*epistēmē*), but neither is it nothing at all. Why can Alcibiades not claim that he knows *justice* just as he knows *stone* or *wood*?

The answer contained explicitly in Socrates' refutation is not altogether conclusive. To illustrate that nothing is so fiercely contested among the many as justice, Socrates points to battles in which Athens has fought, including the battle in which Alcibiades' father was killed, and to the conflicts presented in Homer: the Trojan War in the case of the *Iliad* and Odysseus's confrontation with Penelope's suitors in the *Odyssey*. But do these examples prove Socrates' point? One could argue that it is not justice but love and the jealousy it begets that give rise to the Homeric conflicts (cf. 111e11–112a9 with *Greater Hippias* 294c8–d2).[20] As for the Athenian defeats at Tanagra and Coronea, both were results of Athenian attempts to extend and consolidate power in Boeotia. Of course, claims about justice enter into all of these conflicts at some point, and our understanding of them cannot be complete without consideration of those claims. But reflection upon Socrates' examples prompts us to ask why claims of justice have the character he indicates. That is, what causes the confusion whereby people fiercely disagree over what constitutes the just resolution of a dispute? Why does the same education that taught them to tell a stick from a stone not now serve them in distinguishing justice from injustice?

Some light is shed on this matter by Socrates' other examples of things about which the many disagree. He has Alcibiades consider, "If we wished to know not only what sorts of things human beings or horses are, but also which of them are skilled at running (*dromikoi*) and which not, would the many still be capable of teaching this?" and then, "If we wished to know not only what sorts of things human beings are, but what kinds are healthy and sick, would the many then be capable teachers for us?" (111d6–9, e4–6). Alcibiades agrees in both cases that the disagreement of the many on these matters is sufficient evidence of their being poor teachers of them. But what are the sources of the disagreements? Note an important difference between the two questions: in the first case, the many are asked to say which particular human beings or horses are skilled at running; in the second, they are asked to describe healthy and sick human beings in general. Each requires a kind of comparison. The first requires a comparison of individual people or horses; the second requires a comparison of classes, of one kind of human being (viz., the healthy kind) to its opposite. Now, the many disagree about who is a skilled runner because the prize of honor is at stake. Proud athletes and boasters alike, as well as their families and other supporters, will raise claims to their own skill and disparage potential competitors. The many disagree about the healthy and the sick, on the other hand, because, while there is much at stake for them in this knowledge, they lack the scientific expertise, possessed by the doctor, to be able to identify the essential characteristics of health and sickness.[21]

Each of these examples shares something important with the case of justice. As with skill in running, people and cities will insist on the superiority of their own claims to justice, sometimes at the expense of clarity or honesty concerning others' similar claims. The notion that a war could go some ways toward adjudicating between conflicting claims of justice in the way that a race might be held to determine who is fastest seems bizarre. It has some plausibility only when we consider that in both races and wars, the Greeks tended to believe that the outcomes were determined by the gods. But would the gods really need to do anything in order for the fastest person to win the race, or would their intervention only serve to indicate their favorite?[22] The gods' reasons for favoring one army over another in war are among the most important themes of Homer's *Iliad*, to which Socrates has referred. It is sufficient to say that in either a race or a war, the outcome often seems insufficient to determine the matter in question. One may win a race for other reasons than that one is the best at running, to say nothing of the reasons for which a city might win a war.[23]

There would presumably be less confusion regarding justice if the obstacles to judging correctly were fewer and less grave. The matter is often clouded by the way in which the pursuit of honor and advantage tend to direct claims of justice. But moreover, as with health and sickness, people in general do not give sustained attention to the question of what are the key distinguishing factors separating the just from the unjust. Of course, there are many cases in which most people will easily be able to tell the difference between actual healthy and sick human beings, just as Alcibiades was able to identify deception, coercion, and theft as kinds of injustice. But just as the ability to identify correctly an instance of wood or stone is still far from a complete or scientific understanding of either, so the awareness that a particular act is unjust can be quite independent of any clear knowledge of what makes it so. Our facility with language is deceptive in this way, as the ability to identify members of a class may give the false impression of having an understanding of what unifies the class. It is precisely the extent to which Alcibiades does have some claim to knowledge of justice that prevents him from recognizing his lack of *epistēmē*. And yet, while knowledge of justice in particular, as opposed to stone or wood, is particularly urgent because of how much our good seems to depend on being just, the first book of the *Republic* illustrates that coming up with a clear, consistent definition of justice and injustice proves to be a puzzling and frustrating challenge. It requires long, painstaking study in which most people never engage.[24] One important prerequisite of such a study would be skill in dialectics, that is, the ability to analyze carefully and precisely abstract concepts in speech. This may have been indicated by Socrates' reference to the inability of the many to teach draughts playing.[25]

But we must keep in mind that the confusion of the many concerning justice, their disagreements born of competition over honors and other prizes and from lack of clarity in understanding, only make them *bad* teachers of justice. It does nothing to dispose of the possibility that Alcibiades is right in naming them as his teachers. This means that these confusions and disagreements exist not only between individuals and cities but even within individuals since their education comes precisely from the disagreeing many. For example, Alcibiades believes that unjust war is both unlawful and, at least sometimes, necessary. This is not to say that the just and unjust are taught simply at random. As Socrates quietly reminds us, there are impressive figures who are influential in the formation of conventional opinion concerning justice, such as Homer, who claimed to have been divinely inspired (112a10–b4). But it does mean that Alcibiades is certain to hold hazy and conflicting opinions of justice that he has never adequately expressed or examined. We might praise Alcibiades for his quickness in acknowledging the problem Socrates exposes: he does not object to the suggestion that the battle of Coronea is evidence of the ignorance of the many. That is, he does not respond in spirited defense of the justice of the cause for which his father fought and died. Perhaps the facts that he hardly knew his father and that he has come to revere his adopted father Pericles so highly (see *sumpantōn*, 104b3) make that psychological obstacle less significant. But Alcibiades still has a long way to go before he can turn to a clear-sighted examination of his own ignorance or confusions. For, as the next exchange reveals, Alcibiades does not yet appreciate the full gravity of the refutation he has just undergone.

Upon careful reflection, these Socratic refutations contain a wealth of insight into Alcibiades' concern for justice and indeed into the human concern for justice generally—so much so that Socrates cannot expect Alcibiades to appreciate all of it in the course of the discussion. It seems that Plato's writing is intended both to maintain a clear logic and meaning internal to the dialogue and to provide the reader with food for thought that Socrates' interlocutors cannot reasonably have time to digest. Or perhaps Socrates is planting suggestions and insinuations like seeds in Alcibiades' mind so that certain questions will naturally arise as Alcibiades later reflects on the conversation. If so, we may wonder whether some of the insights we have gleaned into the character of justice from this conversation are ones that Socrates helps Alcibiades elaborate in later conversations, ones that take place out of view between the conversations represented in Plato's dialogues. In any case, we are now able to move forward in this dialogue with a greater appreciation of the character of Alcibiades' concern for and confusion about justice and law. Next, Alcibiades must deal with the paradoxical assertion that he lacks knowledge of the just and unjust things.

## Alcibiades Rebels (Exhortation, 112e1–113d8)

Socrates has performed two refutations, each one purporting to conclude that Alcibiades cannot have knowledge of justice. Given his earlier agreement that the "better" in war and peace is the more just, Alcibiades should now be faced with the troubling conclusion that he is unfit to lead the Athenians. But Alcibiades subtly evinces some skepticism as to whether Socrates' refutations have established what they claim to have established, which Socrates astutely detects. When Socrates attempts to drive the refutation home by asking how it could be likely that Alcibiades knows the just and unjust things, Alcibiades responds, "From the things *you* say, it is not likely" (112d7–10; emphasis added). Socrates recognizes from this response that Alcibiades has not fully accepted the conclusion that he is ignorant about the just and unjust things. He does not consider his own opinions to have been the objects of the preceding examination. Socrates must therefore provide Alcibiades with some preliminary instruction on the meaning, method, and purpose of Socratic refutation. Only then will Alcibiades be able to recognize the course of action prescribed by the refutation's revelation of his ignorance. Thus, this Socratic explanation amounts to an exhortation, a counsel to respond to the refutation with the appropriate measures.

Socrates clarifies for Alcibiades one of the basic precepts of Socratic refutation: it is the answerer, not the questioner, who endorses the opinions put forth in the course of the discussion (113a7–b7). Socrates makes no mention of this principle's important corollary, that the questioner never claims to be revealing his own opinions concerning the matter at hand.[26] It is therefore not Socrates but "Alcibiades, the beautiful son of Kleinias," who has himself concluded, in answering Socrates' questions, that he "does not know about just and unjust things, but supposes he does, and intends to go to counsel the Athenians in the assembly about things he does not know" (113b8–11). Despite his beauty and his family, it has come to light that Alcibiades is not fit for political rule. When Alcibiades halfheartedly accepts this conclusion, Socrates sharpens and repeats it: Alcibiades, according to his own opinion, has "in mind to undertake a crazy undertaking . . . to teach things that [he does] not know, not having taken care to learn them" (113c5–7). This formulation seems to point to a simple solution to the problem that has been discovered: Alcibiades must attempt to learn about the just and unjust things before entering politics. The sensible thing, given the stated purpose of the conversation, would be for Alcibiades to turn to Socrates as a teacher, and we expect Socrates to exhort him, or to continue to exhort him, to do just that.

But Socrates has chosen a strange manner in which to clarify Alcibiades' deficiency in this passage. He seems to have gone out of his way to embarrass Alcibiades, reexplaining the folly of his ambition in harsher terms, calling it "crazy" (*manikon*), even after Alcibiades has owned up to it. He makes it painfully clear that the refutations have not been mere exercises in dialectic but an affront to Alcibiades' sense of worth since they purport to make his belief that he deserves the greatest honor from the Athenians utterly untenable. Perhaps it should be no surprise, then, that Alcibiades does not at this moment turn to Socrates for guidance but rather rebels against him and his refutation. He flees the deeply troubling conclusion upon which Socrates is insisting by rejecting one of its core premises: that the more just is the "better" in matters of war and peace. Now Alcibiades appears ready to embrace a more cynical position: "I suppose, Socrates, that Athenians and the other Greeks rarely deliberate as to whether [things are] more just or more unjust; for they believe that such things are clear, so they let them go and consider which will be advantageous to those doing them. For I suppose that the just things and the advantageous things are not the same, but that it has profited many to commit great injustices, and I suppose that for others who did just things, there was no advantage" (113d1–8).

This outburst brings to mind Alcibiades' agreement, or rather his qualification of the agreement, that he would never advise the Athenians to make war against the just (109c1–3). Then, it seemed Alcibiades was aware that such a war might be deemed "necessary" but effectively denied that its necessity also made it "better" (109c12). Now it is clear that Alcibiades believes such a war could well be advantageous to the instigators despite its being unjust. Does the more advantageous necessarily take precedence over the more just in the determination of "the better"? The obfuscation of this question is a crucial element of the coming refutation.

At this moment, however, we are faced with an interpretive challenge. What is the status, within Alcibiades' own thinking, of the opinion or set of opinions he has just expressed? It may be tempting to think this is an expression of Alcibiades' true view and his earlier acquiescence to the claim that the more just is the better in war and peace was but a part of his sly silence concerning his actual, immoral or amoral opinion. On this interpretation, Alcibiades here reveals that he is more sophisticated and cynical than he had previously let on and that, in fact, he thinks of himself as having "seen through" the concern for justice in politics.[27] But if Alcibiades had been so cautiously concealing his lack of concern for justice, what is it that now causes him to reveal his true position? Perhaps Socrates' aggressive insistence on the refutation's damning conclusion has caused a lapse in Alcibiades' judgment. The contemptuous accusation that he is mad for thinking himself capable of advising the assembly provokes the prideful Alcibiades to an imprudent boast—like a criminal who foolishly explains how cleverly he executed a heist because someone has accused him of being too stupid ever to have pulled it off.

But this interpretation is in need of some correction. The *Alcibiades* as a whole does little if anything to support the notion that Alcibiades is or considers himself to be the sophisticated Athenian whose worldview is marked by the conscious rejection of any necessity, religious or otherwise, to make his political decisions and actions conform to the requirements of justice. Certainly, Athens was home to such men, and the mature Alcibiades was one of them. One need only think of the nameless Athenian envoys who prosecute the "Melian Dialogue" presented by Thucydides (v.85–112; cf. i.75–76, ii.63.2)—a dialogue enigmatically juxtaposed with Alcibiades' generalship[28]—to recall that the city of Athens at its imperial height appeared to be carrying out a daring experiment in hard-nosed political realism. It is clear enough even in the *Alcibiades* that Alcibiades has been affected by this element of his political, cultural, and intellectual surroundings. But Athens was also home to powerful pious sentiments throughout the course of the Peloponnesian War, as Thucydides' narratives convey.[29] Socrates' critique of the many as teachers of justice pointed precisely to the fact that the Athenians were not simply divided into well-defined rival camps concerning justice but were in disagreement with themselves even as individuals—an account that helps make sense of the Athenian vacillations between daring and dread such as they experienced, for example, in the Mytilenian affair (Thucydides iii.49). This inconsistent, even incoherent jumble of beliefs and opinions concerning justice, which Socrates is in the process of exposing within Alcibiades' soul, is what Alcibiades has inherited from the many.

But this means that the cynical view of justice and advantage to which Alcibiades has just given voice is not the fruit of any careful investigation on his part. It is rather one strand in the complex web of opinions and dispositions that has been formed in Alcibiades by the city. For all we know, this is the first time Alcibiades has allowed himself to say these things aloud. So much might be indicated by the fact that Alcibiades thrice qualifies his remarks with "I suppose" (*oimai*), adding a note of tentativeness to his short speech. That these are Alcibiades' own impressions, or the views he inherited from the many, is worth emphasizing from one more point of view. Nowhere in the discussion of Alcibiades' teachers, either in general or with specific reference to his knowledge of justice, is it ever suggested that he has learned anything from the sophists. Indeed, it is made explicit by Socrates that

Alcibiades visited no teachers other than those who taught him to write, to play the cithara, and to wrestle (106e7–9).[30]

As Alcibiades himself emphasizes, he believes the realist view he here espouses to be the common view not only of the Athenians but also of the rest of the Greeks; it is not a view that he thinks is reserved to the shrewd minority who have thought things through. That is, Alcibiades understands himself to be saying no more than what he takes to be obvious to anyone. His appeal is to readily available empirical evidence. Is it not clear that the unjust often prosper? And if being just sometimes means accepting crushing defeat, how can the more just be the better in war and peace? Alcibiades has not been goaded or tricked into revealing a hidden amoralism or cynicism that he inwardly views as his firm and abiding conviction. Rather, we see here his forceful reaction against the intensely distressing conclusion Socrates is pushing him to accept—that he would be mad to think himself a capable adviser—a reaction that relies upon and takes refuge in an argument not without force but that also requires a certain frightening or shameful brazenness that would otherwise prevent him from espousing it. This is probably not the first time Alcibiades has reflected upon the disturbing discrepancy between justice and advantage, but that is not to say he has yet been hardened or jaded by the observation. He is not the criminal who is tricked into confessing. He is more like a man who, having apparently run out of decent means to obtain success, turns with desperate, indignant defiance, but also with trepidation, to the illicit deeds by means of which, he has long suspected in secret, scoundrels often prosper.[31]

The result of his taking this stand is the apparently premature curtailing of the exhortation. It would seem that Alcibiades has failed to face up to the result of the refutations, and so Socrates must mount a new attempt to prove Alcibiades' deficiency and his own ability to resolve it. Before turning to that renewed attempt, however, we might pause to consider whether Socrates' account of the meaning of the refutations (that is, that they are nothing more than expositions of the refuted interlocutor's opinions) is satisfactory. Socrates quietly indicates that the claim is dubious through his reference to Euripides' *Hippolytus*. He paraphrases the line, spoken by Phaedra to her nurse, "These things you hear from yourself, not from me" (*Hippolytus*, 352). In the play, Phaedra has at length provided her nurse with enough clues to guess her dark secret. Socrates, then, suggests that it has indeed been he who has, by subtly guiding Alcibiades in the discussion, allowed him to arrive at a conclusion Socrates himself has had in mind from the start (compare *Meno* 82b9–85c1).

By downplaying his role in Alcibiades' arrival at the conclusions he reaches, Socrates diverts attention away from the question of his own motivation.[32] Hence, in recognizing the inadequacy or incompleteness of Socrates' account of the meaning, method, and purpose of his refutations, we are bound to be struck by this puzzling but crucial question: what is Socrates really up to?

It is Socrates' exhortations in the *Alcibiades* which, by stepping back from the refutations and purporting to explain them, most prompt this line of questioning. It is also in the exhortations that Plato begins quietly to provide some answers to the reader most likely to have taken up that questioning. This first exhortation is extremely brief. As we have said, Alcibiades' rebellion interrupts it before its exhortative character is even made explicit. Accordingly, we are given only the faintest hints here as to the character of Socrates' project. These are provided in the two hypothetical conversations Socrates describes as examples of the fact that it is the answerer and not the questioner who makes assertions in the discussion. In these conversations, Socrates asks Alcibiades about the relative magnitudes of the one and the two and about the letters in "Socrates" (112e10–3a6). What might it mean for these hypothetical conversations to be metaphors for the actual conversation that has just taken place? The question of the relative magnitudes of the one and the two, while apparently trivial, is one that represented an important stumbling block and key transitional phase in Socrates' own philosophic development as he recounts it in the *Phaedo* (97a1–b3). It would seem, then, there is an important question at stake in the subject matter under discussion, which Alcibiades is not yet able to recognize. What might that question concern? Again, we are given only a maddeningly vague wisp of a clue in the suggestion that the discussion may be analogous to one about the letters in Socrates' name: perhaps Socrates is attempting to investigate something about himself.

## Alcibiades Chastened (Speech, 113d9–114b3)

Socrates has ostensibly set out to show Alcibiades that he cannot fulfill his political ambitions without first acquiring knowledge only Socrates can provide, namely, knowledge of the better in war and peace. When that was said to be the more just, Socrates tried to show Alcibiades that he lacked knowledge of justice. But Alcibiades has now petulantly disowned his answer of "the more just" in favor of "the more advantageous," and so the logic of the refutation would seem to dictate that Socrates must show him that he lacks knowledge of advantage. When Socrates begins to suggest that this is what he intends, Alcibiades responds sneeringly, "For what prevents me [from having such knowledge], Socrates? Unless you will ask me again from whom I learned it or how I found it myself" (113d9–e4). By mocking the Socratic procedure of seeking to evaluate his political credentials through the identification of the source of his knowledge, Alcibiades effectively contests the validity of the preceding refutations—not from careful reflection on the soundness of their logic but as a result of his indignation at what they imply about his worth. Socrates, in turn, launches into a scathing rebuke of Alcibiades' childish petulance, in which he first insists he will press Alcibiades to say where he obtained his knowledge of the advantageous and likens Alcibiades' threats to reject this approach to the tantrum of a spoiled brat (113e5–114a4). But Socrates then suddenly and perplexingly changes course, saying now that it is a foregone conclusion that Alcibiades "will not be able to demonstrate that [he knows] the advantageous either from having found it, or from having learned it," and that being "fickle" or "effeminate" (*truphais*) as he is, Alcibiades would no longer "taste the same argument with pleasure." Therefore, says Socrates, he will let the question of Alcibiades' knowledge of the advantageous go and instead ask him to prove "whether the same things are both just and advantageous or not" (114a4–b3). The overall impression of Socrates' harangue, then, is that he could have succeeded by applying the same refutation again with advantage in the place of justice but that he will provide a new set of considerations in deference to Alcibiades' shamefully childish and unmanly rebellion—perhaps even implying that Socrates must be wary of pushing the conversation in too unpleasing a direction lest Alcibiades refuse to continue (cf. 104d7–e3).

But as the sequel will show, Socrates' rebuke is quite effective in getting Alcibiades to own up to his shameful behavior. With Alcibiades having been effectively chastened and subdued, Socrates might well have proceeded down the path he insists Alcibiades refuses to travel: a refutation of Alcibiades' claim to know the advantageous. It thus becomes clear that the change of course in Socrates' speech is not in fact a concession to Alcibiades' recalcitrance since this has been effectively overcome. Rather, Socrates has in mind to expose not just any ignorance in Alcibiades but specifically his ignorance concerning justice: it would not suit Socrates' purpose to refute him simply on the question of advantage, even though it would show, as much as the last refutation, Alcibiades' unreadiness for political life. As we will see, it is precisely Socrates' new question, that of the *relationship* between justice and advantage, that he wants his next refutation to address. Thus, we should not understand this short speech and the preceding short exhortation as results of Alcibiades' failure to appreciate the upshot of the first refutations. It now seems that Socrates *wanted* to bring about Alcibiades' rebellion because it allows him to plunge deeper into the heart of Alcibiades' confusion concerning justice and thereby most fully to awaken him to the gravity of his ignorance.

## The Problem of the Noble and the Good (Refutations, 114b4–116e4)

Socrates' harsh rebuke succeeds in subduing the indignant Alcibiades, whose reaction is rather like that of a shamefaced child: he recognizes with some embarrassment the childishness of the rebellion for which Socrates has berated him. Thus, he replies sheepishly to Socrates' demand to provide him with a demonstration of the sameness or difference of just and advantageous things, admitting his inability to do so (114b4–5). But Alcibiades' shame is not restricted to the way he has behaved: he also appears to regret the morally questionable position he adopted. Thus, when Socrates insists that he defend the thesis that "the just is sometimes not advantageous," Alcibiades calls him "hubristic" (114d5–7). Socrates' *hubris* here lies partly in his aggression toward Alcibiades but perhaps more importantly in his willingness openly to discuss and to explore the possible advantages of injustice. Alcibiades has evinced some awareness of the amoral component of Athenian imperial politics, which he has sketched in an extreme form. But Socrates easily succeeds in calling Alcibiades' hubristic bluff by challenging him to elaborate the brazenly amoral position he has espoused. Alcibiades' discomfort regarding the possible advantageousness of injustice is now such that he no longer wishes to stand by his new claim, and he seems to plead for Socrates to stop pushing him to do so. In fact, the sting of the refutations and of Socrates' scolding are enough to make Alcibiades want to recoil from the discussion altogether. When Socrates proposes to demonstrate "the opposite" of Alcibiades' claim about justice and advantage, Alcibiades at first declines to resume his role as answerer; it is his desire "to be most persuaded" of the advantageousness of justice that draws Alcibiades back into the discussion (114d8–115a1). Hence we can see that Alcibiades really does have an aversion to the opposition of the just and the advantageous he has presented. He is eager to learn of its refutation from Socrates, as is Glaucon, albeit more fervently, in the *Republic*.[33]

Something remarkable emerges in Alcibiades' eagerness to learn from Socrates here. He is now motivated by the moral gravity of the question of justice in a manner at least partially independent from his political ambition. Just as Socrates' decision to take up the question of the relationship between justice and advantage—rather than that of Alcibiades' knowledge of advantage simply—signals a Socratic intention separate from his claim to be able to bring Alcibiades' hopes to completion, Alcibiades' eagerness to pursue this new Socratic question reveals his desire to learn something from Socrates besides what had apparently been promised. This second part of the dialogue, therefore, represents the peak of what we might call Alcibiades' philosophic curiosity. As if to remind us of how apparently distinct this is from what Alcibiades really needs in order to succeed politically, the brief exchange following Socrates' short speech highlights a blind spot from which Alcibiades suffers throughout the dialogue: he does not recognize the difference between teaching and persuading (cf. 113c5–7). He naïvely agrees that since the assembly is made up of individuals, persuading them of the difference between justice and advantage is no different than persuading Socrates, just as a grammarian or a mathematician "persuades" one about the things he knows in the same way he would "persuade" many (114b6–d3). Alcibiades does not understand, has perhaps not even considered, the purpose or power of rhetoric (cf. *Gorgias* 455a2–7). But will his Socratic education in justice somehow help him recognize and remedy that deficiency after all?

Socrates is now ready to refute Alcibiades' claim that the just is sometimes disadvantageous. The change Socrates wants to effect on Alcibiades' position is represented in Figure 1: whereas Alcibiades begins by claiming to believe that the just is sometimes advantageous and sometimes not, Socrates must persuade him that the just is always advantageous. Socrates' strategy can be discerned from the beginning: he immediately introduces the noble, the

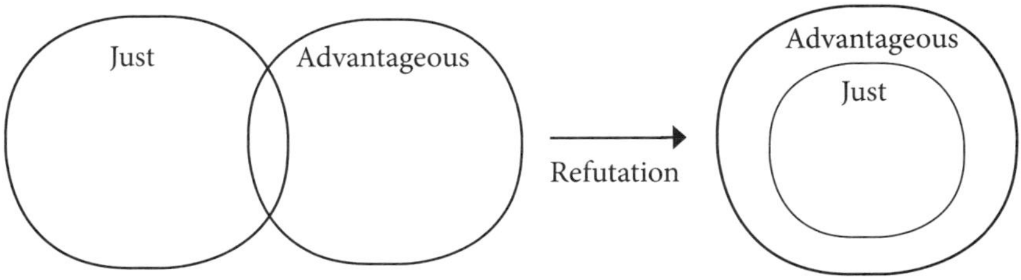


Figure 1. Socrates' Task

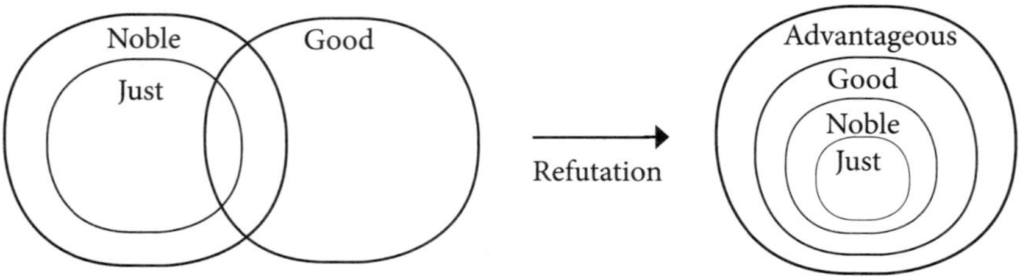


Figure 2. Socrates' Setup

shameful, and the good into the discussion, quickly obtaining Alcibiades' agreement that "all just things are also noble" and never shameful. However, Alcibiades claims to think that noble things are sometimes good and sometimes bad—apparently identifying what is at the crux of his opinion that the just is not always advantageous (115a3–16). Socrates thus shifts the terms of the discussion from justice and advantage to nobility and goodness. The refutation he needs to carry out now is represented in Figure 2. In short, Socrates must demonstrate to Alcibiades—or, rather, show Alcibiades that he already believes—that the noble is always good, and then add the apparently unobjectionable claim that the good is always advantageous. If he can do this, the syllogism will be irresistible: the just is noble, the noble is good, and the good is advantageous; therefore the just is advantageous.

The crux of the matter has thus become Alcibiades' professed belief that some noble things are bad. Ostensibly to clarify what Alcibiades has in mind, Socrates asks whether he means something like "saving comrades or relatives in war" since those who do this are often wounded or killed while those who shirk their duties escape unscathed (115b1–3). Alcibiades affirms that this is the sort of thing he means and agrees also that what is noble in such a deed is the courage, the attempt to save those in need, while death and wounds constitute what is bad (115b4–10).[34] Socrates is thus enabled emphatically to separate courage from death. The former, Alcibiades asserts, is among the greatest good things, the things he most wants for himself—he would "choose not to live if [he] were a coward"—while the latter is among the worst evils. "Life and courage are therefore most opposed to death and cowardice" (115c1–d14). Alcibiades' acceptance of this opposition is the key to the refutation. Socrates makes him see that when we speak of the nobility of saving friends, we are referring precisely to what we admire and honor in that act, and so precisely what we think is good in it—namely, the courage. By highlighting Alcibiades' ardent belief in the goodness of courage or manliness (*andreia*), Socrates is able to draw out his deep conviction that nobility as such—that is, abstracting from any adverse side effects that may happen to coincide with this or that particular noble deed—is always good (115e1–116b1). That the noble is always good is precisely the conclusion Socrates needs to reach; if Alcibiades would accept the additional claim that the good is always advantageous, Socrates could now wrap up his proof that the just is always advantageous.

And yet the manner of Alcibiades' agreement to the conclusion that "none of the noble things, insofar as it is noble, is bad, nor is any of the shameful things, insofar as it is shameful, good," betrays a half-conscious reservation: he answers only, "it appears not" (116a10–b1). To see the likely source of Alcibiades' vaguely felt uncertainty, it is helpful to consider the role of the shameful in the argument. The shameful here calls for special attention because Socrates introduces it along with the noble at the beginning of the refutation but then makes no mention of it until the conclusion just quoted. By largely leaving out the shameful, Socrates obscures an important logical implication of the argument to which he barely points in saying, "If indeed you call [the action of dying and being courageous] bad insofar as it accomplishes a bad, it must also be called good insofar as it accomplishes a good . . . and therefore, noble insofar as it is good, and shameful insofar as it is bad" (115e15–116a4). This would mean that dying, even to save a friend in war, is *shameful*.[35] Yet this immediately strikes us as incongruous: such a death, as Alcibiades would likely agree, is considered supremely noble. But Socrates' key move in the refutation is to deny that death is noble and to say rather that courage is noble and death is bad. As reasonable as this may have seemed at first glance, we must now admit that it fundamentally distorts our experience of the noble. Courageous actions are noble, not despite the dangers they entail and the sacrifices for which they call but precisely because of them. The separation of courage and death to which Alcibiades agrees would seem to contain the thought that acting nobly would be infinitely better if one could only be sure that no sacrifice would be required. But if it were not a call to sacrifice, the action would not be noble. The apparent goodness of nobility springs paradoxically from its badness—or rather, from its badness for oneself.[36] There is an appropriate ambiguity in Socrates' speaking of the good or bad elements of noble or shameful actions: good or bad for whom?

The paradox of the noble consists in the noble's somehow being good for oneself because it requires one to abandon or sacrifice one's own good for the sake of a good that is not one's own. But Socrates leaves virtually all of this unsaid, making clear only that Alcibiades understands the noble to be good and going so far as to suggest that any badness for oneself, any sacrifice, is utterly opposed to the noble. That Alcibiades agrees weakly to the conclusion, then, is not altogether surprising: he is forced to admit that he believes the noble to be good, and yet something about Socrates' presentation must seem to him strangely out of joint with his experience.

As we have seen, Socrates is now in a position easily to conclude the syllogism whereby the just is proven to be advantageous. Before doing so, however, he takes a detour in order to draw out some more implications of Alcibiades' belief that the noble is good. Independently of the preceding refutation, Socrates exposes Alcibiades' belief that those who act nobly "act well" or prosper (*eu prattein*), and that this living nobly or beautifully and well or prosperously provides one with good things and thereby with happiness (*eudaimonia*) (116b2–10). The independence of these conclusions from the preceding refutation indicates that Alcibiades' love of courage is not the only source of his belief in the goodness of nobility. He also believes in a more general way that one cannot live well without being noble and that good things will come to those who do good and noble things. So little are the good and the noble distinguished in this realm of Alcibiades' thinking and belief that failing to notice Socrates' specious logic, he here agrees that the good and the noble are in fact "the same" (116c1–5). But what is revealed most powerfully by this digression is that there is more at stake for Alcibiades in the Socratic refutations than his political career. The very possibility of his obtaining happiness now appears to hang on these questions of the noble and the good.

Socrates finally leads Alcibiades to the conclusion: the good things, Alcibiades affirms, are advantageous, and since the noble things are good and the just things are noble, the just things must be advantageous (116c7–d4). Again, Alcibiades' agreement is rather weak: "It's likely." And then, when Socrates asks whether Alcibiades was not the answerer in the refutation, he says only, "I appear to be, as is likely" (116d5–6). But Alcibiades gives proper expression to his uncertainty only once Socrates pushes him to draw the conclusion that anyone who claims that "the just things are sometimes bad" in advising his city is laughable (116d7–e1). The refutation, which relied heavily on Alcibiades' admiration of courage rather than justice, shifted the conversation's focus to Alcibiades' deep sense that noble virtue could make him happy. In doing so, it abstracted from the question of sound political counsel that sparked it. Now that Socrates reintroduces that question, Alcibiades becomes utterly confused:

"But, by the gods, Socrates, I myself don't know what I mean, but I really seem to be in a strange condition; for when you question me, it seems to me one way at one time, and another at another" (116e2–4). On one hand, Alcibiades admits that the refutation has genuinely exposed his belief that it is good to be noble. On the other hand, he can no more deny now than before the empirical evidence to which he then alluded, to the effect that it is often the unjust who appear to prosper—a consideration that, as noted above, plays a crucial role in providing hard-nosed rationalizations for the audacious policies of imperial Athens. Alcibiades' admission of confusion about justice is the most significant recognition of ignorance the Platonic Alcibiades ever expresses. Socrates must now turn to exhortation so that Alcibiades can be made to see what is called for by such recognition. Before turning to that section, however, we may note that Socrates never fully elaborates the paradoxical character of the noble. It is apparently not his way to lay such things out with total clarity. Rather, he has allowed Alcibiades to recognize a problem by bringing two of his contrary opinions about an important matter to light. Much of the work of examining and dissecting those opinions is thus left to the Socratic pupil, and Alcibiades' ultimate success or failure as such a pupil may be determined in large part by his ability and willingness to carry out thoroughly the necessary analysis of his own beliefs and hopes.

## Alcibiades Fails a Key Socratic Test (Exhortation, 116e5–119c1)

Socrates' exhortation largely leaves behind the substance of the refutation that precedes it and instead takes up an analysis of the disorienting effect the refutation has had on Alcibiades. In this way, Socrates signals that his goal all along has been to elicit the admission of confusion that Alcibiades has just expressed. Socrates now turns to a new question: what would cause someone to answer unwillingly the same question differently at different times, as Alcibiades has? First, he notes that such a person would have to be ignorant of the subject matter in question; Alcibiades' "wandering" (*planasthai*) on the questions of the just, the noble, the good, and the advantageous imply that he lacks knowledge of these things (116e5–117a11). But lack of knowledge is not by itself enough to cause this kind of wandering since someone who is *aware* of lacking knowledge will simply defer to the expert. Alcibiades agrees that he would turn his work over to a chef or a ship's pilot rather than form wandering opinions about how to cook or which way to turn the rudder (117b1–d5). Moreover, continues Socrates, this distinction between recognized and unrecognized ignorance helps us understand the phenomenon of error. For those who err "are surely not the knowers," nor are they those who, knowing they are ignorant, turn their work over to experts. It is those who act with the false opinion that they know what they are doing who are ignorant of their own ignorance and make mistakes; those who are thus ignorant of the greatest things do the greatest harm and are the most shameful. Alcibiades cannot name subjects greater than those about which his own opinions have been wandering—viz., what are "just, noble, good, and advantageous"—and so he admits with concern that he himself has been falsely presuming to know the greatest things (117d6–118b3).

Socrates concludes that Alcibiades "dwells[s] in the utmost stupidity (*amathia*), as the argument, as well as [Alcibiades himself] accuses [him]," and that this is why Alcibiades "rush[es] toward the political things before having been educated" (118b4–8). The ground has been laid for Socrates to draw the conclusion toward which he has been driving: Alcibiades, ignorant of the greatest things, is unready for political life, bound in fact to commit the most egregious blunders if he does not first seek education. Now, in order to make good on his promise and to ensure that Alcibiades turns to him for the education he needs, Socrates must prove that only he can provide it.[37] But this requirement surprisingly entails a kind of undermining of Socrates' claim to Alcibiades' devotion. For by claiming that no one else possesses the wisdom Socrates has to impart, Socrates must imply that Athens's most distinguished and revered statesmen have succeeded despite their lack of this Socratic wisdom. In an ironic twist, Socrates' claim to be Athens's sole educator calls into question the value of his education—unless, that is, Alcibiades has become sufficiently convinced of the sovereign importance and urgency of the ignorance Socrates has revealed in him.

Socrates thus proceeds to claim that "the many of those doing the things of this city" suffer from the same ignorance as Alcibiades, "except for a few, perhaps including your guardian, Pericles" (118a8–c2). The mention of Pericles triggers an insight for Alcibiades. He notes that Pericles is said to have become wise by association with "many wise men, including Pythocleides and Anaxagoras," and that "even now, at his age," he spends time with Damon for this reason (118c3–6). It seems that Alcibiades—who, we recall, has not himself spent time with sophists (106e7–9)—suddenly realizes why actual and aspiring statesmen would want to spend time in study: successful politicians have acquired some knowledge or skill that the rest do not possess. This may be as close as Alcibiades comes in this dialogue to recognizing his need to learn rhetoric (cf. *Phaedrus* 270a3–8). But as soon as Alcibiades shares his insight, Socrates turns against Pericles, and sets out to show that the illustrious statesman is not in fact among the wise. He argues that the wise must be able to make others wise—that "it is a beautiful sign that the knowers know whenever they are able to produce another knower." But Alcibiades is unable to name anyone whom Pericles has made wiser, including himself (118c7–119a7).[38] Now, besides being his guardian, Pericles is the model for Alcibiades' political ambition (104b3–9, 105a7 ff.). If he of all people is not wise, then Socrates would appear to be the only point of light on Alcibiades' horizon. Socrates is therefore ready to ask Alcibiades, "What, then, do you intend to do about yourself? Will you let yourself be as you are now, or take some care [of yourself]?" (119a8–9).

But Alcibiades fails the test. He concludes that since the others in the city are as uneducated as he is, there is no need to prepare and to learn so as to compete with them: "for I know well that, with my nature, I will very greatly surpass them" (119b1–c1). The weight of the refutations no longer presses on his thoughts, and his habitual senses of self-sufficiency and preeminence, no longer challenged, have come rushing back.[39] In fact, his complacency may now be even stronger than it was before, for his exposure to Socrates' critique of the statesmen has given him new grounds for believing that his natural gifts will be enough to propel him to the greatest political heights. Alcibiades' disappointing failure to seek a Socratic education may not, therefore, be the worst of Socrates' problems at present. The one thing that stood between Alcibiades and his pursuit of the vision Socrates had presented in his opening speeches was the suggestion that such a vision could not be realized without Socrates' help. But now that safeguard is gone, and Socrates may have to attempt to curb some of the more dangerous desires he inflamed at the dialogue's opening. Otherwise, it would be difficult to exonerate Socrates of the charge that he made Alcibiades more brazen, more irreverent, and hungrier for power than he had been before.

Alcibiades' failure here marks the midpoint of the dialogue and its most significant pivot. In the section that follows, there are indications that Socrates is starting over with Alcibiades. We shall have to evaluate the extent to which Socrates' renewed attempt to prove his worth to Alcibiades will be guided by the need to reverse some of the more questionable effects of his first attempt. We must admit, however, that it will be difficult to say whether Socrates is changing course so long as we are still uncertain as to what his intentions were to begin with. Alcibiades appears to have failed a Socratic test, but what was Socrates hoping to achieve had he passed? Again, answers to these questions, prompted by the exhortation, are suggested in the exhortation itself. Let us therefore turn back to the exhortation with an eye to discovering something more about Socrates' intention.

In the course of the exhortation, Socrates divides the nonknowers into two classes: those who are aware of their ignorance and those who are not. He does not do likewise for the knowers (117e9–118a3). Why not? Because one cannot be ignorant of the fact that one knows something: if one knows *x*, one *knows* that one knows *x*. Merely to opine that one knows *x* fails to meet the standard of knowledge. Knowledge implies certainty—especially in its typical Socratic opposition to mere opinion. But to assert this is to raise an immediate difficulty: how is certainty to be achieved? If, as Socrates says, those who err do so because they falsely suppose they know what they are doing, it would seem that we should precede all action by confirming that our knowledge of what we are doing is genuine. But how can this be achieved if the professed certainty that one has knowledge is precisely what dooms the one who errs? Socrates provides a method for recognizing ignorance: when one's opinion wanders, it is a sign that one supposes one knows something of which one is ignorant. Incidentally, knowledge of ignorance thus comes to light as a special kind of knowledge; perhaps no knowledge is quite so solid as the knowledge that one does not know something. But as for opinions that do not wander, what can we say about them? Might they not just as easily be persistent delusions as knowledge?

There are some suggestions within the exhortation as to how we might better confirm our knowledge. Possessors of the arts (*technai*)—cooks and pilots are Socrates' examples (117c2–d3)—seem to have a strong claim to knowledge, for they are able consistently to bring about the same good product, effect, or state of affairs. The power of this claim to knowledge is not to be underemphasized. Modern experimental science is founded upon the idea that one has learned something about a phenomenon if one can predict and reproduce it. There is thus an important kinship between the knowledge manifest in modern technology and the Greek idea of *technē* from which it derives its name. But there are some kinds of knowledge that are not apparently obtained by the mastery of an art. Socrates' first questions in the exhortation are whether Alcibiades' opinions change regarding the number of eyes and hands he has (116e7–10). These represent a kind of self-knowledge, but more important, they refer to knowledge ascertained by the senses: what does not *appear* to change, especially when examined from different angles and in different ways, is understood to be fixed and known. One could, of course, raise objections to the certainty of such knowledge, just as one could raise doubts about the knowledge presumed by *technē*, but it cannot be denied that these kinds of knowledge seem to be the nearest things to certainty of which we have experience.

What about knowledge that can be ascertained neither through art nor by the senses? The most striking question posed by Socrates to Alcibiades in the exhortation provides a crucial example: "Do you know of any way you will ascend into heaven?" (117b5). This is a question about whether or not we are destined for any life beyond the present one, that is, about the nature of the human soul and its place in the cosmos.[40] Self-knowledge of the body is relatively easy, but how are we to obtain knowledge, as elusive as it is necessary, of the human soul? And what of Socrates himself? The *Alcibiades* marks the beginning within Plato's dialogues of Socrates' mature philosophic career. It is the first of many conversations Plato presents to us in which Socrates engages young interlocutors in dialectical investigations of moral and political questions. How are these conversations meant to help Socrates as a philosopher? How can they help him find or confirm knowledge about the most important questions?

We noted a statement Socrates makes in the course of his investigation of Pericles' wisdom concerning precisely the question of confirming knowledge: "It is a beautiful sign that the knowers know whenever they are able to produce another knower" (118d6–8). In the context of our present discussion, this statement takes on new significance. For while it is true that Pericles can point to no one whom he has made wise, Socrates himself, at the time of the *Alcibiades*, would seem to be open to the same criticism. If Socrates, as a philosopher, requires a sign or evidence[41] of his wisdom, perhaps he hopes to obtain it by finding a student who is able and willing to follow him along the path that leads up and out of the cave, to confirm for himself the conclusions of Socratic philosophy or else to challenge and refine them. Indoctrination will not do: to produce a believer is not to produce a knower. This helps us understand why Socrates would not with greater clarity explain to Alcibiades the paradox of the noble. Socrates hoped to make Alcibiades wise.

This may also help us answer a question about the exhortation: does Socrates really need to rescind his promise to be indispensable to the fulfillment of Alcibiades' ambitions by pointing out that none of the other Athenians are wise? It would seem that Alcibiades might well be ready to turn to him as a teacher whether or not Socrates should prove himself to be the only one available. Pointing out the lack of wisdom of the Athenians, and especially the statesmen, is not a necessary move for Socrates, but a way for him to test Alcibiades. By effectively rescinding his original promise (as Alcibiades had understood it), Socrates is able to see whether the import of the refutations, as illuminated by the exhortation, has properly set in. Socrates' hope is that Alcibiades' extraordinary ambition can be shown at bottom to be dependent on an unexamined and confused understanding of justice and the noble so that the exposure of the confusion would undermine and redirect the desire.[42] He tries to show Alcibiades that happiness would be unattainable without knowledge of justice, the noble, the good, and the advantageous, supposing that Alcibiades' ambition for political power and fame will not persist if he thinks it a dubious means to perfect happiness. In short, he wants to show Alcibiades that he lacks the grounds to be certain that what he most desires is to be found in politics, implying thereby that a full-scale philosophic investigation of the question of how one ought to live, an investigation that must even press the question of the goodness of political life, must be undertaken.[43] But Alcibiades shrugs off what the refutations had revealed as soon as he notes their apparent irrelevance to the shining but unexamined life he wishes to lead.

In this respect, Alcibiades has let Socrates down. His desire for power, honor, and fame is too persistent and overwhelming, has too great a life of its own, and his concern for the problems Socrates brought to light was too weak by comparison. But the dialogue does not end here, and Socrates' relationship with Alcibiades is only now beginning. Socrates' foresight may be keen enough already to see that Alcibiades will not become wise, but is there still something Socrates can gain from continuing to associate and converse with him? Or does Socrates still hold out some hope that Alcibiades may become truly philosophic? We shall have to turn to the second half of the dialogue with these questions in mind. But whether Socrates knows it at this moment or not, he will have to move on in his search for a philosophic student, and it may not be until he has found such a student that he will be able to furnish the most beautiful evidence of his wisdom by sharing it as fully as is possible. It is our great fortune that he did eventually find at least one such student. Our evidence of Socrates' wisdom is the work of Plato.

Plato does not make political ambition an explicit theme in the *Alcibiades*. The Greek word most commonly translated, *ambition* (*philotimia*, literally "love of honor"), appears only once in the dialogue, in passing, in the section we will come to next.[44] Even the word for *honor* has only been used once thus far, though significantly, as it was in Socrates' accusation that Alcibiades believed he would soon prove to the Athenian assembly that he was worthy of being honored by them as no one had been before. Indeed, the theme of Alcibiades' belief in his "worthiness" (*axia*) may make for a more fruitful focus in the attempt to understand Alcibiades' ambition.[45] A number of questions confront us in the attempt to cast Alcibiades' ambition in these unfamiliar terms, which will help us bring together some key reflections regarding the portion of the dialogue we have covered thus far. What does Alcibiades think he is worthy of? What does he think makes him worthy? And which is more important to him, having his great worth recognized by the Athenians or confirming it for himself?

As to what Alcibiades thinks he is worthy of, we may begin by saying that it is honor. After all, that is what Socrates "accuses" him of believing in his opening speech, and the love of honor is the quintessential feature of ambition as conceived by the Greeks. But Socrates does not hesitate to enlarge upon this characterization in startling terms by imputing to Alcibiades the ultimate aim of achieving universal fame and power. These goals go well beyond that of proving that he is worthy of being honored. They represent, in the context of Socrates' opening speeches, a dramatic elaboration of Alcibiades' desire for self-sufficiency, to be able to "do whatever he wishes," to stand with no authority above him.

These are the lofty aspirations Socrates attributes to Alcibiades, yet even they cannot be said to be the focus of the dialogue. Instead, the conversation thus far has revolved around the question of the qualities in virtue of which Alcibiades considers himself to be so eminently worthy. We learn at the outset that Alcibiades' high opinion of himself is based in part on the superficial qualities for which he has received such great attention: his looks, his family, and to a lesser extent, his wealth. But Alcibiades adamantly maintains that these things do not alone make him worthy of all he desires. He appears to assume, however unreflectingly, what Socrates flatteringly suggests: that he has a soul to match his body and that it will be as an adviser, general, and leader that he will make his great worth evident to the Athenians. But this places a crucial limit on the means by which Alcibiades will be willing to pursue his ambition. It is not at all the single-minded and unscrupulous drive for advancement and acquisition that nowadays often goes by the name of ambition. For unless Alcibiades' desire for fame and power should become unhinged from his belief that he is intrinsically deserving or worthy of them, the path of his political career will be bound by his duty and his ability to enhance the prosperity and glory of Athens.[46]

That Alcibiades has generally given this matter little thought, however, is evident from his lack of reflection upon the substance of his imminent political responsibilities. He has simply assumed he is deserving of the Athenians' honor, an unthinking assumption that has been made possible by the honor he has already been receiving on account of his beauty and status. What Alcibiades, with Socrates' help, begins to sense in the first part of this dialogue is that he may not yet meet his own standard of deserving. Moreover, this is not so much because he lacks the technical expertise to be a great statesman[47] but rather because he is unable to deny—or to sustain his denial—that his worthiness of the greatest goods must ultimately coincide with moral obligation or justice. By drawing upon Alcibiades' own awareness of the contradictions inherent in common opinions concerning the goodness of justice, Socrates is able to make Alcibiades unsure of whether he knows how to be truly and fully worthy of the honors accorded to the greatest leaders.

Alcibiades' previous unquestioning self-assuredness, however, and his failure to think through what would be required to live up to his own evaluation of his great worth may also have precluded his entertaining the notion of seeking political rule through less than honorable means. In other words, there has hitherto been no occasion for Alcibiades to reflect that there might be anything less than perfect compatibility between his own success and the prosperity of the Athenians. We must admit that by the end of this dialogue's first half, it is not clear that Alcibiades will be as insistent about his worthiness of Athenian honor as he was at the outset. On the contrary, he seems to feel himself liberated by Socrates' revelation that wise counsel is not a prerequisite for a successful career in Athenian politics and that his good looks and reputation will likely be sufficient to gain the approval of the assembly. It would seem that the desires for fame, honor, and power indeed have a force in Alcibiades that is separable from his desire to earn those rewards through noble service to his fatherland.

Troubling an indication as this may be, it is still too early to say whether Alcibiades would consider it desirable to become famous and powerful at the expense of the Athenians. Indeed, we have been given no such indication to this point, as Socrates has prudently avoided framing the tension of Alcibiades' ambition in these terms. The question thus far has not been whether Alcibiades will constrain his pursuit of the good by adherence to the demands of justice but whether he will advise the Athenians to do so. The compatibility of his own good with that of his fellow citizens has thus never come under question.[48] For this reason, the necessity or advantage of tyranny or political rhetoric appears to remain completely out of view for Alcibiades. In a way, the closest approach Socrates makes to shifting the emphasis from Athens's rule over its empire to Alcibiades' rule over the Athenians is in his refutation concerning courage. For there, he unexpectedly replaces the justice of Alcibiades' political counsel with the courage of helping friends in war. But we might insist that this is still a question of justice: Socrates' entertaining the idea that it is bad to die saving a friend means that it may be good to benefit at a friend's expense, that is, to be unjust. Should Alcibiades' good come into conflict with that of his friends, would he do better to sacrifice his own so as to avoid what is shameful? To what extent does his own happiness require that he be just? As we have seen, Alcibiades comes to shrug off the uncomfortable weight of Socrates' refutations and does not appear at any point to have seriously considered the possibility that the dissonance between the just and the advantageous might apply to his own relationship to the Athenians.

CHAPTER 2

# THE EXALTATION OF VIRTUE

## (*Alcibiades* 116–135)

The failure of Socrates' exhortation marks the turning point of the *Alcibiades*. The refutations disoriented Alcibiades by showing him that he holds conflicting views concerning "the greatest things"—that is, the just, the noble, the good, and the advantageous—and therefore is likely to err in pursuit of his own happiness. But once Socrates allows Alcibiades to recognize that even Pericles must share in the same ignorance, Alcibiades loses interest in what the refutations have revealed. Until this moment, Socrates had not deviated from his suggestion that the goal he can help Alcibiades to achieve is political success according to the conventional understanding held by Alcibiades himself and perhaps expanded by Socrates' opening speeches. The unexpected conclusion that Alcibiades is here invited to draw is that, in fact, political success ordinarily understood (unaccompanied by Socratic wisdom) cannot guarantee his happiness. Despite this implicit critique of the political life and pointer to philosophy as an alternative, Socrates could not shift Alcibiades' hopes for happiness from one to the other.

Especially when we consider what is suggested by the passage from *Republic* cited in the Introduction it seems as though Socrates sought to turn Alcibiades toward philosophy.[1] Faint but intriguing indications of the motivation for this attempt were given in the course of the *Alcibiades*' central exhortation, in which he suggested that a successful educator to wisdom would have a rare and important confirmation of his own wisdom. But we are still without a clear notion of the point on which Socrates may think his wisdom is in need of confirmation. The one compelling possibility available from the dialogue's first half is the famous Socratic "knowledge of ignorance," which is described most memorably in Plato's *Apology of Socrates*. Given the context of Socrates' caution to Alcibiades concerning this crucial knowledge, it may be especially helpful to recall the emphasis Socrates puts in the *Apology* on his knowing that he knows nothing "noble and good," a particular instance of knowledge of ignorance to which his attention was drawn after a public discussion with a well-reputed Athenian politician (*Apology of Socrates* 21b–d; cf. *Alcibiades* 118c1–2).

But Alcibiades' failure to turn his focus from politics to philosophy means that Socrates may at this moment have a more pressing matter on his hands. One might well fear that the net effect Socrates has had on Alcibiades to this point has been negative and even dangerous. Alcibiades' estimation of his own worth, at one point challenged by the possibility that he was deficient in wisdom concerning justice, has emerged not merely intact but inflated by Socrates' opening flatteries.[2] Moreover, Alcibiades now positively affirms that he deserves Athenian honor and power on the basis of his beauty and family alone—a position that may have been half-implied by his posture at the outset of the dialogue but which was then at least in some tension with his assurance that he was also the most practically capable leader Athens could choose. We can say that Alcibiades has already been corrupted, in that his characteristic belief in his own deserving of Athenian honor has been inflated while his more subterranean belief that his worth is tied to his ability to fulfill some civic duty has been notably weakened. It will be particularly instructive to consider how far Socrates' concern regarding this potential and actual corruption of Alcibiades' ambition outweighs the importance of whatever are his philosophic aims in risking that corruption at all.

## Socrates Renews His Attempt: The Royal Tale (Speech, 119c2–124b6)

The last and longest speech of the *Alcibiades* is preceded by a brief exchange. Just as the dialogue's opening speech was a necessary preparation for the one that immediately followed, the present conversation, following Alcibiades' failure to heed the Socratic exhortation, is a necessary preparation for Socrates' final speech. This preparation is necessary because Alcibiades has returned to his conviction that he needs nothing beyond what his nature has provided him. Socrates must once again provoke Alcibiades to doubt his confidence in the ease with which he will be able to fulfill his ambitions. There are therefore several indications in this section that Socrates is somehow recapitulating the dialogue's opening. But the echoes of Socrates' first speech are mixed with indications that his approach has changed. A case in point is the reemergence of Socrates' *eros* as a theme. Socrates' first response to Alcibiades' rejection of Socratic education is to bemoan how "unworthy" this rejection is of Alcibiades' "looks" and of his other qualities. When Alcibiades asks what he means, Socrates laments, "I am vexed with you and with my love" (119c4–5). In Socrates' opening speeches, he claimed that he "would long ago have abandoned [his] love" if he had seen that Alcibiades was content to go through life with nothing more than his beauty, family, city, and wealth (104e6–8). Moreover, it is here that the theme of Alcibiades' worth reemerges.[3] But whereas Socrates' opening speeches flattered Alcibiades in order to elevate his sense of worth, Socrates now adopts a tone of trenchant sarcasm. His goal appears to be to shame Alcibiades by belittling the level of worthiness with which he has come to be satisfied and to persuade him that some education and training will yet be required if he is to become deserving of, and capable of acquiring, what he most desires.[4]

Socrates accomplishes this by insisting that Alcibiades has fallen short of expectations in deeming it worthy to compete "against the human beings here." Then, when Alcibiades repeatedly asks him to explain what he means, Socrates coyly avoids clarification, responding with an infuriating combination of metaphor and sarcasm. For example, "It's certainly worthy of you to be content if you are better than your soldiers, but not to look toward the leaders of your opponents to see whether you've become better than them, examining and training with a view to them" (119c7–e8). The effect of this is to stir a mounting anxiety in Alcibiades, a fear that he has hubristically overlooked the crucial source of opposition to the fulfillment of his ambition—and therefore, that he has prematurely rejected the Socratic education. Finally, Socrates reveals the identities of Alcibiades' "true enemies." As Alcibiades admits with growing concern, his contest will in fact be against the Lacedaemonian and Persian kings if he is to lead the Athenians, since Athens is often at war with Sparta and Persia. Socrates gets Alcibiades to see that it will not be enough simply to win political victories within Athens. If his career is to live up to the splendid vision he has of it, Alcibiades must come to be known not merely as the leader of Athens but as the one who led her to ever greater glory, which will require military victories. In this way, Socrates effectively reanimates Alcibiades' concern that he may not yet be worthy of what he desires. Alcibiades' complacency regarding the expectation that the Athenians will elect him despite his lack of wisdom is challenged by Socrates' reminder that both his reputation and the very preservation of Athens will depend on his ability to win military victory over formidable enemies.

Socrates' emphasis on the need for Alcibiades to be a good leader and not just a successful politician ushers in one of the major themes of the dialogue's second half: Alcibiades' desire to be a benefactor to the Athenians. We can already detect in Socrates' sarcasm an emphasis on the shamefulness of being a slavish, corrupt, or ineffective leader. Consider, for instance, his mocking suggestion that Alcibiades ought to take after such politicians as "Meidias the quail-striker,"[5] who enter politics in order "to flatter the city but not to rule it" (120a9–b5). Socrates plays on Alcibiades' disdain of flattery, a sentiment related to his naïve ignorance of the need for rhetoric. But this means that Socrates will leave off from his suggestions about the need for rhetoric, which dotted the first half of the dialogue. In this connection, his image of Alcibiades piloting the trireme into battle would seem to be a final reminder of a problem that has not been solved (119d4–e3). He says that Alcibiades must not focus on overcoming his fellow sailors (citizens) but rather on defeating his "true enemies," the pilots (kings) of the other ships (cities). But Socrates also points to the difficulty that this requires prevailing over and "looking down upon" his fellow sailors to such a degree that they do not consider competing with him and instead join him in battle. Yet a warship is no democracy. In a democracy, there are always rivals eager to compete for the highest honors and citizens who are more likely to favor leaders who flatter and indulge their passions than those who, rightly or wrongly, bluntly assert their worthiness of honor and power. It is characteristically paradoxical of Alcibiades' ambition that while he holds the majority of the Athenians to be of little account in comparison with himself, he nonetheless esteems them enough to expect that they will clearly recognize and unquestioningly acknowledge his superiority. Thucydides helps us see that Alcibiades may never have learned the extent to which democratic rhetoric requires a certain pandering or irony for the sake of one's own well-being (cf. vi.16–18 with vi.28.2 and vi.60.1).

Socrates has revealed that Alcibiades' true rivals are the kings of Sparta and Persia. One can imagine Alcibiades' head spinning with shame, embarrassment, and fear as Socrates brings forth from the shadows the enemies he had been concealing, men who cannot possibly be expected to submit to Alcibiades on account of his bare claims of superiority, who wish to dominate him and his fellow citizens, against whom it will be his duty to fight in defense of his fatherland, and whom he will have to overcome if his grandest ambitions are to be fulfilled. But Alcibiades is not yet entirely persuaded: will not these enemies be as lacking in Socratic wisdom as the Athenians? Will Alcibiades' impressive natural gifts, therefore, not still be enough, even without

Socratic education, to win him the glory for which he believes he is destined (120c3–5)? Socrates' original argument for the necessity of Socratic education to political life was confined to the suggestion that without it, Alcibiades would not be able to advise the Athenians correctly with a view to the better—and thus to make himself truly deserving of their honor. Alcibiades' challenge prompts Socrates to reestablish the need for Socratic education or wisdom on new grounds.

Socrates' remarkable two-part response prepares us for his longest speech. First, Socrates obtains Alcibiades' agreement that he is better off believing his enemies to be formidable for he would then take greater care to improve himself (120c9–d8). Second, Socrates says he will show "from the likely things" that, after all, Alcibiades is simply wrong to believe he is superior to his true enemies: the Persian and Spartan kings, descended as they are from the most distinguished ancestors and brought up with the finest educations, are most likely to have become "perfect with respect to virtue" (120d9–e5). This is the first appearance of the word *virtue* (*aretē*) in the dialogue. The procedure of Socrates' speech, will be to show how greatly inferior are Alcibiades' family and rearing to those of his true rivals and thus how sorely lacking in virtue he is. But note what is implied by the two parts of Socrates' reply taken together. Socrates all but proclaims he will be persuading Alcibiades of a salutary falsehood, an exaggerated belief in the might of his rivals that will compel him to take greater care over his own virtue, specifically by pursuing a Socratic education.[6] But this may suggest that Socrates has changed course, for it is not yet clear how long he expects Alcibiades to remain under the spell of this salutary falsehood. It seems he still wishes to educate Alcibiades. But is the education Socrates now has in mind the same one he pointed to by suggesting that Alcibiades must suspend his political aspirations to investigate the relation of the noble to the good? Is the lie Socrates will tell Alcibiades about his "true rivals," then, only a temporary inducement to further puzzling over virtue, to be dispelled and replaced with a clearer understanding in time? Or is Socrates, beginning now, setting out to provide Alcibiades with a different sort of education, one that is not so concerned ultimately to turn back on and dispel the false impressions upon which it is founded, and which is therefore to be a moral education but not a philosophic one? It would then be a beneficial education but, we are inclined to hope and to suspect, not the most beneficial education Socrates has to offer. The character of its benefit to Socrates, in any case, remains enigmatic.

Socrates' clearest purpose in this speech is to bring Alcibiades to shame.

But whereas his previous speech scolded Alcibiades primarily for an *intellectual* failing, that is, for rejecting an argument on childish grounds, this speech will scold him for his hubristic and overweening confidence. Socrates will accomplish this, as he explains, by "setting our things against theirs": by comparing that which Socrates and Alcibiades can claim as Athenians—Socrates speaks now as if they are both in the same predicament (cf. 109d1–8)—to that which belongs to the Spartan and Persian kings. This will challenge a key support of Alcibiades' confidence noted by Socrates in his opening speech but not much discussed since then: the superiority of Athens to other cities (104a7). Beginning with a comparison of families, Socrates has Alcibiades consider that both the Spartan and Persian kings trace their ancestries directly to Zeus through Perseus, by way of Heracles and Achaemenes respectively. Alcibiades retorts immediately that he too is descended from Zeus, through Ajax's son Eurysaces (120e6–121a2). It is in response to this claim that Socrates delivers the dialogue's longest speech. The purpose of the speech is to dissuade Alcibiades of his belief that he is blessed with divine favor, to make him see that he is not himself divine but a mere mortal staring up at his foes as at gods.

The first portion of the speech is dedicated to showing Alcibiades what true divine favor looks like (121a3–c4). Socrates notes that the Persian and Spartan kings are descended from Zeus in unbroken successions of kings, while Socrates and Alcibiades are private men, as were their fathers. As for Alcibiades' own claim to divine ancestry, Socrates casts doubt upon it by juxtaposing it with a fanciful divine genealogy of his own. Moreover, Socrates notes how great the kingdoms of Alcibiades' true rivals are. The Spartan kings rule over Argos and Lacedaemon, and the Great Kings rule not only Persia but often the whole of Asia;[7] not even the noblest of Alcibiades' ancestors possessed land that would be anything but laughable by comparison. From family and land, Socrates turns to the honor in which the foreign kings are held by their peoples. Their queens are guarded—by the ephors in Sparta and by fear alone in Persia—so that there is no doubt as to the purity of the royal bloodlines; Socrates graciously leaves the insinuation about Alcibiades' birth unspoken. All of this serves to undermine Alcibiades' confidence in his own greatness. Socrates does not hesitate to embellish in order to further this effect,[8] and while Alcibiades cannot confirm the veracity of all his claims regarding these remote figures, he can be made to see the distinct lack of evidence suggesting that the gods mean to bestow special favor upon *him*. Or rather, Socrates makes the evidence upon which Alcibiades had already been relying, consciously or not, seem much more ambiguous than it had before.

The next portion of the speech has much the same quality as the first, tracing the birth and upbringing of a Persian crown prince so as to show how splendid are the honors and attention he receives, and thereby to make Alcibiades' own life seem mundane by comparison (121c4–122b8). The prince's birthday is celebrated as a holiday "for the rest of time"; as an infant, he is tended by the king's best eunuchs, who are themselves held "in great honor" for straightening the infant prince's limbs so as "to contrive that he will be most beautiful." By comparison, "the neighbors hardly notice" when Athenians like Alcibiades and Socrates are born, and as an infant, Alcibiades was tended "by a woman nurse of little worth." But as Socrates continues his narration of the rearing of the Persian prince, a new and important element enters his account. The education of the prince is an education in virtue. The prince has four expert "royal tutors," one for each of the cardinal Platonic virtues, and Socrates briefly describes the prince's education in each one. The most striking thing to note about these descriptions is that they are utterly devoid of the paradoxes that riddled the earlier discussions of justice, courage, and the noble. No mention is made of "death and wounds" with respect to courage: it is reduced simply to fearlessness. No mention is made of military counsel with respect to justice: it is reduced simply to honesty.[9] Some preparation for political rule seems to be provided through the education in moderation and wisdom. But in the former case (as in the case of courage), the emphasis is on escaping slavishness and becoming truly free. The education in wisdom is said to include "the kingly things," but the greater emphasis is on Persian religion: the prince learns, from the wisest Persian in the bloom of youth, to serve the gods.

Of course, this account too contributes to the case for Alcibiades' insignificance. His own tutor is "that one of [Pericles'] slaves most useless on account of age, Zopyrus the Thracian." But more important, it introduces the possibility of escape from that insignificance through education in virtue, especially since Socrates notes that Alcibiades' only hope for such an education is "if someone happens to be [his] lover." Alcibiades is thus directed toward Socrates as a teacher of the virtue he needs to compete with his true rivals. Moreover, the image of virtue presented here is of a seamless perfection of soul: perfect freedom, total self-mastery, and divine favor. Socrates gives Alcibiades the impression that the virtuous life is without admixture of evil. We can say that it begins to resemble the highest object of Alcibiades' own ambition. This virtue is acquired through preparation and training in the case of moderation and courage and through some learning in the case of wisdom and justice. Socrates' suggestion that piety and honesty are required for a life of untainted freedom and rule (ironic given the mendacity of Socrates' presentation) is representative of the more conventional civic and moral appearance of the education he now proposes to Alcibiades: the virtuous are rewarded with happiness.

The section of the speech on education makes no mention of the Spartan kings. Perhaps Socrates thought it would be too difficult to distort the Spartan education as he did the Persian since Alcibiades is more likely to have knowledge of Spartan customs. But the Spartans and their legendary virtue have their place in Socrates' speech. Despite the godly aura Socrates was able to give to virtue in his description of the Persian education, the Great King is, after all, a despot. Holding up these kings as Alcibiades' imagined enemies helps foster some humility in him, but Socrates must be careful lest those same enemies become models for emulation in the wrong respects. The passage that follows the education section consists of two lists enumerating the ways in which Alcibiades will find himself eclipsed by his rivals:

> If you wish to focus on (1) wealth, (2) luxuries, (3) clothing and trailing robes, (4) perfumed unguents, and (5) retinues of multitudes of servants and the other Persian refinement, you would be ashamed for yourself if you perceived how far you fall short of them. But if you would wish in turn to focus on the (1) moderation and orderliness, (2) fortitude, (3) good temper, (4) high-mindedness, (5) discipline, (6) courage, (7) endurance, (8) love of toil, (9) love of victory, and (10) love of honor of the Lacedaemonians, you would believe yourself to be a child in each of these things. (122b8–d1)[10]

That these two lists represent ways or features of life to which Alcibiades is attracted is suggested by Socrates' description of the disappointment he would feel upon learning of his inferiority. In other words, the lists suggest two directions in which Alcibiades' ambition might tend.

First, Alcibiades' ambition might drive him to seek money, pleasure, and power. Or rather, if we take the list as a kind of progression, it seems that the desire for wealth in an ambitious soul, especially once that desire has been gratified, may lead to the development of ever vainer and more hedonistic tastes. At the extreme of this list is the possession of multitudes of servants; the ambitious man may come to enjoy and desire greater and greater power simply for the delight in its exercise. At the center of the list is ostentatious adornment. Perhaps the most intoxicating aspect of wealth for Alcibiades in particular is the way it allows him to shine and be admired, to be honored for his magnificence. Of course, Alcibiades' desire to be admired or honored for his adornments, that is, not on the basis of his true merit, is just what Socrates wants to discourage. If this list of Persian possessions partly represents the allure of tyranny for Alcibiades—which would accord with its being associated with the Great King—then we note that tyranny appeals to the love of honor, but honor bought, not earned.[11]

Socrates makes the second list twice as long as the first, which suggests that he wants Alcibiades to give it more attention. Unlike the first, this is a list of qualities of soul and not of possessions. It can be broken into two groups of five, each headed by a cardinal virtue: the first by moderation and the second by courage. These were the two virtues that were said, in Socrates' description of the Persian prince's education, to be obtained through preparation and training, and it is with respect to these Spartan virtues that Socrates says Alcibiades will feel like a child in comparison to his rivals. Socrates may hope that Alcibiades' feeling like a child will intensify his desire to become a man. We learned from the last refutation that courage or manliness, which heads the second half of the list of Spartan virtues, is the most important virtue to Alcibiades. If his ambition will carry him to an emulation of the Spartans, it will be because of his attraction to manliness, his love of victory and of honor. If he fails, it may be because of his lack of what is given under the heading of moderation. Altogether, this list of Spartan virtues, like the list of Persian refinements, appeals to a genuine strain of Alcibiades' ambition, which includes his love of honor. Indeed, it contains the dialogue's only explicit mention of the love of honor, for it is the love of this sort of honor that Socrates hopes to nurture in Alcibiades: honor earned through toil and hard-won victory, through high-minded and virtuous self-control.

These lists appear to indicate that Socrates considers Alcibiades to be at a crossroads. His ambition and love of honor could take him in either of two directions, and Socrates appears determined to guide him toward virtue. Now, one might object on the basis of Socrates' first speech that the danger of Alcibiades' being seduced by wealth and luxury ought to be minimal. For in laying out in the opening speech the qualities and possessions on which Alcibiades prides himself (all of which, incidentally, have been addressed in the present speech), Socrates had supposed that wealth was the least of them (104b8–c1).[12] However, the majority of the remainder of this longest speech is devoted to a discussion of wealth. If Socrates thought that money was relatively unimportant to Alcibiades at the outset, he now has come to think his attempt to educate

Alcibiades will require that he pay significant attention to the question of wealth—or rather, what wealth represents: the desire to be honored for one's power, opulence, and magnificence. This comparison of Socrates' relative emphasis on wealth in these first and last speeches sheds light on the change that has taken place in the interim. Socrates is taking greater caution now than he was before to oppose the tyrannical strain of Alcibiades' ambition.

Socrates' treatment of wealth appears to function much like the rest of the speech (122d1–123c3). He portrays the riches of the Spartan and Persian kings as being so vast as to make Alcibiades' own wealth appear meaningless. That is, to whatever extent Alcibiades' wealth, like his beauty and his family, gives him the impression that he is special and destined for greatness, Socrates' account will help deflate that impression. But clearly that is not quite enough, for while Alcibiades cannot pursue an increase in his beauty or in the greatness of his family so as to remedy his inferiority in those respects, it is difficult to see how recognition of his relative poverty would thwart his attempt to pursue greater wealth. Might not the suggestion that his rivals derive their superiority in part from their wealth cause Alcibiades to strive for the acquisition of as much wealth as possible?

Socrates therefore tinges his description of Spartan and Persian wealth with insinuations that the love and pursuit of it is to be looked down upon as soft or effeminate. For example, he notes that the Spartans receive payment from other cities but that the gold and silver they receive never leaves the city—just as Aesop's fox notices that the footprints lead into the lion's cave but not out. But the secrecy with which the Spartans hoard this money reveals something shameful about it. Their love of wealth represents a decline from the pure military virtue for which they are famous. The lion in Aesop's fable has taken to luring animals into his cave under false pretenses, as he has grown too old to hunt. The Spartans' love of wealth represents their decline from the manliness of force to the dishonorable deceit of fraud. As for the wealth of the Persian king, which truly dwarfs that of any Athenian, Socrates this time omits any mention of luxuries, slaves, or perfumes and instead focuses on the expanse of land the king controls. But what he says about that land is that its regions are named after parts of the queen's wardrobe: the wealth collected from one region would pay for her girdles, another for her veils, and so on. In this way, Socrates makes the vast wealth of the Great King seem almost silly on account of the unserious end to which it is a means. Here, too, Socrates makes the pursuit of wealth seem distinctly effeminate and insinuates that wealth and luxury are frivolous and unworthy of a real man. And yet we might note that this Socratic appeal to Alcibiades' love of courage or manliness is not without ambiguity. The hero of Aesop's fable is, after all, not the lion in his younger days but the cunning, prudent, and female fox. One could say that a great deal hinges on the extent to which Alcibiades can be brought to admire such a hero.[13]

It is fitting, then, that in the remainder of the speech, Socrates describes what he imagines would be the bemused reactions of the Persian and Spartan *queens* upon learning that Alcibiades intends to compete against their sons (123c3–124a7). Socrates has Amestris, mother of Artaxerxes, scoff at the meagerness of the wardrobe of Alcibiades' mother, baffled to think the son of such a paltry woman would conceive of challenging her own son. But then Socrates has her begin to make suggestions similar to the ones Socrates himself had been making. She suggests that Alcibiades' only hopes are taking care (*epimeleia*) and wisdom, and hence she is only more flabbergasted to learn that Alcibiades is barely twenty years old, totally uneducated, and will not even heed his lover's advice to learn, to take care of himself, and to train before challenging the king. She views the very idea that Alcibiades could consider his nature sufficient for the task as insane, just as the Spartan queen Lampido, according to Socrates, would wonder at such a poorly brought-up lad thinking to challenge her son. Socrates has conjured witnesses to confirm his assessment: Alcibiades desperately needs to train and learn if he is to have any chance of political success. That these mocking witnesses are women pushes Alcibiades to follow the manlier strain of his ambition, that part of him wishing to be honored not for his wealth or power but for his virtue.[14] Presumably, he does not reflect that Socrates merely has expressed his own position in the voices of these female antagonists.

The cumulative rhetorical effect of this speech is to make Alcibiades believe that his nature alone and untended, without the hard work of caring for himself and for virtue, and without the pursuit of wisdom in particular, cannot suffice to win him the power, honor, and fame he covets. Concluding his speech, Socrates implores him: "Blessed one, obeying me and the inscription at Delphi, know thyself, that these are our rivals (not those you suppose) of whom we won't overcome a single one by anything other than taking care and art. If you fall short of them, you'll also fall short of becoming a name among the Greeks and the barbarians, which you seem to me to love as no one else [loves] any other thing" (124a7–b6). This art, or "wisdom" as Socrates' Amestris called it, is ostensibly what Socrates proposes to provide through just the sort of "training" that Alcibiades earlier rejected as unnecessary (*askēsanta*, 119b5–c1). Throughout the speech, Socrates allies himself with Alcibiades with the use of the first-person plural. As much as he has been putting Alcibiades to shame by comparing him to the Persian and Spartan kings, he has taken care to present himself as a teacher and lover. In this capacity, he counsels Alcibiades to have the self-awareness to recognize who his true rivals are. Socrates needs Alcibiades to see that his ambition points out far beyond Athens, or that his contest is not "against the human beings here." If Socrates cannot harness Alcibiades' tremendous love of honor, described here as an erotic love of renown, then Socrates will have no hold over Alcibiades, no opportunity to convince him of the importance of virtue. Alcibiades' ambition will be dangerously unfettered. But Socrates' invocation of the Delphic inscription reminds us that the education of Alcibiades is not all that is at stake for Socrates in this association (cf. *Phaedrus* 229c6–230a7); somehow, his own pursuit of self-knowledge through Alcibiades continues.

Socrates' opening speeches in the *Alcibiades* sketched a portrait of young but extremely powerful political ambition, or of its manifestation in an Athenian youth such as Alcibiades. The speech that opens the dialogue's second half, in its careful attempt to lead Alcibiades down the most fruitful path, extrapolates from the initial portrait by pointing to the various ways in which his ambition might develop. As we have seen, Socrates is attempting to motivate Alcibiades both to keep his sights set on the loftiest goals and to take seriously the task of making himself worthy of their attainment. But this adds substantially to our understanding of political ambition by drawing our attention to its fundamental malleability. The desire for fame, which Socrates emphasizes at the end of the speech, can be satisfied in many ways of varying respectability, and more generally, a powerful desire to obtain the greatest goods for oneself is of indeterminate value until one learns to recognize a particular model of its fulfillment as most worthy of emulation.

None of this yet suggests that Alcibiades' ambition could be directed away from politics altogether, but it does imply that even powerful political ambition can begin to dissipate under certain conditions. Alcibiades had already started to lower his sights when he ceased to revere his Athenian political opponents, and Socrates' speech prompts us to consider the attraction to wealth and luxury as a likely and fatal diversion for the politically ambitious soul that has begun to slacken or waver in its insistence on reaching the peak. Socrates appears to think that if Alcibiades is going to be a worthwhile companion, he must not only be in search of fulfillment through political life, but he must be driven to do so with the urgency that characterizes a serious attention to virtue. It is not enough to want to become famous and powerful—Alcibiades must want to deserve these rewards on account of his excellence. Political ambition can survive a diminishing concern for virtue, but such ambition will be degraded and sapped of much of its vigor. Political ambition is at its most powerful when it is fueled by the love of the noble.

## Alcibiades' Unexamined Confusion Regarding the Common Good (Refutation, 124b7–127d8)

Socrates' desire to seek some education for himself through his association with Alcibiades is stated nowhere more clearly than in the passage immediately following his last and longest speech. He now says that he, like Alcibiades, needs an education in order to become "best" (124b7–c3). Socrates speaks as though the two of them are embarking on a common enterprise to take that care of which "all human beings" are in need (124d2–3). But that suggestion is difficult to square with the overall impression of the speech that precedes it, that is, that Socrates will, out of love for Alcibiades, help him to take care of his education so as to supply the wisdom or art that will allow him to compete with his greatest enemies, whose divinely blessed bodies and souls have been molded by the finest royal caretakers. How will this project help Socrates take care of himself? And in what sense will Socrates' and Alcibiades' goals be the same?

One possibility is that Socrates' claim to have need of the same care as Alcibiades, and all other human beings, is ironic. We have already suggested that Socrates may have lost confidence in the project that most involves a shared education for him and Alcibiades, in which Socrates' wisdom is confirmed by Alcibiades' apprehension of it. But even if he no longer thinks Alcibiades can be turned toward a philosophic way of life, Socrates may still be pursuing an education for himself, albeit one that will likely differ considerably in content from the education with which he will provide Alcibiades. That is, Socrates would at this point have two compatible but distinct aims in mind. One would be to continue to promote an education characterized by the salutary lies he earlier suggested Alcibiades ought to believe (120c9–e2), encouraging him to pursue self-improvement through the acquisition of virtue. The other would be to continue to pursue the education he seeks for himself through the confirmation of his own wisdom. But whereas earlier attempts by Socrates to confirm his own wisdom by imparting it to Alcibiades meant that the two men's educations could more simply coincide, the idea that Alcibiades would now be taught to believe what is false means that this

Socratic project cannot continue unchanged. The confirmation of Socrates' wisdom would need to be possible by some other means.

However, it is not certain that Socrates means for Alcibiades *never* to shed his false beliefs about who and what his true enemies are. It could be that the salutary falsehoods Socrates promotes are meant only as temporary spurs to a concern for virtue he hopes will eventually return to the more challenging philosophic investigation begun by the dialogue's central refutation and subsequent, failed exhortation. Of course, even if this is so, Socrates would appear to have changed his strategy somewhat. He would now be taking a more cautious route, encouraging Alcibiades to *be* virtuous but allowing himself some flexibility in the degree to which he will push Alcibiades to *investigate* virtue. In this way, Socrates could be more careful to avoid encouraging the tyrannical strains of Alcibiades' ambition that seem from the most recent speech to have become something of a concern, even as he continues to test the waters of Alcibiades' aptitude and desire for philosophic inquiry. Even in this scenario, however, there would be a question of whether Socrates might still have a strategy for confirming his own wisdom in the event that Alcibiades fails to embrace a philosophic investigation of virtue. For the remainder of this dialogue, at least, Socrates never again prompts Alcibiades to question the goodness of political success but only his ability to attain it.

The question of whether Socrates abandons the project of educating Alcibiades at the midpoint of this dialogue may be one of the most important questions concerning Plato's presentation of their association. If the education that follows is meant simply to be a salutary inducement to virtue, Socrates must be in large part acquitted of the charges of having corrupted Alcibiades. Moreover, Socrates would seem to judge in that case that Alcibiades' political ambition is quite resistant to philosophic challenges to its foundations, or that Alcibiades' desire for honor and power can subsist even in the face of a serious potential critique of their goodness and worth. We should therefore keep in mind the question of whether Socrates was serious in suggesting that he and Alcibiades will each be taking the same care of themselves.

The only way in which Socrates explicitly claims to differ from or surpass (*diapherō*) Alcibiades in this passage is that his "guardian is better and wiser than [Alcibiades' guardian] Pericles." Socrates' guardian, he explains, is "a god, Alcibiades, the very one who did not allow me to converse with you before today, and trusting in whom I say that you will have fame through no one else but me" (124b5–10). Socrates' claim to have access to this god amounts to a claim to have access to some divine wisdom, which appears to govern especially Socrates' own *eros*. It is this wisdom that has allowed Socrates to seek the fulfillment of certain hopes through Alcibiades, and thus the wisdom itself must bear somehow on the character of those hopes. If we are meant to understand that the difference between the educations Socrates and Alcibiades will obtain from their association is represented by the difference between Socrates' god and Pericles, then we can suggest that Socrates' education will illuminate divinity, *eros*, and hope, while Alcibiades will be guided toward a more typical (albeit exceptionally successful) career in Athenian politics—illuminated perhaps by some of the same insights that Pericles learned from his own teachers.[15] However, it should also be observed that Socrates' mention of his god picks up a thread he had left off near the beginning of the dialogue: he here renews his effort to give himself an aura of the divine or uncanny. This may prove especially attractive to Alcibiades to the extent that he continues seriously to be intimidated by the divine favor enjoyed by his "true rivals," and we may be meant to infer that Alcibiades may yet come to find the divinely inspired and wise Socrates to be more impressive and worthier of his attention than Pericles. There can be no doubt, at any rate, that he finds Socrates more intriguing than Zopyrus. Presently, however, Alcibiades responds to Socrates' reference to his guardian god by accusing him of "joking"—an accusation Socrates does not deny.[16] At this point in the development of Alcibiades' attraction to the Socratic depiction of virtue, Socrates' stress on the divine, and indeed on his divinity, still strikes the aspiring statesman as being out of place.

One might begin with the hypothesis that the goal of the final refutation will be no different than that of the previous ones: Socrates wants to make Alcibiades see that he lacks knowledge necessary for the fulfillment of his political ambitions. Indeed, the coming refutation fits that bill even better than the others. For Socrates' earlier refutations purportedly established that Alcibiades lacked knowledge of justice, but Alcibiades was in every case able to turn a blind eye to the suggestion that he was therefore unready for politics. In this final refutation, however, Socrates will show Alcibiades that he has given stunningly little thought to what the purpose of political rule should be at all. Alcibiades will be unable to deny the import of *this* ignorance to his desire to rule, and he will have to turn to Socrates for education. But there is a difficulty with this explanation of the purpose of the final refutation: it would seem that Socrates' speech has already prompted Alcibiades to turn to Socrates for education. The refutation would seem to be superfluous, and therefore a full understanding of its effect will be helpful in determining what has changed in Socrates' strategy.

The structure of this refutation differs somewhat from the previous ones. Rather than begin with a claim that is to be refuted—that Alcibiades knows the just and unjust things, or that the just is sometimes disadvantageous—Socrates presses Alcibiades, through a protracted exchange, to say what the virtue is that he wishes to obtain and what he hopes to accomplish, in concrete political terms, by means of his possession of that virtue. Alcibiades' answers to this Socratic questioning are almost comical in their vagueness; he has thought very little about the practical reality of ruling and how he wishes to go about it. As is his wont, Socrates demonstrates to Alcibiades the imprecision of his answers by suggesting a number of valid but incorrect interpretations of them—the familiar, "Did you mean farmers, shoemakers, etc.?"—until Alcibiades provides some specification. Abstracting momentarily from those intervening exchanges, we can trace the dialectical path up to Alcibiades' key claim in a series of questions and answers (124d9–126c3) (Figure 3).

Figure 3. The Statesman's Virtue

| *Socrates* | *Alcibiades* |
|---|---|
| 1. With respect to what virtue do we wish to become "best?" | 1. That of good men. |
| 2. Good at what? | 2. At the practice of affairs. |
| 3. The affairs practiced by whom? | 3. The noble and good Athenians. |
| 4. Which ones do you say are good? | 4. Those who have power to rule in the city. |
| 5. Whom do they rule? | 5. Those doing business with and making use of each other, as we do in living in cities. |
| 6. Which human beings who make use of human beings do you mean? | 6. Those who share in common in a regime and do business with one another. |
| 7. What do you call a science of sharing in common in a regime? | 7. Good counsel. |
| 8. Good counsel in what? | 8. In better managing and preserving the city. |
| 9. When what is present and what is absent does a city come to be better and to be better tended and managed? | 9. When there comes to be friendship of the people for each other, and when hatred and factional strife are absent. |

This last claim, effectively that Alcibiades wishes to bring friendship to Athens and to banish hatred and faction, becomes the crucial one for the refutation. Socrates will persuade Alcibiades that there are serious problems with this political vision and thus that he does not even know to what end he should direct his political career. But before turning to that refutation, let us briefly consider the winding path that brings us to it.

Alcibiades' first three answers are notably underwhelming. His answers lack any substance; he can hardly describe what it is he actually wants to do as a statesman. The third response is somewhat more revealing than the first two: he wants to take up the business of the "noble and good" men (*kaloi kagathoi*), that is, of the aristocratic class of Athenian gentlemen dedicated to political activity and civic virtue, including military service. It is no coincidence that Alcibiades' admiration for these men comes out in the wake of the speech in which Socrates vaunted the surpassing virtue of his rivals. But Socrates makes prudence or practical wisdom (*phronēsis*) the defining characteristic of the *kaloi kagathoi* and thus quickly shifts all of the emphasis onto the "good" and off of the "noble" (125a3–b8). The question becomes "What are they good *at*?" as opposed, for example, to "Whom are they good *for*?" It is worth noting that there are no mentions of the *kalos kagathos* anywhere before or after this point in the *Alcibiades*. Moreover, with the very slight exception of a few lines at the conclusion of the dialogue (135b7–c1), the noble is never again taken up as the explicit object of Socrates' and Alcibiades' examination.[17] By no means will Socrates attempt to reprise the discussion of the noble and the good that formed the substance of the dialogue's most important refutation. Alcibiades' enduring confusion concerning those matters pervades his responses throughout this refutation, but Socrates does nothing to bring that fact to his attention.

Socrates does not ask for whom Alcibiades will be good, but he does ask whom he will rule. Alcibiades denies that he has in mind to rule those who are sick, sailing, or farming (125b14–19). Of course, he will have to rule over such people; Alcibiades means he will not rule them in their capacities as invalids, sailors, and farmers. He will rule them as citizens, which seems to be a much more exalted thing. But why is that so? Socrates is beginning to coax out of Alcibiades what it is about political life that he finds so alluring—not in the sense of the power or fame that will accrue to him but rather of the characteristics or deeds that he thinks a statesman must acquire or perform to become deserving of those rewards. He is forcing Alcibiades to try put into words what it is about political rule that is so splendid and worthy, but the question of who is ruled causes some difficulty since the ruled are after all nothing more than the collection of ordinary and ordinarily deficient people who happen to inhabit the city. Rule over horses, Alcibiades recognizes, is nothing grand (125b10–11).[18] So what is it about human beings living together in a political community that makes presiding over them so prestigious? Alcibiades' first guess seems to fall well short of the mark. He identifies the utilitarian economic purpose of the political community, the way in which people "make use of" each other in business, that is, the division of labor. Certainly, this is one of the most important functions and origins of political life—Socrates takes it as the starting point for the city in speech of the *Republic* (369c9ff). But Alcibiades is made to see that it does not live up to what he has in mind, as Socrates points out that the ship's pilot and the chorus director each rule over groups of people, organized into classes and ranks according to their tasks, who "make use of one another" by working together toward a common goal (125c6–d6).

Alcibiades sees that rule over partnerships is not enough. He reformulates his response to say that the ruled are those "sharing in common (*koinōnountōn*) in a regime." Thus, Alcibiades turns away from the hierarchical division of labor and conceives of the city as a partnership represented by the "regime" (*politeia*). Now, if this succeeds in doing greater justice to the esteem in which Alcibiades holds the political things, it is likely only because he makes use of the word for *politics*. But vague as it is, his present formulation suits Socrates' purpose. For "sharing in common in the regime" indicates that the citizens *qua* citizens get to share in some important good not reducible to mere economic advantage, that grand common good to which political life seems to be directed. Surely, Alcibiades will have to know at least what this good is if he is to become a successful statesman. We have thus returned to the question of what it is in which Alcibiades will counsel the Athenians—but now the question is not (except indirectly) what will earn him great honors but what will most fully bring about the flourishing of the city. Accordingly, Alcibiades does not speak of war and peace. In the present light, the pursuit and expansion of Athenian empire may appear to Alcibiades too much as a vehicle to his own glory. Alcibiades will instead describe his political goal in terms of "friendship." The friendship he hopes to bring to Athens may strike him as a somewhat nobler expression of his political aspirations, one in which his motives appear more simply virtuous or devotional.

We may note that in order to arrive at the idea that friendship is somehow the ideal end of civic life, Alcibiades had to abstract from the economic division of labor among the citizens. Only then could he articulate a notion of citizenship worthy of the name. But Socrates' analogy of the body to the city, in which he says that the former is well managed when health is present and sickness absent, is given a kind of twist when he repeats the analogy with eyes and ears in place of the body (126a5–b7). This causes us to realize that the good management of a complex whole may require the good condition of its several parts, each with its own narrow tasks to perform and therefore with its own standard of good condition (cf. *Republic* 419a–421c). In coming to express what he takes to be the highest good of the political whole, Alcibiades was forced to lose sight of what is low but necessary within it. His political vision is therefore fundamentally utopian.

Socrates pushes Alcibiades to see this by having him define "friendship" as a kind of agreement or concord (*homonoia*), a definition that in a manner typical of Socratic dialectic, at once puts words in Alcibiades' mouth and, as his assent implies, draws out an important aspect of what he had in mind. Note that when Alcibiades cites friendship as what needs to be present in a well-managed city, he cites *two* things as its opposite: hatred and factional strife. Perhaps this suggests that Alcibiades has a clearer or more vivid idea of what it is he wants to eliminate in the city than what it is he thinks can replace it. Alcibiades sees distressing and unwelcome tension in Athens' bitter partisan divisions, but his vague suggestion that these might be replaced by friendship does not appear to reflect any depth of thought on the root causes of factional political strife. In short, Alcibiades' hopeful vision of politics, though well intentioned, appears rather naïve in its assumption that there can be a resolution of the distressing but deep-seated antipathy in the political arena. Politics has in every place and time—though perhaps especially in democracies—been characterized by disagreement, sometimes profound disagreement, on how the regime ought to be governed. Is there something in the nature of politics that precludes the alternative, a regime in which no disagreement on this crucial question exists? Perhaps it is a vague awareness of this problem that strikes Alcibiades when Socrates begins to elaborate the notion of "concord" by likening it to agreement about numbers, measures, and weights. Political agreement among the rival factions in the city will not be so easy to obtain as agreement about these things, not least of all because they so often involve rival claims to justice (cf. 111e10–112a9). Hence, Alcibiades falls silent when Socrates asks him to name the art that will produce the kind of friendship he has in mind.

In an attempt to salvage the notion of friendship in the city, Alcibiades attempts to reformulate what he means, saying that by "friendship and concord" he means that which a mother and father have with their son, or a brother with his brother, or a wife with her husband (126e2–4). Family members do not promote each other's good or the good of the family for the sake of personal gain. Familial loyalty and devotion seem by their character to imply a belief that one's own good is indistinguishable or at least inseparable from the good of one's family.[19] Hence the family comes to sight as more than the sum of its parts, for the common good that is shared by its devoted members is a good that cannot simply be understood as being composed of the individual goods of each. As a worthy object of devotion, something bigger than oneself, extending forward and backward in time beyond the reach of one's own life, the family can appear to be a great and natural whole, a chorus to which one can add one's own voice in order to become a part of something more splendid and more beautiful than could ever have been accomplished alone. Devotion to the family supports the hope that the soul can transcend the narrow, physical concerns of the body, that there is a higher purpose for it to fulfill, through which it can make itself worthy of the great good it longs for and seeks.[20] Alcibiades senses that devotion to such a common good can provide such fulfillment and more exaltedly still in the case of the city than of the family. Something like this is what he sees as the great good politics can provide, and it is in providing this good to Athens that he hopes to make himself worthy of the honor he seeks.

But Socrates, by means of a surprising argument, is able to persuade Alcibiades that this vision is illusory by reminding him of the division of labor that fragments and disequilibrates the unity of the whole. He points out that a husband will have knowledge his wife does not have ("manly understanding," such as the hoplite's art), and vice versa (the wife has knowledge of how to spin wool, a "womanly understanding"). But this, suggests Socrates, means that there will be no concord between them in these matters and therefore no friendship (127a9–11).[21] Now, Alcibiades' response to this suggestion, "it appears not," is hardly emphatic (127a13). He senses that there is something lacking in this argument, and understandably so since it does not seem that husbands and wives "doing their own things" in the way described will stop them from holding each other dear (127a14–b4). And yet Alcibiades raises no objection, for he is aware that the love between a husband and wife is no argument for the possibility of political unity. As in the family, there will be division of labor in the city. There will be warriors and wage earners, deserving and receiving greatly differing amounts of honor from the city, partaking to different degrees in manliness or courage, the virtue without which Alcibiades would not consider life worth living. There is no political art, no agreement to be brokered, that will make these disparate members of society love each other like a family, and so Alcibiades senses that there is some force in Socrates' point. The only city that comes close to achieving the effect Alcibiades describes is the city in speech of the *Republic*; so it is no wonder that Alcibiades cannot imagine a regime that can overcome the problem to which Socrates points.[22]

But the peak of the refutation is still to come. For Socrates now notes that, not only is it not possible to overcome the division of labor in a city, it is not even desirable! Cities are well managed, agrees Alcibiades, when all within them "do their own things," when different people have different tasks and possess accordingly different knowledge. These are the cities that do "the just things" (127b5–c7). But this means that justice and friendship are mutually exclusive features of the city, for when there is justice, there is no concord; the differing ways of life and differing knowledge and opinions produced by each doing his or her own things make broad political agreement impossible.[23] We note that Alcibiades agrees with Socrates' definition of the just things without hesitation, assuming that justice is a crucial good for the city. Socrates for his part, in accordance with the character of the second half of the dialogue, allows Alcibiades' implicit claim to be able to identify the just to go unexamined. Alcibiades cannot accept the incompatibility of justice and friendship and is therefore left with the impression that the argument that produced that conclusion must somehow have been faulty. Alcibiades admits his ignorance in terms that recall the conclusion of the previous refutation: "But by the gods, Socrates, I don't myself know what I mean, but I'm afraid that my being in a most shameful state has long escaped my notice" (127d6–8). Socrates has exposed the depth of Alcibiades' ignorance concerning the most basic political question: what is the proper end of the city? The manifest relevance of this ignorance to Alcibiades' political aspirations, especially in comparison to the ignorance revealed by the previous refutation, is what causes Alcibiades to feel ashamed in addition to feeling bewildered.

The "royal tale" that initiated the second half of the dialogue showed us Socrates' concern to establish virtue as the explicit centerpiece of Alcibiades' pursuit of political success. This appeared to be a needed remedy to the lowering of Alcibiades' sights upon realizing that no rigorous course of training or education yet separated him from the heights occupied by Pericles. The refutation with which Socrates followed his speech therefore focused upon

Alcibiades' concern for virtue as a statesman. By forcing Alcibiades to express this concern and to submit it to the light of Socratic refutation, Plato has invited us to consider in substantive detail what may be the most important feature of Alcibiades' political ambition, his desire to be a benefactor to the Athenians. It is one thing to say, as we have, that the love of the noble fuels the most powerful and far-reaching political ambition, but it is another to ask Alcibiades to put into words his vision of noble statesmanship.

The most striking thing about Alcibiades' attempts in this refutation, however, is precisely their lack of substantive detail. Alcibiades knows he wants to do good for the city of Athens, but he is virtually clueless as to how he will accomplish this. Upon reflection, however, this perplexity might have been expected on the basis of the dialogue's previous refutation. There, it was demonstrated that Alcibiades lacked clarity regarding his own greatest good (specifically, its relationship to the just, the noble, and the advantageous). It can hardly be a surprise, therefore, that Alcibiades is equally lacking in clarity about the greatest good of the Athenians. From here, Socrates will lead Alcibiades to the familiar Socratic conclusion that virtue is the greatest good for human beings, or is at least its necessary precondition—a conclusion that mostly obscures any possible conflicts between Alcibiades' good and the city's. It will be for us to determine whether the course of education that leads him there is, in the long term, better or worse suited to a true education concerning the noble and the good than the one that explicitly began from the concern for Alcibiades' own happiness. For now, we note that Socrates sidestepped the most serious difficulty in this refutation by refocusing the discussion upon "good men" in the sense of "prudent men," from Alcibiades' initial movement toward the "noble and good men" (*kaloi kagathoi*).

But it would be an exaggeration to say that Alcibiades' concern for his virtue or nobility as a statesman was completely devoid of content. If indeed this concern is, as we have suggested, crucial to the vitality of political ambition, it must have *some* direction, and Alcibiades has given us an idea of what that is. He understands the good of the city, which he will attempt to provide, negatively, in terms of the enmities, rival parties, factions, feuds, and other heated disagreements that create a palpable sense of tension and precariousness. After all, wherever there is charged debate over consequential matters, there is the possibility of misjudgment and error—a lesson from the dialogue's first half. But the awareness of tension falls well short of the capacity to provide resolution. In fact, it is not obvious *a priori* that there is a resolution for every tension, and Alcibiades finds himself giving voice to a stunningly naïve political hope on account of his past failure to think through the primary causes of the political tension that makes him so uneasy.

Yet for all of its simplicity, Alcibiades' answer to the question "What is the good of the city?" provides valuable insight into his political ambition. The desire to bring unity of mind and friendship to the city is, as we have already noted, one of the driving forces underlying the development of Callipolis in the *Republic*. There, the idea that a good city requires *homonoia* appears twice: once under the heading of justice, in Socrates' elucidation of Thrasymachus's argument whereby even a gang of pirates must practice justice internally (351c7–d7), and once under the heading of moderation, which Socrates defines as agreement in the city as to who must rule and who obey (432a6–9).[24] But earlier in that discussion, Socrates stipulates that this agreement among the citizens will require the dissemination of an invented oracular prohibition against the interference of any one class in the business of another (414bff). Alcibiades recognizes that the city will work best—from an economic perspective at the very least—when the citizens work and coexist harmoniously. But he has not yet considered the difficulty that this harmony, to the extent it can exist, must rest upon the general acceptance of certain falsehoods endorsed by the regime concerning the very goods (justice and moderation) it is claiming to provide.[25] A question therefore arises concerning the trajectory of Alcibiades' political ambition. His love of the noble, evident in his desire to be a benefactor of his city, appears to depend upon a certain vagueness in his understanding of what the human good is and the extent to which a regime can provide it, in full, to its citizens. If that vagueness should ever begin to give way to clarity, what would become of his ambition? This type of question is not necessarily answered by Plato in the course of a single dialogue, but we ought to keep it in mind as we watch Alcibiades' political ambition and political understanding evolve over the course of his Platonic appearances. For now, Alcibiades goes no further in resolving his puzzlement than to bemoan his shameful and bewildering ignorance.

## Virtue as Self-Knowledge, the Socratic Project, and the Final Exhortation (Exhortations, 127d9–135e8)

Socrates responds to Alcibiades' lament with encouragement: he is at the right age, says Socrates, to perceive such ignorance; had he perceived it at fifty, it would have been difficult to care for himself appropriately (127d9–e3). Is this an indication that Socrates still sees some potential for Alcibiades to turn toward philosophy? We are at least reminded of the fact that Socrates took particular interest in the Athenian youth, even if he was not always eager to emphasize that fact (cf. *Apology of Socrates* 37d–e, 39c–d with 21b–22e, 23c–d). Socrates mentioned in his opening speech that the god's allowing him to speak to Alcibiades had to do with his age, since the two of them would only have conversed in vain if Alcibiades had not been so full of hope (105e6–106e1). But now Socrates indicates another possible reason for wanting to converse with Alcibiades (and others) at this particular stage of his development: his malleability and openness to revising his opinions and beliefs, namely, by submitting them to rigorous philosophic examination.

However, we cannot know if this is what Socrates has in mind until we see more clearly *how* he is trying to shape or redirect Alcibiades' understanding. To restate a key ambiguity, it is not yet clear whether Socrates intends to guide Alcibiades through a full philosophic investigation of the question of justice. In the most recent refutation, Alcibiades' confidence in the possibility of justice, understood as a broad political common good, was shaken. But what will Socrates do now that Alcibiades has come once again to recognize his need for some kind of education? Even if he should intend merely to moderate Alcibiades' political ambition by helping him see some of the city's natural constraints and limits, it would still make sense for him to say that he is better off recognizing his need for education now than at fifty. We must therefore turn to the dialogue's long final section, Socrates' closing exhortation to Alcibiades, with an eye to the lasting effect Socrates is hoping to have on the youth. Moreover, this exhortation, even more than the preceding ones, will lay out for the careful reader some features of the substance and method of Socrates' own examination.

Alcibiades reiterates his eagerness to learn what he must do, and Socrates' response reminds him that his success is in the hands of the god. Socrates thus maintains a certain caution—he may well be uncertain himself as to how Alcibiades' character and thinking will develop—though without ever indicating any change in the disposition of the divine guardian whose sanction, he claims, is required for this conversation (127e4–8). But there is more to this latest reference to "the god" than another reminder of Socrates' limited liability. At this point, he also refers to his own "divination" regarding the potential benefit to both Socrates and Alcibiades from their association. With this, for the first and only time, Socrates suggests that the divine sanction of his relationship with Alcibiades consists in more than the mere absence of divine opposition: Socrates also claims to possess some revealed and prophetic knowledge. Socrates thus continues to ramp up the uncanny and divine element of his self-presentation. Alcibiades, for his part, does not repeat his accusation that Socrates is joking (cf. 124d1), but neither does he directly address this feature of Socrates' claims. He merely assures Socrates that to the extent his participation is required in the form of answering questions, he can be relied upon.

Willingness to answer questions, however, is not the same as a desire to investigate the questions concerning the just, the noble, the good, and the advantageous, which Socrates had pointed to in the previous exhortation. As he did in that exhortation, Socrates will now suggest a course of inquiry ostensibly designed to remedy the ignorance that has been exposed in the preceding refutation. Hence, Socrates will now proceed to bring a number of new questions and considerations to Alcibiades' attention, beginning with the question of what it means for a human being to take care of oneself (127e9–128a3). The first distinction he makes in this regard concerns "taking care" in the abstract. He distinguishes between taking care of *x* and taking care of *x*'s things, that is, that which belongs or pertains to *x*. Alcibiades has a hard time understanding this distinction but finally accepts it once Socrates clarifies that one cares for something by means of an art that makes it better; but the art that makes the foot, hand, or body better (gymnastics) is different from the arts that make their things better (shoemaking, ringmaking, and weaving). Socrates brings Alcibiades to see that if they are going to take care of themselves, they must come to know what they are in precise distinction from the things that merely belong to them (128a4–129a1).

For the sake of learning how to care for oneself, then, the key question becomes "What is a human being?" Socrates takes up this puzzle first by reference to the Pythian inscription "know thyself," which he previously invoked at the conclusion of his last speech (129a2–4). He thus suggests that the search for the self is mandated by the gods. Through a consideration of the act of conversing in which their own two "selves" are engaged, Socrates leads Alcibiades to the conclusion that the human self is that which makes use of the body. The body is thus understood to be like a tool used by the human being and therefore something distinct from the human being, just as an artisan is distinct from the tools he uses (129b1–e12). Socrates is preparing a dramatic demotion of the body. If the body is not the self but only belongs to the self, then care for the body is not a part of care for the self (according to the first argument about "taking care"). We can begin to imagine the consequences of such a demotion for Alcibiades by recalling the importance of his physical beauty to the grand hopes and sense of deserving or worth he had developed.

Of course, the basis of this demotion is highly suspect. That care for *x* is strictly separate from care for what pertains to *x* is a dubious claim even on the basis of Socrates' examples. Surely shoes help protect the feet if not strictly to make them better. Likewise, the ring beautifies the hand, and it is at least a question whether this counts as improving it. As these considerations show, Socrates' insistence that one must know *what* a thing is in order to make it better is somewhat misleading; the primary thing one would need to know is what it means to make it better, that is, what its good is. We are reminded of Alcibiades' dialectical education near the beginning of the dialogue, which concerned the different meanings of "better" in different contexts and laid the ground for the conclusion that the "better" in a key instance was the more just. A complete examination of care for a human being would require an investigation of the place of the just and the noble in the human good. Turning our attention to the dialogue's concluding section as a whole, the section that ostensibly examines how to care for oneself as a human being, we become aware of a stunning silence concerning what the good of a human being is. That silence is emblematic of the subtle but important difference between the education Socrates now proposes to provide and the one he pointed to at the end of the first half of the *Alcibiades*.

We could also object to Socrates' paradoxical suggestion that the human being is separate from the human body. His argument was that the human being is what uses the body and that user and used are distinct. But this seems to overlook the possibility that the human being is able to use itself or that one part of it is able to use another. Now, Socrates seems to indicate his awareness of this problem when, after getting Alcibiades' agreement that what uses (or "rules") the body is nothing other than the soul, he reintroduces the possibility that body is or is a part of the human being, as though that possibility had not adequately been disqualified: "I suppose that no one would suppose anything but this . . . that the human being is one of three things . . . soul or body or both as the whole thing." But then immediately disqualifying the latter two options on the basis of dubious inferences from earlier agreements, Socrates concludes, "Since a human being is neither body nor both [body and soul], I suppose what remains is either that it is nothing, or if it is something, that the human being happens to be nothing other than soul." Alcibiades appears to take this strange procedure to be a rigorous logical proof that the human being is the soul, but Socrates suggests that the examination has been "imprecise" but "fitting" and that it results in the beautiful (he does not say "correct") belief that the two of them are conversing "soul to soul" (130a1–d10).

To the question "What is a human being?" Socrates has enumerated four possible answers: soul, body, both together, and nothing at all. He does this in such a way as to persuade Alcibiades that the human being is simply the soul, which exercises sovereign rule over the body (129e10–130a3, 130d5–6). But Socrates' indication that the examination has been imprecise means he does not himself consider the argument that has persuaded Alcibiades to be sufficient, and so each of the possibilities he mentions remains potentially valid. Socrates notes that the imprecision in the argument has resulted from their failure to take up a question that was earlier raised and abandoned: what is the self itself (*auto to auto*)? A self is a thing, something one can refer to as "it"; the "self itself" is of the common Socratic form, "the *x* itself," and therefore refers to that by virtue of which all selves can be called selves.[26] Now, how would knowledge of this help us determine what, among the enumerated possibilities, a human being is? Perhaps there is a clue is in the enigmatic suggestion that the human being may in fact be "nothing." By raising this possibility, Socrates suggests that the "human being" may somehow be more illusion than reality, that it is not a self, that there is no "it" to which one refers in saying "human being."[27] Perhaps the combination of body and soul is not in fact a unity in the way the mind perceives it to be. Perhaps not even one or the other alone is truly as much a unity as it seems. Rather, a human being may be more like a galaxy: a number of disparate parts somehow holding themselves in relative proximity to each other, which we regularly or necessarily recognize as a single whole. Or perhaps what is meant by "human being" always includes a soul or mind, the nature of which is a matter of serious uncertainty—especially since the soul or mind is precisely that which appears to confer selfhood on whatever it apprehends, or to be the source of selfhood. Can the soul then correctly be understood as a self? What indeed is the soul? If the nature of the soul does not correspond to the idea of a human being that we inevitably come to hold in our minds, then it would make some sense to say that the "human being" is a fiction. None of these questions or possibilities can adequately be taken up, however, without some understanding of what it means to *be*, or to be a self. This must be grasped before we can draw conclusions as to whether any given thing—such as the human being—is something or nothing. Moreover, it remains to be seen how Socrates' philosophic activity as exemplified in this dialogue constitutes any kind of approach to these questions and problems.

By alluding to the key themes of the fuller, more precise discussion that he elides, Socrates both allows us to work out the questions he has on his mind and gives Alcibiades the impression that they are engaged in a serious philosophic discussion.[28] In fact, it is closer to an indoctrination of Alcibiades in the belief that his soul must become the highest and most serious focus of his life to the virtual exclusion of his body. Of course, this may be a beneficial belief (cf. 120c9–d8), and even a beautiful one, but it has not been demonstrated in the way Alcibiades supposes. In accordance with this indoctrination, the next portion of the exhortation is dedicated to the explicit demotion of all pursuits besides the pursuit of self-knowledge, that is, knowledge of the soul. First, Socrates runs down the arts. The doctor and the trainer know the body but not themselves, while farming and all craftsmanship are all said to be "vulgar" arts, as they provide knowledge not even of the body but of what belongs to it (131a2–b9). Alcibiades welcomes this last conclusion especially; he has, after all, been dismissing Socrates' comparisons of him to tradesmen and artisans throughout the conversation in his struggle to clarify what the political art governs and why it should be exalted. But what Socrates suggests next is more difficult for Alcibiades to swallow. He begins to draw conclusions about Alcibiades' lovers: they did not love Alcibiades himself but his body, which is why they ceased to pursue him once his bloom began to fade (131c5–13). As we have seen, Alcibiades' sense that he is worthy of the greatest goods, of godlike power and fame—itself a crucial source of Alcibiades' ambition—stems in large part from his beauty and from the flattering attention his beauty has garnered him. Hence, Socrates now attacks Alcibiades' ambition directly at its source: the attention he has received says nothing about Alcibiades' worth; it merely refers to something he possesses. It is as if his admirers loved him only for his money (cf. 131b13–c4).

Socrates claims to be the only lover of Alcibiades' soul, citing this as the explanation of his strangeness as a lover, that is, of why he has remained after Alcibiades' other lovers have left. The effect of this revelation on Alcibiades is quite clear: he is adamant that Socrates not leave like the others (131d6). But this means that Socrates now has some real leverage with Alcibiades. Whereas he flattered Alcibiades at the outset of the conversation just to gain an audience with him, he is now in a position to demand something in return for his continued attention and guidance. What he asks is that Alcibiades "strive to be most beautiful"—not in his body, of course, but in his soul (131d7). Alcibiades has now been persuaded that he is not as yet worthy of Socrates' love, and Socrates has, by shaming Alcibiades for his complacency, brought him around to recognizing that he must improve himself. Note that it is the earnest attempt or striving that Socrates demands, not success.

Socrates' concern, as he goes on to explain, is that Alcibiades will become a lover of the *demos* (*dēmerastēs*) and thereby become corrupted. He does not say what this corruption entails, except that it will make Alcibiades uglier or baser (*aischrōn*), but apparently "many and great men among the Athenians have suffered this" (131e10–132a4). Whatever is meant by this corruption, it is clear that the most immediate danger to be addressed is that of Alcibiades being seduced by the Athenian public, which, Socrates says, is "fair of face . . . but one has to look upon it once it has stripped" (132a5–7). We gather, then, that Alcibiades is prone to believing that there is something grand and fulfilling to be won in the Athenians' approval, like a lover enthralled by the beauty of his beloved. But Socrates knows that this beauty is a kind of illusion, an adornment of sorts that can be stripped away to reveal something less impressive—much as Alcibiades' own deficiency has been revealed beneath his own beguiling physical beauty. To avoid corruption, Alcibiades will have to "train first . . . and learn what needs learning in order to go into the things of the city" so that he may "go with an antidote, and suffer nothing terrible" (132b1–3). It thus becomes clear that Socrates wants to hold Alcibiades back from politics long enough to provide him with a certain preparation against becoming enraptured so that the dazzling effect of extraordinary political honors can be counteracted by the knowledge or firmly held opinion that these honors are not what they appear to be.

This is the only use of the word *corruption* (*diaphtharēis*) in the dialogue, and therefore it deserves special attention. Given the suspicion Socrates would later face of having corrupted Alcibiades, it is striking that the only thing he says about corruption here is that he is trying to save Alcibiades from it. It is in fact an instance of a well-known Socratic theme, namely, that the Athenian citizens themselves, Socrates' very accusers, are the true corruptors of the youth and that their corruption consists precisely in what they consider to be good civic, moral, and religious education (*Apology of Socrates* 24c–25d, *Republic* 492dff, 514aff). Socrates is therefore identifying the danger to Alcibiades that lies in his continuing to accept and to adopt the opinions of the Athenians, the expression and promotion of which will win him honor in the assembly. For Socrates to save Alcibiades from this corruption would be to steel him against the corrupting education of the many, especially (if the preceding refutation is any indication) concerning the character and possibility of justice and harmony in the city. But this means that Alcibiades must become uglier and more hated to the city just as he becomes more beautiful and beloved to Socrates by challenging the city's conventions. Socrates' defense against the charge of corrupting Alcibiades here may amount, from the city's perspective, to something of an admission of guilt.

And yet we still do not have a clear idea of precisely what opinions Socrates thinks Alcibiades must challenge and revise. There has, however, been one indication of the substance of the teaching Socrates hopes will help protect him: Alcibiades has agreed that the self-knowledge he must obtain is moderation (*sōphrosunē*, 131b4–5). Moderation—which was the leading member of Socrates' list of Spartan virtues (122c5)—is the first specific virtue clearly endorsed by Socrates in this final exhortation. We might expect Socrates to elaborate by explaining how this moderation will help Alcibiades in the management of the city's affairs and how it will help protect him against the dangers of corruption. From such an account, we could get a clearer impression of the corruption Socrates speaks of by considering what measures he is taking to prevent it. But before Socrates takes up such a discussion, there is a remarkable passage in which Socrates purports to explain the meaning of the Delphic inscription and thus the manner in which one can obtain self-knowledge or moderation.

Socrates' explanation runs as follows. The way for a soul to come to know itself is analogous to the way an eye would come to see itself. Just as the eye must look into a reflective surface, so there must be for the soul an object in contemplating which the soul will come to know itself. In the case of the eye, the very part in which the virtue of the eye—namely, sight—happens to reside—namely, the pupil—also has the properties of a mirror. If one gazes into an eye, one will see one's face reflected, and thus an eye can see itself by looking to another eye in that place where its virtue is found. Likewise, by looking to that part of another's soul where its virtues, namely, wisdom and the like, reside, the soul will come to know itself. Now, this virtue of the soul, by which it knows and thinks or is prudent (*phronein*), is the most divine thing in it. "This in [the soul] is therefore similar to the god,[29] and someone looking to this and knowing everything divine, both god and thought (*phronēsin*), would thus also know himself to the greatest extent" (132c9–133c6).

Let us begin by considering the effect of this explanation on Alcibiades. The upshot would seem to be that Alcibiades must spend his time with Socrates if he is to know himself. Socrates suggests that by contemplating his wisdom and observing the way he thinks, Alcibiades will come to understand what a soul is and will thereby become able to care for himself properly. The account is delivered with a steady crescendo, culminating in the claim that the human soul approaches godliness most by wisdom, knowledge, and thought. Alcibiades is therefore encouraged to believe that what is divine within him can be nurtured and brought out if he is willing to pay careful attention to what is divine within Socrates. Incidentally, it may be at this moment that Socrates' repeated claims to have access to a divine power or divine wisdom will strike Alcibiades as more serious than he had previously suspected or at least more important given Alcibiades' current impression that his greatest political battles will be waged against divinely favored kings (cf. 124d1). Moreover, the elevation of the soul that has been the theme of this exhortation now takes on a significant new dimension. If there had been any doubt at the moment when Socrates first differentiated the soul from the body, there can be none now: souls are not physical beings, and therefore neither are we. Socrates has Alcibiades direct his focus intently on those features of human experience, of knowing and thinking, that often and for many seem to announce their connection to a world beyond what is disclosed by the senses, an invisible reality that intersects mysteriously with the visible one, and to powerful beings who seem to order and oversee the whole. Alongside Socrates' exhortation to moral virtue, then, Alcibiades is now given a jolting inducement to piety.

But there is much more to this exchange than its effect on Alcibiades. The *Alcibiades* is punctuated by reminders that Socrates too is seeking an education in his relationship with Alcibiades. The first exhortation contained a hint that Socrates was seeking self-knowledge (113a4–5). In the second exhortation, it became clear he was concerned with confirming his wisdom, albeit by a means that appeared to become closed to him shortly thereafter (118c7–d8, 119b5–c5). Earlier in this final exhortation, Socrates raised but did not pursue some intriguing questions about the nature of the human being and of the soul (130a5–c7). Now, as the exhortation approaches its conclusion, Socrates lays out a method for a soul to come to know itself through an examination of wisdom and the divine. The suggestion that this account is meant to describe the method and substance of Socrates' own philosophic project can also help us solve the puzzle of his introduction to the account. Why does he say that it will be an explanation of the Delphic inscription "know thyself"? It is hardly reasonable to think that this pithy imperative implied anything like the elaborate account of the pursuit of self-knowledge that Socrates goes on to explain. But the Delphic Oracle is an important figure for the Platonic Socrates: in the *Apology of Socrates*, he claims that his refutations of statesmen, poets, and craftsmen were motivated by an attempt to test the veracity of the god's pronouncement that no one was wiser than Socrates. Now, if one wishes to place this twenty-year-old Alcibiades in the category of statesmen, one can say that Socrates' refutations of him were in the service of his Delphic mission. But it is more illuminating to note that Alcibiades is the first and most famous member of another group: the beautiful, ambitious, aristocratic Athenian youths for whose corruption Socrates was tried and executed by the city. The account Socrates gives here, then, may indicate the way in which his association with these youths was also a part of his project to test his own wisdom.[30]

It may be tempting to suspect that this account is merely an elaboration of our earlier suggestion that Socrates wishes to confirm his wisdom by making others wise. But the analogy of the eye seeking its reflection in another eye does not quite bear that interpretation. The reflecting eye is in one way active and in another way passive. It is active in that it is gazing back into the eye that gazes into it. Socrates will watch Alcibiades watching Socrates. More concretely, Socrates will observe Alcibiades' process of knowing and thinking as Alcibiades attempts to grasp Socrates' wisdom. But the eye is passive in that it does not become, but merely reflects, that which it sees. Socrates will examine Alcibiades' development as it is exposed to a Socratic education in an attempt to see his own wisdom confirmed (or "reflected"). In particular, Socrates will attempt to understand that which appears to be most "divine" in the soul, that is, its capacity for scientific and practical thought, by means of an investigation of everything divine (or, we may say, the divine itself), which will take place through the observation of Alcibiades. Thus, Socrates' encouragement of piety in Alcibiades comes at exactly the moment when he signals to the careful reader the most important reason for that encouragement. We can therefore make the following tentative suggestion as to the purpose of Socrates' education of Alcibiades in the second half of the dialogue. On one hand, it is a genuine attempt to direct Alcibiades away from his more dangerous tendencies and to protect him from the form of corruption alluded to above. On the other hand, it is an education that will allow Socrates to observe closely the human soul in the active pursuit of happiness through wisdom or prudence, and as its attachment to virtue and piety grows and changes. It is thus, as Socrates himself says, an attempt to gain self-knowledge by learning about "everything divine, both god and thought."

Socrates has by now convinced Alcibiades that he needs a Socratic education in virtue before he can begin his political career. As noted above, this is not because the goodness of such a career has come into doubt but rather because Alcibiades has become convinced that he is destined to fail if he does not take care to become as excellent or virtuous as possible. What remains is for Socrates to explain how that attention to virtue will allow him to succeed where he otherwise would have failed. Socrates will appear to fulfill his promise after all, having something to offer Alcibiades without which his ambitions would go unfulfilled. But as Socrates' arguments in this section are relatively weak, Alcibiades' failure to object will testify to the strength of the conviction Socrates has instilled in him that nothing is more important now than care for the virtue of his soul.

Socrates begins by renewing his agreement with Alcibiades that moderation is self-knowledge. Then, for a moment, he comes close to raising a crucial question that has been left unaddressed throughout this final section: "So if we neither know ourselves nor are moderate, would we be able to know our things, and among these, both *bad and good* things?" (133c18–23; emphasis added). By specifying the bad and good things, Socrates reminds us that the most important function of self-knowledge must be the ability to provide oneself with the good and avoid the bad (cf. *Charmides* 174a10 ff.). But Socrates immediately ceases to speak of the bad and the good for oneself, and it becomes clear that Alcibiades has already been sufficiently persuaded of the key suggestions: that virtue is the human good or at least its necessary and sufficient condition, and that vice stands likewise with respect to the bad. As the dialogue winds toward its conclusion, Socrates increasingly makes virtue the *sine qua non* of all human happiness. Rescinding his earlier concession to doctors, trainers, farmers, and craftsmen, who were said to be immoderate in lacking self-knowledge but still to have knowledge of the body and its things, Socrates now says that *only* moderation can provide knowledge of oneself, one's things, and the things of one's things. Moderation is also therefore necessary, Alcibiades agrees, if one is going to have knowledge of the things of others or of cities; the immoderate man can never be a statesman or a competent household manager, but lacking knowledge of what he does, he will err, do badly, be wretched, and make those wretched on whose behalf he is acting (133d1–134b3).[31] Nothing worthwhile, it would seem, can be accomplished without moderation.

Furthermore, continues Socrates, this means that it is not the wealthy man who avoids the greatest misery but the moderate man. We thus see a return of Socrates' attempt to weaken Alcibiades' attraction to wealth (though Alcibiades' lukewarm response to this claim may be a troubling sign in that regard).

Socrates extends this conclusion to the city: building walls, triremes, and dockyards will not make the city happy if it lacks virtue. This seems to supply the knowledge of which the last refutation showed Alcibiades to be ignorant. The purpose of political rule is to provide virtue to the citizens, which is why a good statesman must be virtuous (134b4–c7). With this exhortation to virtue now explicitly connected to the end or purpose of political rule, Socrates at last begins to make explicit the danger his teaching and preparation are meant to curb in Alcibiades: "Therefore it is not authority or power (*archēn*) to do what you want that must be provided either to you or to the city, but justice and moderation . . . and it is by acting justly and moderately that both you and the city will act in a manner dear to the god (*theophilōs*)" (134c9–d2).[32] The power to do what he wishes, a power that borders on or points to omnipotence, is what Alcibiades admires in Pericles, according to Socrates' opening speech, and what Alcibiades covets for himself (104b3–8, cf. 105a7–b7). It is Alcibiades' desire for this power, his belief that he can become effectively omnipotent by ascending to the highest political rule, that is here Socrates' concern, and it is in his expression of that concern that he reintroduces justice as a key political virtue without which no statesman can succeed, linking this virtue to piety. So concerned is Socrates that Alcibiades come to see this as necessary, that Socrates guarantees Alcibiades' happiness and that of the city if he and it act uprightly and do well, "looking toward what is divine and bright" (134d3–e2). If such a guarantee is seriously intended, it quietly casts doubt on the possibility of acquiring the virtue Socrates speaks of.

While the corruption of the city's education may pose the greater danger to Socrates' philosophic project, Alcibiades also risks straying, partly on account of Socrates' philosophic challenge, toward what we surmised was represented by the attraction to Persian luxury in Socrates' longest speech. Accordingly, Socrates consistently opposes virtue to the pursuit of wealth here in the exhortation's culmination. It appears that the desire Socrates now wants to curb in Alcibiades is the same one he was willing to inflate in his opening speeches. Thus, in his final formulation of the "godless and dark" behavior that Alcibiades must avoid, Socrates calls the object of this desire by its name, finally making explicit that the two paths between which Alcibiades must choose are those of virtue and tyranny (134e4–135b5). This would suggest that the "love of the *demos*" to which Socrates earlier referred opens the door to tyrannical urges: desire for tyranny is the pole toward which democratic statesmanship will naturally incline if it is not properly constrained. The power and honor granted to the statesman by the city only make more insatiable his desire for power and honor. This insatiable desire is what Socrates described in his opening speeches in saying that Alcibiades would never be satisfied if he could not "fill all human beings" with his name and his power. The antidote Alcibiades must have in hand in going to lead the city, then, is a powerful belief in the goodness of virtue and the impossibility of happiness without it, and in the calamity that will befall him if he should pursue his tyrannical urges—and that means a sober awareness of the illusory hopes and desires fostered by the acquisition of great power and honor from the *demos* (134e8–135b1).

Concluding the exhortation, Socrates now makes explicit Alcibiades' need to submit to him as a teacher. It is better, nobler, and more fitting, agrees Alcibiades, for the bad and slavish, until they acquire virtue, to be ruled by their virtuous superiors. Alcibiades admits with overwhelming shame that he is in a state befitting a slave (135b7–c11). Our suspicion regarding the dialogue's central exhortation is confirmed: Socrates does not need to prove that he is the *only* one able to educate Alcibiades in order for Alcibiades to agree to turn to him for education. Needless to say, Socrates does not here repeat the test that forced him to abort the project of the dialogue's first half. He does not for a moment allow Alcibiades to suspect that Socratic education in virtue is unimportant for political success. The dialogue does, however, conclude with what appears to be another failed test. Socrates asks Alcibiades if he knows how he will escape his condition, and Alcibiades answers, "If you wish it, Socrates." Socrates says this answer is not "beautifully spoken" and corrects it: "If the god wishes it" (135c12–d5). Alcibiades' response would have been better had it reflected an appreciation of the training and discipline to which Socrates had often pointed, or of the piety Socrates had been attempting to foster in him, or of the need for moderation as self-knowledge that was the theme of the final exhortation. Instead, he seems to attribute to Socrates a wondrous power to bestow upon him the great goods he desires. Socrates' foisting of the responsibility for Alcibiades' success onto the god is partly a prudential measure: he does not want to bear the brunt of the blame when his education turns out not to fulfill Alcibiades' ambitions. But it also indicates the emergence of a remarkable dynamic: Alcibiades now looks to Socrates as to a god. And perhaps more important, Alcibiades responds to the Socratic correction by affirming in his own name that Socrates' divinity will be responsible for Alcibiades' fate (*legō dē* 135d7). Thus, Socrates at last succeeds—though only after fully persuading Alcibiades of the profound necessity of acquiring virtue for the sake of happiness—in getting him to acknowledge the power of his god (cf. 103a4–6, 124b8–d1).

Alcibiades feels he must now win Socrates' favor and warns him that they will likely be changing roles: it will be Alcibiades attending to Socrates from now on (135d7–10). Socrates responds strangely: "O well-born one, my love will not differ from a stork's if, having hatched a winged love in you, it will be tended by it in turn" (135e1–3). Perhaps this is an indication of what Socrates sees as the best case for Alcibiades now. His own love for Alcibiades—or whatever that represents—likely will not bear the fruit he hoped it might. Alcibiades will not be a philosopher. But Alcibiades' newfound affection for Socrates means that Socrates can hope at least to have the benefit of his loyalty and service. Indeed, should Alcibiades become powerful in the city, this loyalty would be of no small benefit. Moreover, Alcibiades' agreement to devote himself to Socrates and his commitment to "begin from this moment to take care of justice" mean that the Delphic quest for self-knowledge through the examination of Alcibiades' soul can continue (135e4–5). And yet, Socrates' concluding reply reveals some serious concern: "I wish that you would continue to do so; but I dread—not from distrusting something in your nature, but from seeing the might of the city—that it will overpower both me and you" (135e6–8). Socrates is not confident that Alcibiades will be able to continue to concern himself with justice; the might of the city, which would seem to refer to the seductive power of the *demos*, will be too much for Alcibiades to resist.

The end of the *Alcibiades* is a reminder that corruption—especially in the context of Socrates' alleged corruption of Alcibiades—is a more emphatic theme in Plato's presentation of this relationship than simply ambition. Of course, corruption here means in part the corruption of grand ambition, but we have now learned there are at least two distinct senses in which Alcibiades' ambition is in danger of being corrupted. As the concluding portions of the dialogue clearly indicate, Socrates wants to avoid fanning the flames of Alcibiades' tyrannical desires. This was already becoming clear in Socrates' speech about the Persian and Spartan monarchs, as Socrates' new and unexpected emphasis on wealth seemed designed to discourage Alcibiades from pursuing power in the form of despotic luxury. But the very last lines of the *Alcibiades* suggest there is another danger, this one connected to the dialogue's only explicit mention of corruption. Alcibiades is in danger of being lured away from Socrates by the promise of honor from the *demos*, which stands in direct tension with Socratic education insofar as it requires the unthinking adoption of the city's conventional (and confused; 110d5ff) opinions concerning the just, the noble, the good, and the advantageous.

The challenge Socrates faces, then, is to discourage those desires in Alcibiades that most threaten to nourish or become tyrannical ambition without squashing his ambition so much as to permit him to become complacent in his love of the *demos*. The dangers of a tyrannical Alcibiades to Athens, to Alcibiades himself, and to Socrates as his teacher are obvious enough. The danger of an Alcibiades corrupted by the Athenians would seem to have most to do with Socrates' philosophic pursuit of self-knowledge as described in his account of the Delphic inscription. To study the effects of exposure to Socratic education on moral and religious opinions, Socrates needs Alcibiades to continue to attend to that education and therefore to feel some abiding need to learn something about virtue and the soul. As we saw at the end of the first half of the dialogue, the strength of Alcibiades' desire for honor from the *demos* is a significant obstacle for Socrates in this respect. But this means that Socrates might not be simply vindicated by the reflection that he is trying to save Alcibiades' ambition from corruption. As we noted above, being corrupted by the Athenians would be viewed by the Athenians themselves as being well educated—and while this education may contain the seed of the desire for tyranny, it may also include measures that effectively restrain that desire by making it inseparable from a desire to benefit the city. That is, if Socrates were simply to leave Alcibiades to his pursuit of democratic honors, that very pursuit might provide the necessary security against any inclination to rule tyrannically. But all through the dialogue, Socrates has been engaged in the risky project of drawing Alcibiades' ambition out beyond—but not too far beyond—its democratic horizons.

All along, however, Socrates has deployed one important tactic that may serve to protect Alcibiades simultaneously against both threats of corruption: the inducement, subtle at first but becoming explicit by the end of the dialogue, to piety. Socrates has, almost from his very first words to Alcibiades, presented himself as a lover whose unusualness is somehow connected to a special understanding of and relationship to the divine. His portrayal in his longest speech of the divinity of especially the Persian king forms a part of this effort, as it suggests to Alcibiades that he may need some divine support in order to contend with his "true rivals." In the dialogue's closing exchanges, it becomes clear that fostering a sense of piety in Alcibiades could be an important means by which Socrates can restrain some of Alcibiades' nascent tyrannical desires—a suggestion supported, as we shall soon see, in the *Second Alcibiades*. But Socrates' attempt to encourage some concern or curiosity in Alcibiades regarding the gods, their sanctions, and their punishments also forms a part of his project to find confirmation of his own wisdom. As a practical matter, and as has already been suggested, Alcibiades' felt need for divine support may help keep his gaze fixed upon Socrates and his strange revelatory claims. More substantively, however, Socrates pushes Alcibiades to see his happiness or fulfillment, the good of his soul, and his virtue as being intimately bound up together. As a result, Alcibiades' attention to Socratic education will be focused upon the question of how a life of virtue is to lead to or constitute human happiness—as Alcibiades' repeated assent throughout the closing portions of the dialogue suggests he thinks it does—and especially the extent to which the existence of gods who reward and punish might support or complicate these same matters. Socrates' explanation of the Delphic imperative to seek self-knowledge suggests that he is particularly keen to observe Alcibiades' evolving opinions regarding these questions. Self-knowledge seemed there to refer especially to the fundamental Socratic question "What is a human being?" and confirming his own wisdom concerning this question requires careful attention to the matter of the human soul and its good and therefore its place in the cosmos.

All of this, however, leaves quite unclear the extent to which Socrates' education will continue to challenge Alcibiades' opinions concerning the just, the noble, the good, and the advantageous. If Socrates still intends to maintain Alcibiades' interest by showing him the unworthiness of sharing and promoting the opinions of the Athenians in order to win their honor, what will prevent Alcibiades' disenchantment with the *demos* from diminishing his desire to serve them and accordingly turning him ever more toward tyranny? One possibility is that Socrates still hopes for Alcibiades to recognize in philosophy a critique of political life that will curb his political ambition altogether—but the conclusion of the first half of the *Alcibiades* is not encouraging with respect to that goal. Another possibility, as we have already noted, is that the pious fear instilled in part by Alcibiades' Socratic education could make the pursuit of tyranny a frightening proposition even as demagoguery loses its appeal—but the sustainability of that approach will depend rather heavily on the extent to which Socrates intends to leave the pious inclinations he fosters in Alcibiades unperturbed by his philosophic investigations. Perhaps Socrates' most valuable asset in his dangerous attempt to keep Alcibiades away from demagoguery and tyranny simultaneously is the hopefulness that characterizes Alcibiades' youth. Youthful hope for happiness, drawn upon by Socrates at the peak of the dialogue's central refutation (116b7–8), insists on the possibility of perfect human fulfillment in a way that becomes less clear or less common with age (cf. 127d9–e3). This fact is deeply understood and powerfully made use of by Socrates, who brings Alcibiades' hopes to a fever pitch by the end of their first conversation. But how long will these hopes remain at their highest under the pressure of Socratic education?

As things stand now, Alcibiades' high hopes run through Socrates, with his half-promise of divine assistance toward the acquisition of virtue, freedom, and happiness (135b7–d6). We shall have to see how these hopes appear by the time the *Second Alcibiades* begins. But there is one aspect of Alcibiades' Socratic education, evident a bit more in the first half of the *Alcibiades* than in the second, that we must continue to bear in mind: the need for and power of rhetoric for a democratic statesman, which Alcibiades seems naïvely to lack at this point. In this connection, one aspect of Socrates' presentation of the Persian and Spartan kings and queens, not mentioned above, bears emphasis. The royal bloodlines, Socrates noted, are protected by keeping all men but the king away from the queen. The ephors guard her in Sparta; fear alone in Persia (121b5–c4). At issue here is the question of how a political leader can successfully subdue competitors and usurpers. Alcibiades' "true rivals" are absolute monarchs, who have on their side overwhelming force in one case and fearful religious devotion on the other. The democratic or Athenian way, emphasized by Socrates as Alcibiades' only hope to become worthy (123d2–4), is through rhetoric. If Alcibiades cannot be stopped from pursuing his happiness in politics, teaching him to succeed with rhetoric rather than by force may be the best way to moderate his ambition.

CHAPTER 3

# RESCUING ALCIBIADES

## (*Second Alcibiades*)

*Alcibiades*/*Second Alcibiades* is not the only pair of Platonic dialogues to feature the same interlocutors, nor is it the only pair with both parts named after the same person. It is, however, the only pair of dialogues in which the title of one suggests that it cannot be understood apart from the other. The *Alcibiades* can stand alone, but the title *Second Alcibiades* implies that the dialogue's purpose and meaning are not fully discernible without reference to the *Alcibiades*.[1] What, then, is the relationship between the two? Obviously, the *Second Alcibiades* is set at a later date. We know this because the *Alcibiades* presents the very first conversation between Socrates and Alcibiades, and so the *Second Alcibiades* cannot have taken place before it. But how much time passes between the dialogues? One portion of the conversation in the *Second Alcibiades* implies that Pericles, who died around the time of the end of the siege of Potidaea in the year 429 BC, is still alive (143e8 ff).[2] The *Second Alcibiades* must therefore be set between the *Alcibiades* (when Alcibiades is nineteen years old, so around 431 BC) and the death of Pericles only two years later. Furthermore, it is important to note that Socrates and Alcibiades were on campaign together in Potidaea for much of those two years.[3] And while it is not impossible that the *Second Alcibiades* takes place abroad, Plato gives us no positive reason to think it does. This in itself is reason for thinking that the conversation takes place before Potidaea and thus only a few months after the association of Socrates and Alcibiades began.[4]

As far as we know, then, the *Second Alcibiades*, like the *Alcibiades*, takes place before its title character's infamous political career has been launched. It is, however, set after the beginning of Alcibiades' education at Socrates' hands or at least after their agreement that such an education would be undertaken. The *Alcibiades* ended with the suggestion that Socrates would need to provide Alcibiades with an education in virtue—piety, justice, wisdom, and moderation understood as self-knowledge—in order to prevent him from being seduced by the dark temptations of demagoguery or tyranny. And yet some doubt was raised as to the possibility of Alcibiades' success in completing such an education on account of the overwhelming strength of his political ambition and desire for the admiration of the *demos*. By presenting a second glimpse of Socrates and Alcibiades, then, Plato invites us to search for evidence of changes in Alcibiades' opinions and disposition. If we can identify some effects of the Socratic education on Alcibiades, we can attempt to infer what the character and purpose of that education may have been. In addition, we must try to determine whether the conversation of the *Second Alcibiades* itself forms a part of that educational project.

A final note about the sequence *Alcibiades*/*Second Alcibiades* before turning to the latter's opening section. The traditional subtitles of these dialogues, apparently assigned by a thoughtful Platonic scholar in the two or three centuries following Plato's death,[5] are *On Human Nature* and *On Prayer*. Each title suggests two things. The former suggests both that Alcibiades is presented as an exemplary specimen of human nature—a human being, we can say, whose natural hopes and desires have been allowed to grow and flourish in the most favorable possible conditions—and that Socrates is attempting to answer the core philosophic question "What is a human being?" (129e9). Likewise, the latter suggests both that our model of human nature will now be portrayed in the condition that gives rise to a turn to prayer and that Socrates' investigation will focus on the spiritual posture of his interlocutor. All of this bears emphasis at the outset because, while prayer is indeed the framing theme of the *Second Alcibiades*—the drama of the dialogue revolves around Socrates' successful bid to discourage Alcibiades from the prayer he was on his way to make—the details of the discussion make it easy to lose focus on the theme of prayer per se. In particular, the dialogue is memorable for Alcibiades' open contempt for the imprudence of the many (139c6–9, 145a8–10, 146c8–10)—a sentiment at odds with his earlier insistence that the *demos* can never be won over by anything but good counsel grounded in knowledge (*Alcibiades* 107a10–c12)—and especially for what appears to be his candid acknowledgment that tyranny must be counted among the greatest goods (141a5–b8). Indeed, these details will be crucial for our understanding of the development of Alcibiades' political ambition. But we must keep in mind the theme of prayer if we are to grasp the meaning of the *Alcibiades* dialogues taken as a pair.

## Prayer, Prudence, and Madness (138a–140d)

The *Second Alcibiades* opens on Socrates intercepting Alcibiades on his way to pray "to the god" (138a1–3). Alcibiades acknowledges that he intends to pray, but when Socrates remarks upon his sullen or angry countenance, noting that Alcibiades is "looking to the ground, as if concerned about something (*ti sunnooumenos*)," the latter replies cagily, "And what would one be concerned about?" (138a4–6). Alcibiades is not forthcoming about what is troubling him. Either he does not think Socrates will be able to help him, or he is ashamed or embarrassed to reveal his thoughts.[6] But Socrates replies as if he has at least an idea of what is troubling Alcibiades: "The greatest concern, Alcibiades, as it seems to me. Since, by Zeus, don't you suppose that, of the things we happen to pray for in private and in public, the gods sometimes give some but not others, and to some people but not to others?" (138a7–b4). This consideration can be said to represent "the greatest concern" because it points to the question of the relationship between human beings and gods. The frequent inefficacy of prayer might be interpreted as evidence against the existence of gods or at least against the existence of providential gods who care about our well-being. Of course, it cannot be considered to be a proof that no (or no such) gods exist, but it does suggest that if there are gods who listen to our prayers, they are not content to grant all of our requests. Some human beings appear to be favored over others, and so the question of what the gods want from us is also raised by the phenomenon of unanswered prayers. Socrates' terse response thus raises the questions "Are there gods?," "Do they care about us?," and "What do they want from us?," that is, the theological questions that weigh most heavily in the consideration of the key philosophic one: "How ought I to live?"

Alcibiades responds with emphatic assent to Socrates' intimations about "the greatest concern" (138b5), leading us to suspect that he is occupied, at least in part, with one or all of the questions raised above. It is likely that Socrates' education of Alcibiades has been the cause of his coming to consider such questions. As we will see, Alcibiades' opinions about what is good in human life generally and in political life specifically have undergone significant changes since his first conversation with Socrates. But not all changes in one's opinion about what is good prompt a turn to prayer. In attempting to determine what precisely has prompted this turn in Alcibiades, it is important to note that the particular changes that have taken place in his opinions are ones that make him uneasy. So far, then, we can tentatively suggest that Alcibiades' prayer is the result of some new uncertainty about how to live that has in turn raised questions about the divine.

Having confirmed that Alcibiades considers the frequent inefficacy of prayer to be a problem, Socrates suddenly takes the conversation in an unexpected direction. He now suggests that the problem with the frequent inefficacy of prayer is not the difficulty of getting what we want but the danger that we might get what we ask for. "Much foresight," says Socrates, is needed to avoid praying unwittingly for "great evils, supposing they are goods," at just the time "when the gods happen to be in that disposition in which they give what one happens to be praying for" (138b6–9). From the outset, then, Socrates appears concerned to caution Alcibiades against taking prayer too lightly, especially if there remains any confusion as to what is good and what evil, and for so long as he is uncertain as to what disposes the gods to answer prayers. This advice appears to assume what the act of prayer generally implies: that praying opens up a line of communication between human beings and gods. Of course, there may be gods who consider our thoughts and desires at all times, not just in prayer, and this may be commonly believed even by those who imply by praying that requests to the divine must be submitted under special circumstances. But Alcibiades has not questioned the traditional understanding of prayer and of the performance of religious rites: we learn at the end of the dialogue that he has brought a wreath for the god to whom he had intended to pray. Alcibiades may have come to have some grave questions about the relationship between gods and human beings, but his questioning is characteristically partial. There are some conventional beliefs he does not think to doubt.

Socrates' caution highlights two dangers of prayer. We have been considering the danger that arises from not knowing what disposes the gods to favor a given supplicant: there is uncertainty as to what the gods want, and so their demands must not be taken lightly. On the basis of this advice one should avoid *testing* the gods, for example, by saying, "Let Zeus strike me with a lightning bolt if he does not wish for me to be a tyrant," since precisely this may anger the gods, while the results of such a test could never be conclusive. (It is not clear how or how well Socrates applies this advice to his own activity.) It is the other danger of prayer, however, that Socrates goes on to emphasize: namely, the danger that we might accidentally pray for the bad, thinking it is good. Socrates illustrates this danger with the example of Oedipus, who "is said to have suddenly prayed that his sons divide their patrimony with the sword" (138b9–c2). By this choice of example, Socrates calls to mind the depictions of gods and human beings characteristic of tragedy, in which it is quite unclear to what degree anyone has control over his or her own fate. Of course, it is typical of tragedy for the heroes' fates to be attributable to their own *hubris*, but this very *hubris* is the cause of the fulfillment of prophesies that suggest their fates were already determined. Tragedy thus gives meaning to the inevitability of human suffering by suggesting that our suffering has divine or cosmic significance. Socrates is right in saying of Oedipus that instead of cursing his sons, "it was possible for him to pray for some relief from the evils present to him" (138c2–3). But this abstracts from the significance of his suffering and his curse: Oedipus blinds himself and has himself exiled in order to purify himself and Thebes of his monstrous deeds, and it is on account of the injustice of his sons that he curses them. If Oedipus's actions affirm the tragic understanding of human significance, Socrates' warning against Oedipus's misunderstanding of good and bad is a warning against assuming that there is any such significance. It is a call to consider and address the possibility of human insignificance and meaninglessness. Perhaps we can even go so far as to say that Socrates' opposition to Oedipus's mistake puts Socrates on the side of comedy as opposed to tragedy.

How much of this does Alcibiades understand? He responds by calling Oedipus a madman, asking "Who do you think would dare to pray for such things if he were healthy?" (138c6–8). Alcibiades does not consider that Oedipus's deeds may represent a characteristically human reaction to great misfortune. Instead, he casts doubt on the validity of Socrates' concern by pointing out that healthy, sane human beings do not curse their own families and therefore that Alcibiades need not worry that he will make such a mistake. But Socrates forces him to clarify what he means by "madness." Alcibiades first agrees that being mad is opposite to being prudent and then that there do seem to be both imprudent and prudent human beings (138c9–d3).[7] Alcibiades, though he scoffed at the suggestion that he ought to worry about exhibiting the *madness* of Oedipus, at least acknowledges the existence of *imprudence* among human beings and therewith the danger that he might fall prey to it. Might it be that he considers the possibility of imprudent prayer to be a more genuine danger than that of mad prayer? Socrates suggests that the two of them examine who the prudent and imprudent are (138d4). Most relevant would seem to be the question of which group Alcibiades himself belongs to. The surprising conclusion of this examination is that madness and imprudence appear to be the same thing, for just as one can be sick or not sick but nothing in between, all who are not prudent are imprudent—but Alcibiades has already agreed that the opposite of prudence is madness "and how could two things," namely, imprudence and madness, "be opposite to one?" (138d7–139b11).

Alcibiades does not recognize the crucial misstep in this argument; Socrates will expose it in a moment.[8] But the identification of imprudence with madness serves to bring the question of Alcibiades' own condition to the fore. Alcibiades dismissed Oedipus on the grounds that he was mad as opposed to sane, and no one would claim that Alcibiades is insane. But Socrates shifts the opposition to that of imprudence and prudence, implying that prudence, not mere sanity, is what is needed for the correct identification of good and bad and thus for safe prayer. Thus, Socrates' faulty argument may yet establish a conclusion worth considering: the errors of the merely imprudent may not be so far removed from the follies of madmen as they seem (cf. Xenophon, *Memorabilia* 3.9.6–7). That Alcibiades may himself be in the situation of a madman, however, seems from his easy dismissal of Oedipus not to be on his mind. In light of the *Alcibiades*, then, in which Socrates noted that it is only after recognizing one's ignorance that one can attempt to remedy it, Alcibiades appears still to be living in the fog of a kind of imprudence. We see Alcibiades' lack of understanding in this regard even more clearly when Socrates reveals that Alcibiades has come to refer to the majority of people in the city, both those his own age and his elders, as madmen (139c3–9). As we have noted, this opinion seems to be the result of exposure to Socratic philosophy; one might think, for example, of the famous analogy of the cave in the *Republic*. But Alcibiades' attitude here suggests that while he has been quick to recognize the errors of others, he has failed to see how he himself suffers from the same ignorance that afflicts the many.

Socrates makes this misunderstanding of Alcibiades' even starker by getting him to realize that the way in which he conceives of the city as full of madmen cannot be accurate. He asks, "Do you suppose we would safely share the city with so many madmen, and that we would not long ago have paid the penalty by being struck and pelted and undergoing the very things madmen are likely to do?" and Alcibiades responds, "So how does it stand, Socrates? For it's likely not as I supposed it was" (139c10–d6).[9] That it gives Alcibiades pause to consider that living in the city is appreciably different from living in an insane asylum shows the thoughtlessness of his assessment. He has not understood what truly makes them mad, and thus he has failed to diagnose himself as sharing their madness. For Socrates and Alcibiades each will pay a penalty to the city: they will be accused and convicted of injustice and impiety. The city is a cave after all, and Alcibiades, whatever critique of it he has adopted notwithstanding, is still very much living within it. It is because Alcibiades has failed to understand the true argument for the similarity of imprudence to madness that Socrates will now be able to persuade him that there is a greater distinction between them than he had supposed.

Socrates elucidates the mistake in the argument to which Alcibiades had agreed by a series of illustrations. Gout, fever, and ophthalmia are all types of sickness, but no one of them is identical to the whole of sickness; shoemakers, builders, and sculptors are all craftsmen, but no one of their arts is identical to the whole of craftsmanship (139d8–140c4). Similarly, says Socrates, madness is only a part, albeit the greatest part, of imprudence, but imprudence and madness are not therefore the same thing. This argument has the potential to soften Alcibiades' contempt for his fellow citizens: many of them might suffer only from mild forms of imprudence. Socrates identifies a number of types of imprudence less severe than madness, saying that some such people are called "'silly' and 'thunderstruck.' Of those wishing to name them with the most euphemistic names, some say 'great-souled,' others 'good-hearted,' and still others 'guileless,' 'inexperienced,' and 'dumb' . . . but all these things are imprudence" (140c5–d4).[10] The analogy to craftsmanship even suggests it may be beneficial for the city as a whole for each citizen to share in some part of imprudence or thoughtlessness. After all, if liberation from the most problematic kind of imprudence requires that one take up a Socratic examination of oneself and of the city, then prudence can belong only to the philosopher and to those with sufficient natures who have had significant exposure to philosophy. The arts, which are made possible by the city and which in turn make the city worthwhile for the citizens, require imprudent practitioners whose lives must be more or less circumscribed by their activities (cf. *Apology of Socrates* 22c9–e1, *Charmides* 162e7–163e11).

But while the analogy of imprudence to the arts suggests that imprudence may have its benefits, the analogy to sickness reminds us of the cost the citizen must pay for the city's useful and beautiful works or of the insufficiency of those works to provide the good. The key point in Socrates' differentiation between imprudence and madness comes when he asks Alcibiades whether all sickness is ophthalmia. Strangely, Alcibiades replies, "Clearly not, as it seems to me at least; and yet I am at a loss about what I mean" (139e8–9). Why does he hesitate on this seemingly trivial point? Perhaps Alcibiades has become wary of the sting of Socratic refutation and senses that Socrates may be setting a trap (cf. *Alcibiades* 116e7–117a2, *Memorabilia* 1.2.47). He agrees to push forward in the argument once Socrates, quoting Homer, suggests that they investigate as "two together" (140a1–2). But perhaps Alcibiades was right to hesitate over this question. For it may be that while all sickness, clearly, is not ophthalmia, all imprudence may be a kind of blindness. The sections that follow will help us understand that suggestion by revealing the most important things Alcibiades has not been able to see.[11]

## Politics, Eros, and the Greatest Goods (140d–143b)

Socrates suggests that he and Alcibiades should return again to "the beginning of the argument," specifying that he has in mind the question of who the imprudent and prudent men are (140d6–8). One might object that the very beginning of the argument concerned the questions regarding prayer that Socrates first pointed to. But as Socrates goes on, he has Alcibiades agree that the prudent are those who "know what things they ought to do and to say," whereas the imprudent know neither and therefore do and say what they ought not (140e1–9). To speak of what one ought to do and say, however, is to raise the very question we drew out of Socrates' opening reflections on prayer, that is, the question of how one ought to live. Hence we can see that as Socrates and Alcibiades have now defined prudence, it requires above all an understanding of the relationship such as it is between gods and human beings. This alone should suffice to indicate the rarity of the virtue of prudence in its highest or Socratic form.

Socrates now explains his invocation of Oedipus by saying he is to be counted among the imprudent human beings since he said and did what he ought not to have said and done. What separates Oedipus from the majority of people, however, is that he prayed for things he supposed were bad for himself, whereas there are many people, says Socrates, "who are not in a rage as he was, and do not suppose they are praying for bad things for themselves, but good" (140e10–141a4). Socrates thus draws a distinction between two ways in which people choose the bad for themselves: on purpose and out of ignorance. Since Oedipus is the example of the former and since Alcibiades claimed that Oedipus was mad, we are tempted to say that what distinguishes madness among the forms of imprudence is the knowing, willing pursuit of or prayer for the bad (e.g., in the spirit of vengeful anger) as opposed to the accidental choice of the bad through ignorance or error. But it must be admitted that it is the "madman" Oedipus who presents the more serious challenge to Socrates on the question of prudence. If Oedipus knowingly chooses the bad for himself, then he at least correctly distinguishes the good from the bad. The disagreement between Oedipus and Socrates, then, is not over what is good and what is bad, but whether one ought to choose what is good for oneself or what is bad for oneself. Socrates has asserted that Oedipus is among the imprudent in the sense that he does and says what he ought not. But might not Oedipus make the same accusation of Socrates? Their disagreement hinges on an evident difference between their understandings of how the will of the gods must inform our decisions about how to live. Perhaps the difficulty in meeting the challenge of Oedipus is reflected in the fact that Socrates himself never says that Oedipus is mad. The crux of the matter may lie in the "rage" that Socrates says possessed Oedipus when he cursed his sons.[12]

But while the case of Oedipus is complicated by his clear-sightedness regarding the good and bad things, Socrates now accuses Alcibiades of the more ordinary sort of imprudence. He claims that if the god to whom Alcibiades had intended to pray were to appear to him beforehand and offer him "to become tyrant of the city of Athens"—or, if Alcibiades should think that paltry, then over all the Greeks or all of Europe, or even that everyone come immediately to perceive "that Alcibiades, son of Kleinias, is tyrant"—Alcibiades would go away pleased, as having hit upon "the greatest goods" (141a5–b6). To this accusation, Alcibiades replies, "I suppose I would, Socrates, as would anyone else if such things should happen to him" (141b7–8). This is surely the most shocking and most memorable moment of the dialogue. Despite the *Alcibiades*' having closed with Alcibiades accepting Socrates' condemnation of tyranny, he is now clearly open to it.[13] It even seems that this passage answers one of the dialogue's central dramatic questions: for what was Alcibiades on his way to pray? But if we are precise, we should say that an offer of tyranny from the god to whom Alcibiades had intended to pray would obviate the need for Alcibiades' prayer, whatever it was to be.[14] At any rate, the shift from the desire to be a counselor and to bring friendship to his community to the desire for a god to grant him tyranny over the Athenians goes together with the contempt for the *demos* that is evident in his characterization of the many as imprudent or mad. Disillusionment with democracy, perhaps especially with Athenian democracy, has led Alcibiades to think that tyranny may be as good as or better than democratic statesmanship. But that is not a conclusion that a youth such as Alcibiades, who had had such enormous hopes for his career as an Athenian general and politician, would freely and happily accept. Most significantly, such a conclusion would require Alcibiades to accept the need for injustice in politics, not only in dealing with other cities—we know from the *Alcibiades* that he has flirted with that idea—but in dealing with the Athenians themselves.

Alcibiades' ready acknowledgment that the divine offer of universal tyranny would delight him and obviate his need for prayer is met with an elaborate Socratic warning. Socrates sets up his first major speech of the dialogue by eliciting Alcibiades' agreement to a pair of clarifying qualifications concerning the hypothetical divine offer: Alcibiades would not exchange his life or soul (*psuchē*) for tyranny over all the Greek and barbarian lands, nor would he accept it if he were only "going to make bad and harmful use" of it (141c1–8). Once Alcibiades has agreed to these stipulations, Socrates proceeds to remind him of just how frequently human beings acquire the objects of their prayers only to pay for them with their lives or with such misery as to negate any goodness they might otherwise have obtained.

Socrates' speech cites three examples that illustrate the danger of imprudent prayer: Macedonian tyranny, Athenian generalship, and parenthood. In the first case, he refers to the beloved (*ta paidika*) of the tyrant Archelaus, who loved tyranny no less than Archelaus loved him, and who killed Archelaus "in order to be a tyrant and a happy man" but was in turn killed only three or four days later by "some others" (141d7–e3). Next, he describes the plight of the Athenian *strategoi*: some are now exiles, others have lost their lives, and even those who seem best off must not only brave fearsome dangers on campaign but are "besieged" by the sycophants at home no less than by their enemies abroad, so that the prayers of some of them express regret at ever having become a general at all (142a1–b1). Finally, of those who pray for and beget children, Socrates says that those whose progeny are "thoroughly rotten" go through life in pain, while others come to wish that even their good children had never been born after having been robbed of them by misfortune (142b3–c3). And yet, says Socrates, one rarely finds anyone who would cease praying for these things or refuse them if offered, and the many, when they acquire what they seek only to be harmed by it, soon recant their prayers (142c4–d4).

Socrates concludes that the imprudence of human beings—their ignorance of what they ought to say and do—is a great cause of their misery, and he claims to marshal the authority of Homer in defense of that conclusion, suggesting it may have been said "truly" that human beings blame gods in vain in saying their evils come from them; " 'but they [i.e., human beings], by their own'—one must say either 'reckless wickedness' or imprudence—'have pains beyond what is fated'" (142d4–e1, cf. *Odyssey* 1.32–34).[15] In the passage Socrates quotes, Zeus is referring to Aegisthus, who murdered Agamemnon and married his wife Clytemnestra, even though he had been warned by the gods that Orestes would take vengeance upon him should he do so.[16] But Socrates' suggested emendation of the Homeric verse is of no little importance. In the original, Zeus condemns human disobedience of divine command. By suggesting the substitution of imprudence (*aphrosunais*) for sinfulness (*atasthaliaisin*), Socrates makes the passage appear to support the clearest strain of his message to Alcibiades: one must be prudent—have knowledge of what one ought to do and say—before praying for or pursuing any ends, lest their attainment bring more harm than good. That this message is not simply Homeric is further suggested by the fact that the prayer Socrates recommends to Alcibiades is not from Homer, nor is anything like it uttered by any Homeric character. It is rather from an unnamed "prudent poet," who prayed, infers Socrates, on behalf of himself and his mindless friends who "were doing and saying what was not best, but seemed to them so": "Zeus King, give us the good things (*ta esthla*) both when we pray for them and when we don't, but ward off the terrible things (*ta deina*) even when we pray for them" (143a1–3). This, says Socrates, is a "beautifully" and "safely" spoken prayer (143a4–5).

Alcibiades' admission that he considers universal tyranny among the greatest goods is thus followed by a Socratic speech that ostensibly aims to demonstrate the inadequacy of his reflection on the goods he is pursuing. The most pressing suggestion of the speech is that Alcibiades' pursuit of the good is misguided, as Socrates' story about Archelaus's usurper clearly suggests that tyranny alone does not constitute the greatest good. Indeed, the short-lived ruler is said to have killed Archelaus so as to be "a tyrant and a happy man." He succeeded in the former, but his emphatically unhappy end provokes us to ask which of the two goals, or of the two components of his goal, was more important. If tyranny should in fact be understood only as a means to happiness, then Alcibiades is likely confused in counting universal tyranny among the greatest goods. It is happiness that should be striven and prayed for, not a potentially deficient and disastrous means toward it. But perhaps it must be said that tyranny is not a means but an indispensable component of happiness or the greatest good, at least for Alcibiades.[17] There would still be an important lesson here for Alcibiades insofar as he has failed to see tyranny as a good that is incomplete and unstable. Praying for or accepting tyranny would be a dangerous proposition in that it invites the possibility of calamitous unhappiness by failing to insist on obtaining whatever else is needed to secure and complete the good.

Socrates' story contains a further suggestion that the good provided by tyranny is inherently incomplete. While it is true that Archelaus's beloved is said to have "loved" (erotically desired; *erasthenta*) tyranny, this very love is directly compared to Archelaus's love of him. Any attempt to suggest that the shortness of the usurping beloved's reign and life is the only thing that marred his happiness must account for the fact that his erotic striving has a counterpart in a man who had acquired and successfully maintained tyrannical rule for many years. Not only did the successful tyrant Archelaus have an erotic longing comparable to his beloved's desire for tyranny, but his possession of tyranny did not even provide him with a successful means to the end he so passionately sought, namely, the affection of his beloved—in fact, it was his very undoing.[18] At least in the case of tyranny, then, we are led to wonder whether a full account of its goodness does not require a full examination of *eros*—a suggestion confirmed by the inclusion of offspring in Socrates' catalogue of goods commonly but imprudently prayed for.[19] In what sense and to what extent does erotic desire direct us, as we divine or suspect it does, toward the good? Both Archelaus and his beloved find only disaster in their erotic pursuits, and the example of Archelaus himself suggests that his counterpart would not have been satisfied even if he had "succeeded."

Alcibiades' response suggests he has failed to see the furthest-reaching suggestions and questions that could be provoked by Socrates' speech. He appears to agree with what he understands Socrates to have said and to think this agreement unproblematic. He says that Socrates has spoken beautifully and agrees that human beings falsely assume they are up to the task of praying for the best things for themselves and not the worst. "This I understand: how many evils ignorance is the cause of for human beings whenever, as is likely, we forget our own selves because of it both in doing and, in the extreme case, praying for what is worst for ourselves" (143a6–b5). Indeed, this may seem to be a kind of regurgitation of Socratic teaching, of something like the argument Socrates had made in the *Alcibiades* to the effect that ignorance of ignorance is the source of error and wretchedness for human beings (116e7ff). But Alcibiades gives no indication here that he has become convinced of his own ignorance regarding the good. He does not, for example, take the safe prayer of Socrates' prudent poet as a solution to his problems, which it seems would be necessary, at least for the time being, if he had come to doubt his own ability to identify the ends he should pursue. In fact, Alcibiades' apparent silence following the speech (see *mē siōpa*, 143a5) and his apparent lack of any interest in Socrates' prudent prayer suggest that he does not think Socrates has offered any guidance with respect to the "greatest concern" with which he is preoccupied on his way to pray. His distress about the gods is not that they may give him what he asks for, however safely or dangerously he asks, but whether they will hear or care for him at all. In short, Alcibiades' response shows no sign that he thinks Socrates' speech has taught him anything he had not already learned. Most important, his disposition toward tyranny does not appear to have changed.

Perhaps we can even go so far as to say that Socrates' speech was, in Alcibiades' ears, little more than a recapitulation of what has turned him to prayer in the first place. Whereas Alcibiades was supremely confident at the outset of the *Alcibiades* in his self-sufficient capacity to fulfill his political ambitions, he has since then clearly become concerned that he may lack what is required to ascend to the loftiest political heights on his own. To see why he has turned to the gods for help and not to Socrates, we must consider further Alcibiades' underwhelming response to Socrates' speech.[20]

Alcibiades' failure to object to Socrates' characterization of Athenian generalship is particularly striking. Socrates concludes his discussion of the Athenian generals, the best of whom he claims face greater dangers at home than they do on campaign, by noting, "If these dangers and toils were such as to lead to benefit, there would be an argument [for praying for or accepting generalship]; but as it is, it is quite the opposite" (142b1–3).[21] Would the young interlocutor of the first *Alcibiades* have acquiesced to this remark? We might well have expected Alcibiades categorically to reject the suggestion that the prospect of danger and hard work alters the desirability of becoming a general. We might have expected him to object that it is precisely the toil and braving of dangers that make generalship such a rare and splendid honor and that the required sacrifices, up to and including or especially death on campaign, only further exemplify the nobility and thus the glory of the general.[22] In his first conversation with Socrates, Alcibiades said he thought courage so great a good that he "would choose not to live if [he were] a coward" (115d5–7). Why does he not say here, against the thrust of Socrates' whole speech, that *courage* is required for those who wish to secure the greatest goods, that dangers must be braved but that the braving of dangers is at all events what makes life worth living?[23]

Alcibiades' silence about courage or nobility following Socrates' speech illuminates a key feature of the exchange preceding Socrates' speech. As we have seen, Alcibiades agrees that he would decline the divine offer of tyranny if it required him to give up his life (or soul, *psuchēs*) since that would render him unable "to make use" (*chrēsthai*) of the Greek and barbarian territories he was being given (141c1–5; cf. *Alcibiades* 129d11). By contrast, Socrates stresses in the *Alcibiades* that Alcibiades would rather die than accept anything less from "the god" than universal fame and power (105a6, 105c2–4). That Alcibiades now not only agrees but clarifies and elaborates in his own words that it is nonsensical to give up one's life or soul in exchange for the greatest good suggests that he has given some thought to the utilitarian argument lurking behind Socrates' refutation concerning the just, the noble, the good, and the advantageous (*Alcibiades* 115a1–116d6). Never in the *Second Alcibiades* does Alcibiades use any form of the word for *justice*. The word for *noble* or *beautiful* barely appears at all, though twice at the conclusion of Socrates' speech: Socrates says the prudent poet has spoken nobly, and Alcibiades in turn suggests that Socrates has spoken nobly (143a4, 7).[24]

Alcibiades no longer sees in courage an unambiguous solution to the problem Socrates has raised concerning the riskiness of pursuing the greatest goods or to the problem of ignorance and error that Alcibiades has learned to recognize. If this is indeed because noble sacrifice, such as was considered in the central refutation of the *Alcibiades*, no longer appeals to Alcibiades as it once had, then we are closer to understanding why he has become willing to admit openly to a desire for tyranny (as he refused to do in the *Alcibiades*, 106c2–3). The combined effect of Alcibiades' lowered esteem for the *demos* and his exposure to a critique of noble devotion has been to give life to the possibility that the fulfillment of his ambitions will require the compromise of his moral and political scruples. However, the associated undermining of courage has apparently sapped Alcibiades of his confidence in his self-sufficiency. His turn to the gods therefore arises from a complex psychological situation. Even if the gods exist, listen to prayer, and are able to help Alcibiades get what he wants, how will they look upon his newfound openness to unscrupulous political practices? Do the gods not condemn injustice and, as Socrates suggested at the end of the *Alcibiades*, tyranny above all? If the god to whom Alcibiades was going to pray were to offer him tyranny, says Socrates, it would not only obviate his need for prayer but would even replace his concern with joy. Such an experience would both allow Alcibiades to circumvent the mortal dangers that beset the path to political supremacy and secure the divine sanction for tyranny of which he must otherwise be unsure.

In the absence of such a revelation, however, what possibilities exist for Alcibiades? In particular, is there anything that can be provided to him by the man who has in fact appeared to him on his way to pray to the god? To restate a crucial feature of the passage we have been considering, Alcibiades is remarkably resistant to recognizing Socrates' insistence on the importance of reconsidering the goodness of the political life he passionately desires. That insistence becomes especially evident when we note that Socrates' description of the ills that befall the best of the Athenian generals reads like a brief summary of Alcibiades' future career. But is there yet some education that Alcibiades can fruitfully obtain short of the most demanding philosophic critique of his erotic political ambition? The answer to this question may depend upon the answer to the question raised by Socrates' emendation of the Homeric verse. Is it, after all, sinfulness or imprudence that brings to human beings "pains beyond fate"? If Socrates' proposed correction is ultimately well grounded, then what Alcibiades needs most is to become prudent. Political prudence may be what most truly succeeds where courage, or courage without prudence, is liable to fail. It may be especially lack of prudence that explains the sad political and other failures Socrates cites in his speech. But political prudence, which Socrates may be willing and able to provide, is hardly a safeguard against the more profound danger indicated by Homer's Zeus. And it is with respect to this danger that Socrates, as much as or more than Alcibiades, may be in need of an education (cf. *Alcibiades* 124c1–2).

The revelation of Alcibiades' openness to tyranny that led into Socrates' speech provides a window on Alcibiades' political ambition that parallels the Socratic accusation that initiates the *Alcibiades*. In both cases, Plato points to rule and renown as the imagined ends of Alcibiades' political aspirations. Of course, the version in the *Second Alcibiades* is more shocking since it mentions tyranny by name and since it gives us Alcibiades' own testimony rather than Socrates' mere allegation. More shocking still, if taken in comparison to the *Alcibiades* as a whole, is that there has yet to be any clear indication that Alcibiades' tyrannical ambition is still tempered by a desire to earn his fame and power honorably, by being a benefactor of the Athenians. This is not to say that that desire has disappeared in Alcibiades. We shall soon see that it is still active. Rather, we note here that Alcibiades' apparently diminished emphasis on virtue and the noble, which has come together with his loss of confidence in the prudence or understanding of the *demos*, has not been enough to dislodge his belief that the greatest goods are the fame and power that can only be obtained through political activity. Some kind of tyrannical ambition is after all a possible result of a noble ambition that has been undercut in this critical way. But it is also important to note that Alcibiades does not appear as bold or as vigorous here as he did in the *Alcibiades*. His desire for the greatest goods remains strong, but without his belief in the happiness guaranteed by virtuous devotion, he is at a loss for how to proceed. A vital attachment to the noble not only helps ensure that the objects of political ambition remain lofty enough to inspire great devotion; it also supports a strong and consistent belief that those objects can be obtained by virtuous activity.

## Morality, Piety, and Philosophy (143b–144c)

Socrates' failure to get Alcibiades to examine the goodness of the political life, or to see the need to do so, does not necessarily mean that Alcibiades cannot be discouraged from the pursuit of tyranny. After all, Alcibiades is still in need of help, lacking as he does a solution to his apparent loss of conviction that courage and nobility are enough to ensure his happiness. Seeking the gods' help to remedy his deficiency is no foolproof solution. The very idea seems to have been provoked by, and then strengthened in turn, a moral and psychological backlash against all that is implied by his disenchantment with the Athenian *demos*. That is, serious openness to the pursuit of tyrannical power, however well justified, has provoked in Alcibiades some moral and pious concerns, and the attempt to allay those concerns by seeking divine support cannot be free of the worry that the danger will thereby only be exacerbated.[25] Thus, at a moment when tyranny has become thinkable for him, but courage imprudent and the character of the divine uncertain, Alcibiades is potentially open to a Socratic *deus ex machina* purporting to be able to resolve his dilemma. As has already been suggested, some offer of an education in political prudence might appear especially valuable to Alcibiades at this moment, and nothing prevents Socrates' arguing that such prudence is deeply at odds with tyrannical rule, if not, as he has attempted to suggest in the past, with political life as such (*Alcibiades* 134b3–6).

But we noted in the *Alcibiades* that Socrates has something more at stake in getting Alcibiades to take up a rigorous philosophic self-examination. To have Alcibiades as a philosophic companion would be for Socrates an opportunity to test his wisdom by attempting to teach it. As we have seen in this dialogue, the wisdom in question may pertain most importantly to the question of how one ought to live, especially as that question is shaped by the character of the relationship between the human and the divine. We also took from the *Alcibiades* the suggestion that even if Socrates could not make Alcibiades wise, Socrates might still learn something by studying the development of Alcibiades' thinking as he is exposed to Socratic wisdom. In the section of the *Second Alcibiades* following Alcibiades' failure to recognize Socrates' most profound critique of his political ambition, we have an opportunity to consider the extent to which Socrates is still willing to provide Alcibiades with pointers and invitations to genuine philosophic questioning, as well as the manner in which Socrates may yet learn from Alcibiades by observing what things change and what things remain the same in Alcibiades' disposition toward piety and justice.

Following Alcibiades' reaction to his speech, Socrates makes an unexpected suggestion. He proposes to Alcibiades that a man[26] wiser than the two of them might accuse them of "not speaking correctly in blaming ignorance so indiscriminately," unless they would additionally specify what the ignorance is of and for which people in which condition such ignorance might in fact be something good (143b6–c3). Alcibiades is understandably taken aback. He did not expect to hear Socrates suggest that ignorance could ever be better than knowledge (143c4–5). When Alcibiades, swearing by Zeus, disagrees on this point, Socrates reassures him that he will nonetheless not accuse Alcibiades of wishing to do to his mother what Orestes and Alcmaeon are said to have done to theirs (143c8–d1).[27] Alcibiades' shock at this bewildering and unwelcome turn in the conversation is evident in his reaction: "Hush, by Zeus, Socrates!" (143d2). The tone of this startled reaction is notably religious. Besides the oath by Zeus, Alcibiades chastises Socrates with the imperative "Hush!" (*euphēmei*), which is more literally translated as "Speak well!" in the sense of "Don't blaspheme!" But Alcibiades' agitated plea for pious speech (or silence) is met by comical levity from Socrates, who calmly objects that Alcibiades is wrong to hush someone who says he would *not* be willing to kill his mother rather than someone saying the opposite, "since it seems to you to be such an extremely terrible matter that it is not to be spoken of so flippantly" (143d3–7). It is as if Socrates pretends to be oblivious to the reason for Alcibiades' distress.

But what is the reason for that distress? If Alcibiades' reaction strikes us as understandable or even familiar, that is only more reason to think carefully through what motivates it. The religious language in which his reaction is expressed suggests that Alcibiades is giving voice to a deep-seated pious fear. In particular, he seems to evince a belief that the gods forbid the mere discussion of certain matters, especially the most monstrous injustices. Socrates' reply makes clear that the context of the discussion is irrelevant for Alcibiades: one must no more speak of not committing matricide, according to the belief implied in Alcibiades' reaction, than of committing it. There may be something reassuring in seeing Alcibiades react so strongly against the mention of a heinous crime.[28] However seriously Alcibiades may be considering a life of tyranny, he is still guided and constrained on some level—a level deeper and less examined than that on which his critique of noble sacrifice has emerged—by a powerful sense of moral obligation. However, it must also be said that his sudden reaction against Socrates' speech in this context serves as a vivid illustration of the way in which the pious fear that attends deep moral attachments precludes the possibility of a philosophic examination of that very fear. For what cannot in any context be spoken of cannot be rigorously examined. And although the specific question of matricide is in no special need of thorough examination here, we can see that Alcibiades has not learned to subject his most deep-seated moral and pious beliefs to philosophic analysis. Willingness to risk exhibiting some measure of *hubris* in speech is necessary if one is going to test one's beliefs against the standard of reason, regardless of whether the ultimate result of the test is to support or overturn the original belief. We see again here the import of Socrates' emendation of Homer: the Homeric Zeus condemned wickedness while the Socratic Zeus condemned imprudence. The former likely prohibits probing inquiry into the reasonableness of pious obedience, whereas the latter may well require it.

Could it be that this resistance to philosophic scrutiny of the most deeply felt moral concerns is what is really at the core of Alcibiades' inability to doubt the goodness of the political life? Is it possible that his overwhelming desire for fame and power is fundamentally related to some kind of moral or pious commitment? Socrates may be pointing the way to an exploration of such possibilities, for it is especially at the moment when he comes up against the limits of Alcibiades' capacity for self-examination that Socrates provides himself with an opportunity to consider that which Alcibiades cannot investigate in himself. This helps explain why Socrates chose to introduce the subject of matricide with such a jarring non sequitur. Alcibiades is thereby caught off guard and reveals something about his pious fears that must remain largely hidden most of the time. It is particularly interesting that evidence of these fears is elicited by the mention of heinous injustice. The line of argument that Socrates will now pursue will go even further in clarifying the connection between Alcibiades' piety and his morality.

Alcibiades, prompted by Socrates, denies that either Orestes or anyone else would dare to do "any of these things" if he were prudent and knew what was best for himself to do (143d7–e2). Alcibiades thus appears to believe that the most abhorrent deeds are always imprudent and that they never constitute the best course of action for oneself. No circumstances, no matter how extraordinary, could ever make matricide advisable. This in turn points to the belief that one always comes to harm if one behaves immorally—at least in the case of the most extreme transgressions—whether because some divine or cosmic forces see to the proper administration of justice or because immorality is fundamentally incompatible with human well-being. The poets, for their part, seem in one way to attest to Alcibiades' view, since both Orestes and Alcmaeon were tormented by the Furies. But Orestes was commanded by Apollo himself, through the Delphic Oracle, to avenge his father's death by killing his mother. And as we were reminded when Socrates earlier quoted the *Odyssey*, Homer's Zeus considers Orestes' murder of his stepfather Aegisthus, at least, to have been just punishment for the latter's *hubris*.[29] Alcibiades, however, does not hesitate for a moment in denouncing Orestes as ignorant of what is best. He thus affirms that nothing, not even divine command, can trump the most solemn moral imperatives.

But if Alcibiades truly believes this, as it seems he does, then his plan to seek divine sanction for the pursuit of tyranny is deeply misguided, for according to the opinion we have drawn out from Alcibiades' responses, not even divine sanction could redeem a life of injustice. That Alcibiades holds such a view may be of great interest to Socrates. For the fact that Alcibiades' newfound openness to tyranny was followed by a turn to prayer might have led one to conclude that he believed just the opposite: that moral absolutes are subject to revisions and exceptions issued by gods to particular human beings. From the point of view of the need to determine how we ought to live, it would be quite important to know what led Alcibiades to suppose that the gods might be such as to be willing and able radically to undermine or transform the moral order. As it stands, however, it seems that Alcibiades has not overturned or even examined his belief that moral absolutes are in fact unalterable, even by gods, which goes to show how confused he must be if he is thinking of praying for tyranny.

Socrates now brings this confusion to the fore by having Alcibiades imagine a scenario in which he is suddenly overtaken by the opinion that it is better to murder Pericles (143e8–144a2). Alcibiades' reaction to this suggestion is notably different from his reaction to the mention of matricide. When Socrates interrupts his own narration of the hypothetical murder plot to get Alcibiades' agreement that "when a thought occurs to someone who is ignorant of what is best, nothing prevents his thinking that even the worst thing is best," Alcibiades agrees emphatically (144a4–7). Perhaps Alcibiades had contemplated precisely this kind of unjust means to the attainment of political power, which then caused him such deep concern and stirred his piety as a kind of backlash.[30] If so, Alcibiades here indicates that he has been tempted by the prospect of committing what even he considers to be the "worst" evils, thinking them momentarily to be "best." But after having touched this nerve in Alcibiades, Socrates winds his way to a rather strange conclusion. He first points out that Alcibiades would never kill Pericles if he should always fail to recognize him at the crucial moment (144a9–b10) and then presents this as proof of the proposition that ignorance of certain things and for some people may be better than knowledge (144c6–10).

Alcibiades' reactions to Socrates' conclusion are understandably reserved (144c8, 11). From the point of view of the ambitious but perplexed Alcibiades, these last Socratic reflections have offered little in the way of practical guidance. Alcibiades has acknowledged a serious difficulty: part of him is tempted to take up an immoral pursuit of political power, while another part of him thinks that such a pursuit would be irredeemably imprudent. Socrates, in the name of a "man wiser than you and me," has advanced the practically useless observation that a kind of selective amnesia would act as a safeguard against Alcibiades' execution of unjust and therefore imprudent designs. Since Alcibiades cannot himself make use of this observation, we must wonder whether its true meaning has rather to do with what Socrates might hope to achieve by means of persuasive speech. This suggestion would accord with Socrates' indication in the *Alcibiades* that certain false beliefs can be more conducive to self-improvement and self-discipline than the truth (120c9–d8). The image of the assassin Alcibiades who is suddenly unable to recognize his illustrious target corresponds to the suggestion that Socrates will not change his mind or deceive Alcibiades about the plan he intends to carry out—a plan that may be immoral, imprudent, or both, but at any rate is born of some kind of ignorance—but might hope to instill in him a further ignorance or confusion that would make the plan impossible to carry out. The question remains as to whether Alcibiades is meant ultimately to transcend his belief in Socrates' noble lies or to remain immersed within them.

We can try to make these general suggestions specific by applying the advice of the "wiser man" more directly to Alcibiades' present condition. The general principle states that one who thinks the bad is good is better off being ignorant of the means to the desired end. Alcibiades holds the opinion, though not without qualification, that tyranny is good. At the moment, he is inclined to seek support—or at least a token of indifference—from the gods. Alcibiades might thus be better off being unable to recognize the presence or absence of divine signs. If at length Alcibiades should come to be more keenly aware of the problem of *eros* to which Socrates' speech had pointed, and thus to see that any erotic pursuit is characterized by the exaggeration of the imagined self-sufficiency or perfection to be obtained—that is, if he finally takes up a full examination of what he believes to be the greatest good—then perhaps Socrates would direct him back to a deeper consideration of what was revealed by this most recent exchange. If Alcibiades is concerned to know whether or not to fear the gods' prohibitions in the wake of his loss of esteem for the judgment of the *demos*, he would do well to consider that concern in the light of his pious or moral condemnation of the deeds of Orestes. As for Socrates himself, who we must recall was equally chastised by the "wiser man" for failing to consider adequately the contingent advantages of ignorance, he has already observed the crucial fact. He must have noticed that Alcibiades' pious fear proved in the end to be fundamentally a moral fear. Having made that observation, Socrates can now turn to the task of providing Alcibiades with an interpretation of the wiser man's praise of ignorance better suited to Alcibiades' safety, self-improvement, and, in the best case, education.[31]

## Democracy, Statesmanship, and the Science of the Best (144d–147d)

Socrates' attempts to get Alcibiades to recognize his own imprudence by calling the goodness of what he desires into question have failed, at least for now. But Socrates can still attempt to have a moderating influence on Alcibiades by curbing his desire for tyranny. If it is the critique of the *demos* that has turned

Alcibiades toward the pursuit of tyranny, then a softening of that critique might return him to a desire for high democratic office. In fact, Socrates has already prepared such a softening by his denial that imprudence is simply identical to madness and by his suggestion that ignorance may in some cases be beneficial rather than harmful. By returning to this strain of his argument, Socrates lets us see that the attempt to show Alcibiades his own imprudence, beginning with his accusation and long speech, was something of a digression. That digression helped us see more precisely the present limits of Alcibiades' ability to follow the path of Socratic philosophy and, more important, allowed Socrates to investigate the relationship of Alcibiades' piety to his morality. But if Alcibiades cannot come to appreciate the full meaning of the critique of imprudence by turning that critique on himself, he can at least be made to have greater sympathy or less contempt for the imprudence of his fellow citizens.

Socrates' task is therefore to convince Alcibiades that the ignorance of the many is not in fact an evil but a good. To do this, Socrates introduces the notion of what he calls "the science of the best" (*hē tou beltistou epistēmē*). He begins by saying, "The possession of the other sciences, if one [of them] should be possessed without that of the best, is probably seldom beneficial, and most often harmful to the one having it" (144d4–7). Socrates then proceeds to lay out something like the argument he made in the *Alcibiades* regarding the role of knowledge in human endeavor: whenever we intend to speak or act, we necessarily "suppose we know or actually know" whatever it is we are about to say or do (144d7–e1). Alcibiades' agreement here is expected (144e2), echoing as it does his own articulation of the dangers of ignorance, which he gave in response to Socrates' earlier speech. Hence, Socrates will argue that the ignorance of the many is beneficial since they are without the "science of the best" they would otherwise need to make good use of knowledge. But before drawing this conclusion, Socrates extends the notion that actual or supposed knowledge must precede all action in a direction not explored in the *Alcibiades*. "The public orators (*hoi rhetores*)," says Socrates, "either knowing how to advise or supposing they know, advise us on each occasion, some concerning war and peace, others concerning building walls and furnishing harbors. In a word, as many things as the city ever does with respect to another city or itself by itself, all of these come to be from the advice of the public orators" (144e3–145a2). Socrates thus portrays the orators or rhetoricians in the assembly as being the singular decision makers for the city, their knowledge or ignorance effectively determining the success or failure of the city's business. These orators, in this presentation, are to the city as the intellect is to the human being.

As we have already noted, Alcibiades, in his first conversation with Socrates, denied that the assembly could be swayed by anything but the best advice. He thus betrayed a naïve ignorance of the power of political rhetoric. We also noted that by the time of the *Second Alcibiades*, he has clearly lost his optimism concerning the wisdom of the many, and the cynicism that has taken its place has given rise to his openness to tyrannical power as an alternative to democratic leadership. Recognition of the imprudence of the many has disheartened Alcibiades with respect to what it is possible to accomplish in a democracy, but Socrates' portrayal here of the power of the rhetorician—which, in its own way, follows from the imprudence of the many—has the potential to reopen the possibility of effective democratic leadership. In the picture Socrates has presented, there is no suggestion that the *demos* has any role in the decision making of the city. The people merely constitute the material that the public orators shape and direct. Socrates has not yet shown if or how this insight directs the aspiring statesman definitively to democratic leadership over tyranny, but he has at least prepared the way for an argument in favor of rhetoric as a uniquely powerful political tool if used within the framework of a democracy.

Having prompted Alcibiades to reassert his opinion that the many are imprudent and the few prudent, Socrates begins to explore the standard to which Alcibiades looks in making this claim (145a6–12). Of course, Socrates had already defined the prudent as those who do and say what they ought to do and say, and the context in which he did so led us to suggest that that definition of prudence implied knowledge of the divine above all. But now that Socrates has (at least temporarily) left behind the attempt to get Alcibiades to recognize the depth of his own imprudence, a more narrowly political conception of prudence is fleshed out. The man is not prudent, Alcibiades agrees, who knows how to advise but not whether or when it is better to do so; nor is one who knows how to make war, but not when or for how long it is better; nor is one who knows how to kill someone or take his money or exile him from his fatherland, but not when and to whom it is better to do so (145a11–b11).

This discussion reminds us of the exchange in the *Alcibiades* in which Socrates led Alcibiades to the conclusion that the better in matters of war and peace is the more just. The discussion of the *Alcibiades*, however, was confined to the question of how Alcibiades could be a good adviser in matters of war and peace, whereas now even the one who knows how to advise is said to be potentially imprudent. Why should the prudent man have to decide "whether" to advise or not? The clearest answer is indicated by the inclusion of killing, confiscation of property, and exile on the list of political affairs in which the prudent man must be an expert. The prudence described here is not simply that of the *stratēgos*, that is, of the man who must persuade the assembly on matters of war and peace, but of one to whom the tools of the tyrant are as open to consideration as those of the democratic statesman. In this context, we note the other great difference between this discussion and its counterpart in the *Alcibiades*: Alcibiades here agrees without hesitation that the science of the best in all the matters discussed is the science of the beneficial (145c1–4). The answer given previously, that the better in political affairs is the more just, is no longer mentioned.

But if the discussion of prudence, up to this point, has contributed to the dialogue's disconcerting insinuations about Socrates' influence on Alcibiades, the concluding definition of the prudent man forces us to reconsider Alcibiades' disposition toward tyranny. He now agrees to Socrates' summary statement that "we will call him prudent who is a sufficient counselor both to the city and himself to himself" (145c5–8). Alcibiades' endorsement of this description of the prudent man reveals both the half-heartedness of his commitment to tyranny and his continued commitment to civic-spirited ends. Alcibiades does not reply, as would seem to be required by the immediately preceding reflections, that the prudent man must only sometimes be a good counselor to the city but a dictator at other times, nor does he suggest that the ruler's good is in any tension with that of the city. And if we reconsider what seemed like Alcibiades' agreement moments ago that prudence required the employment of tyrannical means, we find first that his agreement on those points was not as emphatic as his agreement to this last description of the prudent man and also that it is not clear that he was endorsing those tyrannical methods. Rather, he agreed that one who *misuses* the ability to kill, rob, and exile cannot be prudent.

Socrates' latest portrait of prudence, then, seems the best conceived to suggest a solution to Alcibiades' present dilemma. Prudence thus understood does not require the extreme and fearsome measures of tyranny by suggesting that the ruler's good is increased at the expense of the citizens. It merely recognizes the dangers faced by a good adviser of the *demos* and includes such "self-counsel" as may be necessary to avert or thwart those dangers. We may wonder whether Alcibiades realized all that was at stake in admitting that the prudent man may sometimes have to consider "whether it is best" to be a counselor (145b1–2). But as to the crucial question arising from his acknowledgment that the prudent man possesses a "science of the beneficial"—namely, for whose benefit does he rule?—Alcibiades appears ready to accept the answer, "for his own good and the city's." The notion of prudence to which, under Socrates' direction, Alcibiades is now attending is one that would most simply fill the void left by the critique of courage and noble devotion.

Alcibiades is now primed for an argument in favor of democratic statesmanship that will provide the basis for a common good between statesman and city. Socrates begins his argument by turning from the arts of ruling he had been describing to subordinate military, athletic, and otherwise competitive arts: horsemanship, archery, boxing, and wrestling. Socrates asks whether it seems to Alcibiades to be necessary "that the one who is a knower (*epistēmona*) of something concerning these [arts] also be a prudent man (*andra*), or will we say that he is in need of much [more]?" (145c9–e1). Of course, Alcibiades strongly affirms that this man falls far short of prudence; none of the arts Socrates mentions enables one to be a more capable adviser to the city.

Indeed, this criticism probably resembles the critique of the many that Alcibiades has come to espouse. The very *demos* that governs the city is composed of thousands of artisans whose areas of expertise have no bearing on the political art. But now Socrates has Alcibiades imagine a city made up of *only* these sorts of people: "So what sort of regime do you suppose would be made of good archers and aulos players, and the other athletes and artisans besides, and mixed in with these those we just now spoke of who know war-making itself and killing itself, and in addition rhetorical men blowing political hot air, and all of them without the knower of the science of the best, i.e., when and to whom it is better to do these things for each one?" (145e3–146a). Alcibiades admits this would be a poor regime, and Socrates elaborates by describing how everyone would attempt to apportion the greater part of it to himself out of a love of honor, giving preference to the practice of his own art over all the others (146a2–7). Each man would thus "have utterly failed to hit upon the best for the city and for himself in many things which, I suppose, he had trusted to opinion without mind (*nou*)." This is the city in which one *would* be "struck and pelted" from all sides, as if living among madmen (cf. 139d10–e4). Such a regime, Alcibiades agrees with an oath by Zeus, would be "full of disorder and lawlessness" (146a8–b4).

This mention of law makes even more striking Socrates' abstraction from justice in discussing the science of the best applied to the regime. For justice is the standard to which the citizens look in determining what are the lawful and unlawful applications of the arts Socrates has mentioned, both the violent athletic and military arts and, just as important, the rhetorical and political arts. By eliding the importance of justice, Socrates' allusions to "the science of the best" conceal his judgment that a full understanding of the good at which politics aims is impossible without a philosophic analysis of justice. But it is also Socrates' abstraction from the need for knowledge of justice that allows him to present to Alcibiades a vision of the city that offers an opportunity for successful and fulfilling statesmanship. For Alcibiades can take Socrates' vague statement of the city's need for a leader possessing the science of the best as an endorsement of his own qualification to rule so long as he believes that he is or can be such a leader. That is, insofar as Alcibiades does not take the dystopia Socrates has described to be a description of Athens—and Athens is, after all, governed by law—he must draw the conclusion that competent leaders *are* at the helm. Pericles, for example, would come to light for Alcibiades as a possessor of the science of the best. Recall that in the *Alcibiades*, the claim that Pericles did not possess the wisdom required by politics was Socrates' bid to turn Alcibiades from a more political to a more philosophic pursuit. The reestablishment of contemporary Athenian statesmen as competent leaders in this section reflects Socrates' concession, however partial or temporary it may be, to the irrepressibility of Alcibiades' political ambition.

Socrates brings his demonstration to a close by drawing from his dystopian example the conclusion at which he claimed he would arrive, namely, the suggestion of the "wiser man" that ignorance of some things is good for some people in certain conditions. To this end, Socrates has Alcibiades reaffirm several of the important points that had been agreed upon. Before attempting to act or speak, one must either suppose one knows—or else really know—what one intends to do or say; if this knowledge or supposed knowledge is accompanied by knowledge of the beneficial, such a person will profit his city and himself; but the many are imprudent and the few are prudent, and the many fall short of what is best in many things by trusting in opinion without mind (146b5–d1). All of this allows Socrates to conclude that "it is therefore profitable for the many neither to know nor to suppose they know, if indeed they will be more eager to do the things they know or suppose they know, doing harm by acting more often than they benefit" (146d2–5). On the basis of this argument, Alcibiades finally agrees that knowledge can be harmful rather than beneficial (146d7–e3).

Thus, Alcibiades seems to have been convinced that the ignorance of the many, which has been a great source of his recent distress, is in fact to their advantage. But if he had considered Socrates' argument more carefully, he might have noticed its inadequacy. Imagine that we took Alcibiades aside at this moment and asked him to relay to us what Socrates had just explained. "I have learned," he would say with some relief, "that the ignorance of the *demos* is not such a deplorable thing as I had supposed." If we should ask him why not, he would reply, "Because ignorance is to be preferred in that majority of citizens for whom knowledge would be more dangerous." "And what knowledge," we would press, "has Socrates shown to be particularly dangerous?" "Knowledge of the arts," Alcibiades would recall, "such as horsemanship, archery, boxing, wrestling, and rhetoric." "But," we could then insist, "the *demos* is not ignorant of these arts! The city *is* full of horsemen, archers, boxers, wrestlers, and ambitious rhetoricians, and they *do* all vie for the city's honor. So how can it be that Athens is not a chaotic dystopia?" "Well," Alcibiades would reply, feeling suddenly ill at ease, "the order and lawfulness of the city must be due to the guidance of legislators and statesmen who possess the science of the best." Tactfully passing over the dubiousness of this suggestion, we could finally reply, "Be that as it may, the ignorance that Socrates has convinced you would be better for the city than knowledge cannot possibly be the ignorance in the *demos* you have been lamenting these past few months. For Socrates has purported to show no more than that the many would be better off lacking precisely the knowledge of the arts that they possess. Whatever has been the ignorance you have come to deplore in the Athenians has by no means been shown to be beneficial."

Alcibiades' failure to recognize this difficulty is due to the attractiveness of the possibility Socrates has now laid out. Socrates' earlier insight, which had surprised Alcibiades, that the city does not appear to be full of madmen, can now be interpreted by Alcibiades as reflecting the prudent guidance of its leaders. Alcibiades is being allowed to suppose that the imprudence of the individual artisans, alluded to in Socrates' analogy of imprudence to craftsmanship (140b7–c3), can be overcome by a statesman who directs the considerable powers of the citizens in a unified manner toward a common goal. A great partnership can thus emerge between the *demos* and its elected leader, in which the capable leader can harness the power of the city and lead it to greatness, thereby obtaining glory both for himself and for his fatherland. Perhaps this will require a sophisticated rhetorical approach, but the statesman's rhetoric will be used for the good of the citizens who are too imprudent on their own to recognize what is truly in their interest. Incidentally, this means that in order for Socrates' vision of politics to be viable for Alcibiades, Socrates may have to instruct him in the art of rhetoric. But most important, it means that Socrates is now obscuring the way in which his dystopia is a description of Athens. As we noted when Socrates initially claimed the city might not be full of madmen, both he and Alcibiades will eventually "pay the penalty."[32] Thus, in a masterful twist of Platonic irony, Socrates is applying the lesson that ignorance is beneficial to those who lack the science of the best to Alcibiades by having him misunderstand that very lesson.

As if to make this irony still sweeter, Socrates now applies a rhetorical flourish of his own: "It is necessary for both city and soul that intend to live correctly to get hold of this science [of the best], just as plainly as a sick man needs a doctor or one intending to sail safely a pilot. For without it, however much more splendidly the wind of fortune blows, whether for acquiring money or for bodily strength or any other of such things, so much more is it necessary, as is likely, that errors come to be from them" (146e4–147a4). Of course, Alcibiades is thinking of himself as the doctor or pilot of the city, failing to realize that it is his own soul that is in need of Socrates as its doctor or pilot. But now Socrates makes a strange digression, musing that the poet was right who accused someone by saying that "he knew many things (*erga*), but he knew all badly" (147a5–b4). As we will soon learn, this is a quotation of Homer's lost mock epic, the *Margites*, which followed the misadventures of its title character.[33] When Alcibiades quite reasonably objects that the passage does not seem to be relevant to the present conversation, Socrates explains, "But he speaks enigmatically, best one, both he and nearly all other poets. For the entire poetic art is enigmatic, and not to be understood by just any man; and in addition to its nature, it is such that, whenever it takes hold of a man who is jealous and does not wish to reveal himself to us but to conceal his wisdom as much as possible, the thing is manifestly exceedingly difficult to understand, whatever it is that each of them thinks" (147b7–c5). Socrates then goes on to give his solution to the alleged Homeric riddle. Homer, whom Socrates calls "the most divine and wisest poet," could not have meant that Margites knew everything badly since Homer was well aware that it is not possible to know badly. Therefore, Socrates surmises that Homer disguised his meaning by replacing "bad" with "badly" and "to know" with "he knew" so that Homer's true meaning was, "He knew many things, but it was bad for him to know all of them" (147c6–d5). Socrates does not say how Homer indicates that the knowledge was bad "for him." That problem aside, however, Homer thus supports Socrates' thesis: the foolish are harmed by what knowledge they have.

Why in the world does Socrates go out of his way here to describe the enigmatic character of poetry and then to propose this far-fetched interpretation of a Homeric verse? Perhaps we can begin by noting that Socrates calls Homer the wisest poet. When Socrates introduced the suggestion that some ignorance might be beneficial for some people, it was in the context of the hypothetical objection of someone wiser than both him and Alcibiades. Now Socrates tells us that "nearly all the poets" conceal their wisdom by writing enigmatically. Socrates was not a poet; Plato was more like a poet than Socrates. Was Socrates perhaps too open with his wisdom? Was it a mistake, for example, to expose Alcibiades to the critique of democracy that comes with illuminating the folly of the *demos*? And if so, does the poetic Plato help him conceal his mistake? Socrates here gives us an example of how one can uncover the true meaning of an enigmatic poet. Socrates knows two crucial things: he knows that Homer is divine and wise, and he knows that it is impossible to know badly (*kakōs epistasthai*). He is therefore able to conclude that Homer cannot have meant what he said when he said that Margites knew all things badly. Can we perhaps use this example to help us understand the meaning of the wise Plato's strange digression at this point in the *Second Alcibiades*?

Socrates notes that it is impossible to "know badly." By this he appears to mean that to know something badly would be to know it wrongly. But this is not knowing; it is falsely opining. Of course, Margites does not *know* he is opining falsely: he believes he has knowledge. It was with respect to just this type of dilemma that Socrates, in the *Alcibiades*, pointed the way toward a consideration of a serious difficulty: how can one ever be certain that one's professed knowledge is not in fact false opinion? To take the most important example from the *Second Alcibiades*, how can one know if one has finally obtained the indispensable "science of the best"? We have noted that the true science of the best would have to include knowledge of justice, which in turn takes us back to our reflections from the beginning of the dialogue: the question of how we ought to live, of what is "best" for a human being, depends heavily on what we can conclude about the gods. Obtaining a science of the best, without which, as Socrates points out, all of one's learning and skill will likely be employed in a manner harmful to oneself, involves a very serious and daunting challenge. Or rather there is a question as to whether there can be a "science of the best," a body of fixed knowledge that can determine what one ought to say and do in any circumstance, or whether we must instead rely at every turn upon prayer and divination to reveal to us the wills and whims of the gods.

The *Second Alcibiades* helps us see some of the most serious challenges to Socrates' knowledge of the good or the best by allowing us to see what stood in Alcibiades' way of that same knowledge. Alcibiades was unable critically to examine his attachment to political life and his pious fears or the moral beliefs indicated by those fears. Exposure to a powerful Socratic critique of democracy, supported by Socrates' compelling arguments for the unmatched importance of knowledge and prudence, was enough to stir up in Alcibiades the troubling thought that tyranny may be preferable to democratic statesmanship. But this possibility did not sit well with Alcibiades since he remained attached to what is shining and attractive in democratic politics: the belief that one can earn the highest political honors and the loving admiration of one's fellow citizens by being a great benefactor to one's fatherland.[34] Alcibiades has a deep sense that human life is most fulfilling when it is devoted to a great political good. His grave doubts about the prospect of pursuing tyranny represent, as it were, the other extreme of this same sense: the ominous fear associated with the prospect of harming those to whom he feels he ought to be most devoted. Alcibiades' belief to this effect is reflected in his reaction to Socrates' nonchalant introduction of the theme of matricide. It is never in one's interest, says Alcibiades in that context, to do great evil. Not even the gods, in Alcibiades' view, seemed able to change that fundamental moral fact.

The consideration of this complex of beliefs in relation to the science of the best may provoke some questions. What is the source of the apparently universal human belief that the greatest human goods are to be found in acts of great devotion? How could its validity be confirmed? And if it should prove valid, to whom ought one's greatest devotion be directed? It could be that it is above all pious devotion and obedience to divine will (as described, for example, by Homer's Zeus earlier in the dialogue) that is best for human beings and that the widely shared sense that this is so is somehow delivered to us by the gods, as well as communicated through interpreters such as Homer (the "most divine poet"). If Alcibiades' pious fears as illuminated earlier are well grounded, then Socrates' philosophizing, in its willingness or need to indulge in irreverent and hubristic speech, may be grossly imprudent. If we are right in thinking that Socrates considers the philosophic life, especially in contrast to the political life, as the life consistent with the science of the best, we must ask how he will respond to the challenge posed by the view that the political life accords more completely with the divine demand for human devotion. It is in response to this purported demand that the insight noted above may be the most relevant: that Alcibiades thinks of morality as a standard beyond the reach of the gods. This would at least suggest that if the coincidence of the human good and human devotion is communicated to us by the gods, then it is apparently on account not of divine whim but of fixed necessity. Investigation of the character of that necessity might then prove profoundly revealing.

Before moving on to the final section of the *Second Alcibiades*, it is important to correct the tentative assessment of the state of Alcibiades' ambition given above in the wake of his affirmation of openness to tyranny. Then, we had still received little if any indication that the desire to be a benefactor to the Athenians continued to motivate Alcibiades. Now we have two pieces of evidence that, while hardly as arresting as his proposal to make the Athenians love each other like a family in the *Alcibiades*, confirm the persistent operation of his concern for justice and noble devotion. The first is his strong reaction against the discussion of matricide, and the other is his passing agreement that the prudent man advises both for the sake of his own good and for the city's. For all that he appears to have altered his position on, for example, sacrificing one's life for a noble cause, Alcibiades still seems not to have been able to recognize the possibility that the devoted service of the public benefactor and the single-minded pursuit of one's own greatest good may not ultimately be compatible. It is at least conceivable that were he fully to recognize the importance of this possibility, he would finally turn to Socratic philosophy with awareness that the question of the greatest good must be examined from the ground up. As far as we can see, Plato has given no indication that the political character of Alcibiades' ambition could survive the suspension or abandonment of his desire to be a great benefactor. The love of the noble is not easily discarded, and its role in the phenomenon of political ambition, even when that ambition has taken an apparently tyrannical turn, is not to be underestimated.

## Prophecy, Socratic Religion, and the Fate of Alcibiades (147e–151c)

Alcibiades, in giving his assent to Socrates' assessment of Margites, agrees that ignorance can indeed be beneficial (147e1–2). Immediately afterward, however, he notes that it also seems to him as it did before—that he is still on some level persuaded by the Socratic argument that knowledge is always better than ignorance (147e4). Alcibiades cannot hold the argument underlying Socrates' qualified praise of ignorance firmly in his mind, which is understandable given that the version of that argument that has most convinced him (regarding the ignorance of the many in the city) was flawed. Socrates takes this opportunity to remind Alcibiades of how dangerous it is for him to pray. "So still even now, if the god to whom you happen to be going to pray, becoming visible to you, should ask you before you prayed for anything if it would be sufficient for you that something of those things that were said in the beginning should come to be, or if he should turn it over to you yourself to pray, how in the world (*ti pote*) do you suppose that you would hit upon what is propitious either in accepting the things given by him or by praying yourself that they come about?" (148a2–7). Although Socrates had to abandon his most serious attempt to get Alcibiades to recognize his imprudence and thus his unfitness for prayer, his success in arguing for the benefit of the many's imprudence, because it has led to *aporia*, has allowed him once again to challenge Alcibiades directly. Socrates' arguments purporting to undercut the critique of the *demos* that had been a source of Alcibiades' concern have necessarily intensified the dubiousness of praying for tyranny. Alcibiades therefore admits, with an oath "by the gods," that he needs to take great care not to pray for evils supposing they are good, only to have to recant soon after (148a8–b4). Finally, Socrates has succeeded in getting Alcibiades to question the prudence of the prayer he was about to offer.

Why has stopping Alcibiades' prayer been so important to Socrates? It is one thing to note that Alcibiades' prayer is an indication of what he most deeply desires, but if that is the only relevance of Alcibiades' prayer in this dialogue, then it should not matter so much to Socrates whether or not Alcibiades prays. Rather, he should then only be concerned to change Alcibiades' opinion about what he ought to pursue. And yet Socrates has now drawn our attention for the second time to the question of what it would take to get Alcibiades not to pray for tyranny. He has now raised this question twice in the context of an imagined scenario in which the god to whom Alcibiades was going to pray intercepts him. This, as was indicated above, resembles the action of the *Second Alcibiades* itself, with Socrates intercepting Alcibiades and persuading him not to pray. But all this only emphasizes the fact that Socrates' goal here has been not only to change Alcibiades' mind about tyranny but to stop him from praying. Understanding this aspect of the dialogue is the task to be taken up in this final section.

After reminding Alcibiades of the nameless poet's prayer recited earlier in the dialogue, Socrates now delivers the dialogue's longest speech. His initial reminder, however, emphasizes only the poet's counsel that one pray "to ward off the terrible things," while making no mention of the prayer's asking for "the good things" (*ta esthla*, 148b5–7cf. 143a1–3). Alcibiades has come to see how easy it can be to pray accidentally for something that one soon after views as bad, but he has not understood to the same degree just how far he is from seeing clearly what is good. The speech then begins with Socrates' claim that the Lacedaemonians use a prayer very similar to the one Socrates had mentioned, either in emulation of its unnamed author or because they had independently observed the same things as he had (148b9–c3). But their prayer, in Socrates' brief description of it, is slightly different both from the prayer Socrates originally suggested and from his partial summary of it moments ago. He says that the Spartans' prayer includes nothing beyond "telling the gods to give them the noble things in addition to the good things (*ta kala epi tois agathois*)" (148c4–5). The Spartan prayer is not as careful as the prudent poet's. It assumes that the noble and good things are compatible, whereas the prudent poet's version remained agnostic about this, asking for the somewhat vague *esthla* rather than either *kala* or *agatha*.[35] Moreover, the Spartans' prayer is to "the gods" generally, apparently presuming that they are in agreement. The prudent poet may have been indicating his recognition of the difficulty that arises from the gods' disagreement in praying simply to "King Zeus."

Nonetheless, Socrates attributes the Spartans' unmatched (though not perfect) good fortune to their use of this prayer, noting that to whatever extent it has not been effective, this is a result of the gods' sometimes giving the opposite of what is prayed for (148c5–d2). The first part of Socrates' speech, then, praises a prayer not quite as agnostic as the "safely and beautifully" spoken one he presented earlier but close to it. He would like Alcibiades to adopt such an agnostic attitude as much as possible. But he makes sure to note, as he did at the very beginning of the conversation, that the prayer will never be perfectly successful. Socrates thus guards preemptively against disillusionment with the pious outlook he wishes Alcibiades to adopt.

The next portion of Socrates' speech is the recounting of a relevant story he has heard "from some old men" (148d3–4). The first part of the story runs as follows. The Athenians and the Spartans were at odds, misfortune "always" befalling the Athenians in their land and sea battles so they could never get the upper hand (148d3–7). Distressed and at a loss, the Athenians took counsel and decided to send to Ammon to ask what they needed to do to turn the tide of the war.[36] But they also decided to ask him something else. The Athenians wanted Ammon to explain why the gods were giving victory to the Spartans when the Athenians, of all the Greeks, sacrifice the most and the most beautifully, adorn their offerings in their temples as no one else does, have the most expensive and most august processions every year, and "spend more money than all the other Greeks combined," while the Spartans care so little for the gods that they sacrifice maimed animals and generally give the gods insufficient honor despite their having just as much money as the Athenians (148d7–149a6).

The Athenian request is marked by a kind of *hubris*. First, they send not to a Greek god but to an Egyptian one, as if to suggest dissatisfaction with the Greek gods' handling of their affairs.[37] And then, in addition to their request for guidance, they demand an explanation for their shabby treatment, as if the gods owe them fair treatment. On one hand, this indicates an understandable, perhaps even necessary, assumption that the gods deal justly with human beings. But on the other hand, it presumes that the Athenians are correct in what they think the gods want from them: honor, in the form of splendid spectacles and expensive adornments. In effect, the Athenians assume the gods will be pleased by the kinds of things that please the Athenians. Their demand for an explanation from Ammon suggests they are not so much subordinate to the gods as mutual partners with them, exchanging and sharing benefits as each is able. By contrast, the Spartans seem to assume nothing about what the gods want except what they know from tradition, which they blindly follow. They do not dare to interpret the gods' desire for burnt offerings on the basis of an assumption that the gods are like themselves but obligingly give what is required of them without question. The Athenians seem to want to make the gods rational, both by interpreting their desire for tribute according to what they understand about such desires generally and by insisting that there be a good reason for the gods' failure to reward their sacrifices over the Spartans'. Socrates, too, in his investigation of the divine, holds the purported activities and decrees of the gods to the standard of reason and is not satisfied to submit to divine or moral imperatives without adequate justification. To the extent that the Spartans are meant to be the object of emulation for Alcibiades, Socrates' story is an allegory for the difference between his own way of life and the way of life toward which he is directing his young interlocutor.

Another major theme of the story is the difficulty of interpreting the results of our requests and prayers to the gods. Socrates concludes his story by recounting the oracular reply. The prophet speaking for Ammon gives to the

Athenians' twofold request a single answer: "To the Athenians, Ammon says the following things. He says that he would rather have the Lacedaemonian *euphēmia* than all of the sacrifices of the Greeks put together" (149b2–4). Socrates says the reason for the prophet's saying no more than this is clearly that the god did not allow it (149a8–b1). This unsubstantiated claim of a divine prohibition against any more elaborate proclamation is followed by Socrates' speculation as to how the terse oracular reply should be interpreted: "It seems to me," he explains, "that the god meant by *euphēmia* nothing other than [the Spartans'] prayer, for it really surpasses the others' by far. For some other Greeks, after having offered cows with gilded horns, and still others, after having given votive offerings to the gods, pray for whatever it should happen to be, good or bad. So the gods, having heard them blaspheming, do not accept their expensive processions and sacrifices" (149b5–c6). Socrates' interpretation of the oracle, of course, supports his endorsement of the Spartan prayer. But the very fact that he has to speak of how "it seems" to him shows it is not a clear or conclusive matter. Ammon may, for example, mean to indicate that he simply prefers the Spartans to all of the other Greeks. In that case, there would be no hope for the Athenians, and their pious observance would simply be in vain. Indeed, this is the suggestion Socrates now makes regarding the Trojans in reciting some Homeric verses: the gods did not answer the Trojan prayers because the Trojans were hateful to them (149c8–e3).

So why does the prophet give such an ambiguous reply? Of course, by saying that Ammon did not allow the prophet to say more than he did, Socrates may simply be referring to the enigmatic character of oracular replies in general. But does this mean the gods are intentionally enigmatic, withholding their counsel from human beings? The question reminds us that Socrates has in fact already suggested an explanation for the enigmatic expressions of human beings believed to be divinely inspired. This was in reference to the poetic art. But Socrates never suggested that the reason for the enigmatic character of poetry was that the gods forbid the poets to write more candidly. Rather, he suggested that the poets often jealously conceal their wisdom by means of their enigmatic writing. In fact, it is striking that Socrates was silent in that context regarding the suggestion that the poet is channeling or communicating with gods or muses, except perhaps for his calling Homer "the most divine and wisest poet."[38] But does Homer's being "divine" indicate that he is inspired by the gods? Or does it not rather suggest that he somehow *is* the gods? Perhaps the quiet suggestion in the case of the poets, which would have to be considered in the case of Ammon's prophet as well, is that the wisdom they are concealing is in large part their invention of the gods with whom they claim to communicate. The enigmatic character of both poetry and prophecy, then, would be necessary in part to make the claim to divine inspiration difficult or impossible to disprove.

But a danger arises from the great ambiguity that remains concerning the will of the gods. Vastly different interpretations of what the gods want can arise, as is exemplified in the differences between the Athenian and Spartan sacrifices, which seem ultimately to reflect the customs and dispositions of the people who perform them. What is more, the Athenians' "bad luck" in their war with Spartans aroused their indignation and even made them turn partially away from the traditional Greek gods. It is this danger arising from the ambiguity in the gods' responses to our prayers that may be the most important reason for Socrates' wanting to reform Alcibiades' piety *before* he goes to pray. Had Alcibiades either prayed for tyranny or attempted to test the gods through prayer to see if they would endorse or condemn an unjust pursuit of political power, he might very well have found a way to interpret the results of his sacrifices and prayers as supporting tyrannical ambition. To be sure, such a conclusion on Alcibiades' part would, as we have seen, only represent one stratum of his confused understanding of the divine, the deepest level of which is his firm belief that the gods cannot make the most heinous injustice good for human beings. But one can imagine that belief becoming eclipsed and distorted by the temptation of fantastic power and fame together with whatever in the Socratic critique of devotion still moves Alcibiades. Socrates must therefore provide Alcibiades with an understanding of the divine that does not admit interpretations according to which tyranny can receive divine sanction.

It is fitting, then, that the foundation of the religious teaching that Socrates gives Alcibiades is *euphēmia*, since we saw that Alcibiades still strongly feels the need for *euphēmia* not only in prayer but in ordinary conversation. And, after all, it is *euphēmia* in this sense of keeping speech within the limits of pious reverence, and not the use of Socrates' invented prayer, that provides the most straightforward interpretation of Ammon's oracle: the Spartans speak piously, while the Athenians invite and produce sophistry and philosophy. By tweaking this sense of *euphēmia* with his emphasis on the nameless poet's prudent prayer, Socrates at once draws on and shapes what Alcibiades most deeply senses the gods require. Socrates' intention is made evident when he says "it would be terrible" if the gods considered gifts and sacrifices instead of whether one's soul is just and pious (149e6–150a1). In a formulation given soon afterward, Socrates switches to speaking of justice and prudence, giving the impression that prudence and piety are in perfect harmony and saying now that it is the prudent and just man who knows "what he ought to do and to say both to gods and to human beings" (150a6–b3). Socrates thus pushes Alcibiades to listen above all to the intuition he has that what the gods demand primarily is justice. It is important that Alcibiades not perceive the gods as taking bribes (149e2–4, 150a1–6).[39]

There is one important puzzle left to consider in this speech: it concerns Socrates' quotation of Homer. As it turns out, Socrates is not in fact quoting Homer but inventing Homeric verses. He recites one invented verse, paraphrases a real verse from the *Iliad* out of meter, and then adds three more verses of his own. In Socrates' version, the Trojans make a massive sacrifice, but the gods do not wish to accept it, for the people of Priam are hateful to them (149d3–e1). The passage in the *Iliad* in which the prose line can be found in verse, however, simply speaks of the smoke from the Trojan campfires wafting up to the sky; there is no mention of a sacrifice nor of the gods' disposition toward Priam or the Trojans. This is the third time in the *Second Alcibiades* that Socrates has emended Homer, but the first time he has done so in verse and passed it off as authentic. Perhaps this is not meant to be an emendation but an exemplification of the problem that Homer's enigmatic writing presents. It invites the interpretation, expressed explicitly by Socrates' additional lines, that the gods simply take sides without concern for our prayers and sacrifices. It is Socrates who must interpret the "Homeric" verses as supportive of his own claims that the gods care only for the justice and piety of one's soul. Perhaps we can see in Socrates' frequent references to the poets throughout the dialogue that his project of reforming Alcibiades' piety faces a tremendous challenge in its need to combat the traditional notion of piety supported by the authority of the poets.

Alcibiades' response to the speech suggests he has been persuaded. He says "it would not be fitting" for him to disagree with "the god" (150b5–7). But Socrates, in the dialogue's closing exchanges, expresses serious doubt concerning Alcibiades' ability to adopt the religious teachings Socrates has been offering. Reminding Alcibiades of his acknowledgment that he is in danger of praying for bad things he thinks are good, and thus blaspheming, Socrates now suggests that the safest course for Alcibiades is not to pray at all (150b8–c7). Socrates explains this by saying he does not think Alcibiades will be willing to use the Lacedaemonian prayer on account of his "greatness of soul, the noblest of the names for imprudence" (150c7–9). Alcibiades' disinclination to use the Spartan prayer makes him like the Athenians of Socrates' story. Greatness of soul, as Socrates is here using the term, suggests a kind of *hubris* characterized by ungrounded assumptions about the relationship of gods to human beings. Alcibiades cannot be trusted to adopt Socrates' religious teaching because he will be unable to maintain the Spartan style of humble, pious obedience. Desiring greater and more splendid things, he will inevitably recover his desire for political fame and power.

Just as Socrates suggested that Alcibiades could not be deterred from praying unless he were offered the fulfillment of his grandest political aspirations, Socrates himself must now appear to offer something of this sort if he is to stop Alcibiades from praying. Indeed, this has always been the source of Socrates' power over Alcibiades: the promise that only Socrates could provide him with what he needs for his greatest hopes to be fulfilled. Socrates therefore suggests that Alcibiades needs to abstain from prayer until he has learned "how he must be disposed to gods and to human beings" (150d1–2). When Alcibiades coyly asks, "When will this time be at hand, Socrates, and who will be the teacher? For I think that I would be most pleased to know who this human being is," Socrates replies equally coyly, "He is the one concerned about you" (150d3–6). Socrates does not say what he allows Alcibiades to think, that Socrates will himself be willing and able to teach him what he still needs to learn. Socrates even explains what this would be, saying that someone must first remove the mist from Alcibiades' soul—just as Athena removed the mist from Diomedes' eyes to let him distinguish gods from men—and only then "apply the things through which you will recognize bad and good (*esthlon*)" (150d6–e3). But if the one who "is concerned" for Alcibiades is foremost Alcibiades himself, then Socrates here indicates the hard work of philosophic self-examination that Alcibiades would have to undertake in order to cure himself of his imprudent misunderstanding of how he ought to live. Socrates cannot, as he lets Alcibiades believe he can, bestow clarity upon him as if by divine revelation, or as Athena did for Diomedes. Alcibiades would need to take a much harder look at the roots of his piety than he has been willing to until now—to learn to distinguish between gods and mortals—if he is to have a chance at properly discerning the bad from the good. That is, if Alcibiades is to distinguish the good from the bad, that which ought to be prayed for from that which might be prayed for in error, he must first clarify his thoughts concerning the human and the divine, mortality and immortality. Athena allowed Diomedes to avoid fighting in vain against the gods; more careful reflection upon what separates human beings from gods might allow

Alcibiades to stop pursuing in vain what mortals cannot obtain. But even Diomedes misused the power Athena granted him by attacking Apollo on the battlefield (*Iliad* 5.432–7).[40]

Alcibiades pledges his obedience to whomever his teacher might be, and Socrates replies that it is "amazing how much zeal he has for you" (150e5–151a2). To Alcibiades, this must sound like an affirmation of Socrates' willingness to educate Alcibiades, whereas in reality it is probably a reflection on how eager and yet how unable or unwilling Alcibiades is to learn. But Alcibiades agrees to put off his sacrifice, and Socrates praises the safety of this decision (151a3–6). The result of the dialogue is that Socrates has at least bought himself some time. Alcibiades has once again become convinced that Socrates can provide him with something he lacks and without which the pursuit of his political goals will be in vain. But the problem of Alcibiades' failure to distinguish god from man is made most evident by his final action in the dialogue: "I will crown you with this wreath, since you seem to me to have given advice nobly; but to the gods we will give both wreaths and the other lawful things whenever I should see that day coming. And it will come before long if they are willing" (151a7–b3).[41] This is a clear indication that Alcibiades hopes for Socrates to provide him with something beyond what Socrates can truly offer. Thus, Socrates has won Alcibiades' affection for the time being on account of his "noble" advice, but there is a grave question as to what will happen if Alcibiades should once again become disillusioned with the hopes Socrates has here rekindled. The conversation has been a success—but perhaps only a temporary one.

This sense of foreboding is expressed most strongly by Socrates himself in the dialogue's closing words. Socrates accepts the wreath, claiming it is a good omen just as Creon believed Teiresias's wreaths to be a good omen in Euripides' *Phoenician Women* (151b4–10). In the scene from which Socrates quotes, Teiresias is arriving in Thebes from Athens, where he has been honored with the first fruits of victory for prophesying that Athens would prevail over Eumolpus and the Eleusinians. In keeping with his censure of looking to gifts received rather than to the soul of the giver, Socrates clarifies that it is in fact Alcibiades' opinion of him (not the wreath) that he takes to be a good omen (151b11). But as in Euripides' play, the sign of victory in one battle is not a guarantee of easy victory in the other. Socrates has won some kind of victory in getting Alcibiades to look to him as to a god. But whatever battle Socrates is fighting in which that represents a victory, there is another battle that will yet be difficult to win. Socrates ends with the enigmatic words, "I would wish to become victorious over your lovers" (151c2).[42] We must turn to the *Symposium* to determine whether the battle Socrates has won is in fact the battle for Alcibiades' enduring allegiance.

The *Second Alcibiades* portrays its title character in the immediate wake of some significant intellectual transformations, the manifestations of which we are compelled to see as the effect of Socratic influence. One element of Alcibiades' character, however, reflects an unbroken thread connecting the *Alcibiades* and *Second Alcibiades*: the impermeability of his political ambition to Socratic critique. Alcibiades' recalcitrance is most immediately evident in the fact that he continues unreflectively to assume that (divinely sanctioned) political rule over a great number of people would constitute "the greatest goods" (141b5–7).[43] Amazingly, Alcibiades is not even aware that Socrates might have grounds for disagreement. Socrates has not yet made clear to Alcibiades that he considers the life of philosophy superior to the political life, although his argument to that effect, as reported in the *Symposium*, is alluded to here in his speech about tyranny, generalship, and parenthood. Philosophy is never mentioned in the *Alcibiades* or *Second Alcibiades* (cf. *Symposium* 218a2–7). From the beginning of their association through the end of the *Second Alcibiades*, Socrates has come no closer to revealing the true goal of his education than he did at the midpoint of their first conversation; he has been forced to maintain the pretense that his aim is to help Alcibiades become famous and powerful.

Socrates refers to this resistance in Alcibiades as a type of imprudence known as "greatness of soul" (*megalopsuchia*).[44] It is this quality, Socrates claims, that makes Alcibiades unable to use the prudent or Spartan prayer, which would imply acknowledgment of his total ignorance of the good and thus *a fortiori* of whether political life is good or bad. We may get some help in understanding this by considering the starting points of Aristotle's discussion of *megalopsuchia*: "The man seems to be great-souled who deems himself worthy and is worthy of great things," "and if of the greatest things most, then it would concern one thing most . . . that which we assign to the gods, which men of worth aim at most, and which is given as a prize for the noblest deeds; such a thing is honor" (*Nicomachean Ethics* 1123b1–2, 15–20). Here Aristotle treats greatness of soul unambiguously as a peak virtue (1123b26–27), which makes his account difficult to reconcile with the Platonic Socrates' only mentions of it (*Second Alcibiades* 140c9, 150c8). Some helpful contrast is given in the description of the character of youth in the *Rhetoric*, in which Aristotle says, "They are great-souled, for they have not yet been humbled by life, but are inexperienced in necessities; and deeming oneself worthy of great things is greatness of soul, and this belongs to the hopeful" (1389a31–33), without claiming that the great-souled man is correct in his self-assessment. It was on account of Alcibiades' teeming hope and his opinion of his great worth that Socrates claimed, in introducing himself, finally to be able to begin their association.

But if Alcibiades was to satisfy Socrates' own greatest hopes, it could only be by means of an adequate examination of his sense of worth and the honor he hoped to win. If Alcibiades' greatness of soul is a kind of imprudence, and if imprudence is ignorance of what one ought to do and say, then Aristotle helps us see that Alcibiades' great imprudence is his failure to consider whether or in what sense honor is truly the greatest good.[45] Despite his lowered esteem for the *demos* and his newfound wariness of noble sacrifice, Alcibiades continues to aspire to be a good counselor to the Athenians. This contradiction is at the root of his perplexity in the *Second Alcibiades*. Alcibiades entertains the possibility of tyrannical rule as a way to obtain honor without having to flatter the *demos* or to risk falling victim to its imprudent and violent whims. He contemplates living an unjust life because justice may require sacrifices that would impede or preclude the fulfillment of his ambitions. But Alcibiades' flirtation with evil makes him very uneasy, especially because he has begun to feel as though the attainment of the highest ends he seeks cannot lie fully within his unaided mortal reach. Socrates has brought about a crisis in Alcibiades culminating in the collision of his need for divine support and his need to compromise his morality. What Socrates is able to discern in the midst of this crisis is that Alcibiades' pious fear arises most of all from his belief in the inviolable nature of moral obligation. The only way for Alcibiades fully to resolve his dilemma would be to examine this sense of obligation. And because he continues to feel and to fear that he cannot be worthy of the greatest goods if he should defy the demands of morality, the scope of his examination would have to encompass honor, that great good of which he most passionately desires to be worthy.

Alcibiades' imprudence, however, can be understood in two different ways. As we have been considering it, his imprudence consists in his ignorance of the ends he ought to pursue. He has not adequately grounded his opinion that what he covets and seeks to obtain in political life, whether it be power, wealth, honor, or any combination of these (cf. *Nicomachean Ethics* 1124a17–19), is the greatest good, to which his most serious and diligent efforts ought to be directed. It is this fundamental imprudence that has continued to resist Socratic critique. But prudence, that is, knowing what one ought to say and do, can also refer to the deft calculation of means to any given end. This narrower sense of prudence may fail to live up to the name of virtue. But what Alcibiades seems to need when Socrates intercepts him on the way to pray is precisely a version of this kind of prudence, a particularly powerful version that we may call political prudence. The *Second Alcibiades* thus contains a critique of political prudence insofar as its development and use often imply a lack of reflection upon the proper ends of human striving. But this connection is not a necessary one. The fate of Socrates reminds us that the philosopher has a need for political prudence—to garner praise and avoid blame, for example—to say nothing of what may be required for Socrates' educational project. An understanding of rhetoric must make no small part of the political prudence Socrates possesses. Hence, Socrates meets at least one crucial criterion of the qualified teacher of political prudence (cf. *Alcibiades* 111a11–b1).

As for Alcibiades, his perceived need for political prudence has arisen as a result of Socratic reflection. In the *Alcibiades*, he was blissfully unaware of the difficult and even dangerous tasks that stood between him and the attainment of the ends he required. Having given little if any thought to what he would need to *say* to the assembly, he imagined that his mere appearance before the Athenians would be enough for them to be certain he was deserving of the greatest honor (*Alcibiades* 105a7–b7). But when the city appears, as it has come to appear to Alcibiades, to be full of madmen, there is no assurance that one's worth will be justly recognized. Instead, political life is seen to be beset by dangers. Alcibiades' incredulity at Socrates' suggestion that the city is not full of madmen is justified by Socrates' later admission that the best Athenian generals are besieged by their own compatriots. And where the more naïve Alcibiades may have seen in these dangers an opportunity to display his courage and noble devotion, the more cynical Socratic pupil can see only a dispiriting obstacle to the fulfillment of his ambitions.

Political prudence, therefore, may seem to Alcibiades to promise the solution he had tentatively been seeking in divine support. What he would need to learn from Socrates is, in the best case, the ability to control and manage the passions of the Athenians or, in any case, to predict them (cf. *Republic* 493a4–e1). Incidentally, Alcibiades does seem eventually to have learned to do this. His ability as a politician to sway people's opinions when possible and to elude their grasp when necessary was more impressive on the whole than his strategic and tactical acumen as a military leader. The *Second Alcibiades* portrays him after the recognition of his insufficiency to the task of navigating democratic political life but before he has acquired the shrewdness and confidence born of political prudence. In the midst of this *aporia*, Alcibiades has turned almost simultaneously to the gods on one hand and to injustice on the other, raising the question of the relationship of justice to piety. Socrates is therefore in a position to intervene: he holds out the promise of prudence to Alcibiades but not without redirecting his efforts to the more familiar and comfortable territory of democratic politics. Of course, the democratic politics Socrates describes have a cynical edge: he describes the orator as the mind of the city, controlling the dumb flesh by means of rhetoric and law, and directing it toward its (and the ruler's) own good. But tyranny, by the end of the dialogue, is completely taken off the table, and Socrates renews the call for justice and piety, which, he implies, must always coincide (149e8).

But as we have seen, Socrates' virtuous-sounding exhortations at the close of this dialogue are not without an invitation to searching critique. Are justice and piety as simply harmonious as Socrates appears to imply? What force, for example, should one ascribe to the argument that "it would be a terrible thing if the gods focused on our gifts and sacrifices but not on the soul, that one should happen to be pious and just" (149e6–a1)? Socrates presents this statement as though it were enough to dispose of the troubling possibility to which it alludes, but in fact it does no more than express a fear or fearful possibility. To be sure, it is a particularly important possibility. It may be just this fear or possibility that has been gripping Alcibiades in his contemplation of tyranny. The question therefore arises, is it Socrates' intention that Alcibiades should simply accept the surface inducement to justice and piety, or does he want Alcibiades to think critically about the Socratic exhortation and thus about the relationship of his own piety and morality? Probably, he is open to both possibilities, presenting his wisdom in a manner that is, after all, akin to the enigmatic presentation of the poets. If Alcibiades is to succeed in following the thread of Socrates' teaching concerning prayer, for example, he must return to and reconsider Socrates' presentation of the safely and beautifully spoken prayer of the prudent poet, determine what if anything could be deficient about such a prayer, conclude what the gods would have to be like in order for it to be sufficient or deficient, and, most of all, examine the source of his own claims about the necessary imprudence of certain breaches of morality.

For Alcibiades successfully to complete such an investigation would fulfill Socrates' own greatest ambition as we discerned it in the *Alcibiades*: it would be "a beautiful sign" of his own wisdom. The challenge to piety and to justice that necessarily accompanies such an investigation, however, could exacerbate the turbulent transformation that Alcibiades' political ambition has been undergoing. This may be yet another reason why Socrates is intent on diverting Alcibiades' attention away from prayer altogether until he can more fully be brought to distinguish the bad and the good (150e2–3), that is, to become prudent in the fuller sense. However, if the most important consideration with respect to prudence in the fuller sense is what one ought to do and say with respect to the gods, then it may not be possible to avoid exposing Alcibiades to the dangers in question. The difference between the sight given to Diomedes by Athena and that which Socrates proposes to help Alcibiades achieve may be less than it seems at first. Therefore, Socrates may have to remain content with Alcibiades remaining in the midst of partly beneficial delusions. It should be noted, however, that piety was not to be among the virtues for which Alcibiades would become most famous. At least for the sake of political prudence, Alcibiades may indeed have learned the lesson conveyed by Socrates' account of Ammon's prophet.[46] The setting of the *Symposium* and the subject of Alcibiades' speech therein promise to clarify the question of Socrates' effect on Alcibiades' piety.

Before turning to Plato's depiction of the mature Alcibiades, however, we should take a moment to consider his one remaining depiction of the *young* Alcibiades, which is presented in the *Protagoras*. We have left this discussion until after our exploration of the *Second Alcibiades* because Plato defies any attempt to determine with certainty which of the two comes first, but leaves no doubt that the *Alcibiades* and *Second Alcibiades* are to be taken together. That the *Alcibiades* takes place before the *Protagoras* is clear because Alcibiades is portrayed in the latter, together with the infamous Critias, as an eager attendee at the sophist-filled house of Callias, while in the former his education has not yet strayed beyond the traditional and respectable Athenian curriculum and he appears to recognize for the first time that a further education can provide an edge in politics.[47] But does the *Second Alcibiades* precede or follow the experience Alcibiades has at Callias's house? The *Protagoras* is a complex, philosophically rich, and lengthy dialogue in which Alcibiades is, for the most part, a silent observer. This means that a proper understanding of the place of the *Protagoras* in Plato's presentation of Socrates and Alcibiades requires a full interpretation of that dialogue in which we consider at every turn how Alcibiades is likely to be affected by the discussion—a task that takes us too far astray to be carried out here.

Nonetheless, an attempt briefly to summarize the relevant details can help us speculate about the place of the *Protagoras* in Plato's presentation of Socrates and Alcibiades. The *Protagoras* describes an encounter between Socrates and Alcibiades in the course of which Socrates, by his own admission, "did not pay attention" to Alcibiades and even "often forgot" about him on account of his greater interest in the wise Protagoras (309b7–d2). Socrates may therefore have said things it would have been best for Alcibiades not to hear, at least given the course of education along which Socrates had been carefully leading him. For example, the main argument Socrates makes in the *Protagoras* is that virtue cannot be taught—an argument that completely undercuts his bid to teach Alcibiades virtue. Of course, Socrates ends by claiming to have reversed his position in the course of the dialogue since he ends with the claim that courage is wisdom concerning what is terrible and what is not and thus must be teachable *qua* knowledge (360d4–361c2). But reflection upon the case of courage in particular, especially in its form as a science of measurement concerning pleasure and pain, would not have been likely to bolster Alcibiades' belief in the goodness and advantage of noble or courageous sacrifice (357a5–b3, 359e1–360a6).

In light of these reflections, it is tempting to interpret the events of the *Protagoras* as being responsible for (and therefore, of course, preceding) Alcibiades' dourness and concern at the outset of the *Second Alcibiades*. Alcibiades' turn to prayer could be explained as the result of his loss of faith in Socrates' ability as a teacher to impart the virtue he needs to succeed, and the course of Socratic education that appears to have come between the *Alcibiades* and *Second Alcibiades* may in fact have been the lesson Socrates inadvertently imparted by discussing courage, piety, poetry, pleasure, the noble, and the good with Protagoras in Alcibiades' presence. But other considerations weigh against this conclusion. The primary and explicit feature of Alcibiades' role in the *Protagoras* is his repeated and successful effort to ensure that the discussion proceed on Socrates' terms (336b7–d5, 347b3–7, 348b1–c4).[48] There is no sign in the *Second Alcibiades* of the rhetorical touch and dialectical quickness that Alcibiades displays in his manipulation of the discussion in the *Protagoras*. In fact, it seemed by the end of the *Second Alcibiades* that Alcibiades was only beginning to grasp the importance of honing his skills as a speaker for the sake of democratic statesmanship.[49]

The difficulty in placing the *Second Alcibiades* on one side or the other of the *Protagoras* may serve the purpose of reminding us that the most important comparison is between the *Alcibiades* and its sequel. If we put too much weight on the suggestion that Alcibiades' turn to prayer was a reaction to what he heard and contemplated in and after the *Protagoras*, we might forget that Socrates *wanted* Alcibiades to be more concerned with piety and the gods, and ended their first conversation with strong encouragement to that effect. That is, we might confuse the *Second Alcibiades* for an exercise in Socratic damage control and fail to see its place in the planned course of Socrates' education. More than an explanatory device for the action of the *Second Alcibiades*, the *Protagoras* is best taken as a vivid reminder that Alcibiades' association with Socrates took him into the active and turbulent world of Athenian political-intellectual life.

CHAPTER 4

# A PUZZLING RETROSPECTIVE

## (*Symposium* 211–222)

Interpretation of the *Alcibiades* and *Second Alcibiades* requires careful comparison. The similarities in setting and literary form, the proximity of the dramatic dates, and the numerous pairs of parallel passages direct the interpreter to trace the trajectory of the brief but impactful Socratic education that took place in the unnarrated interim. Alcibiades' other major Platonic appearance does not follow the same pattern. The *Symposium* is not a private conversation between Socrates and Alcibiades; Alcibiades does not even join the party until most of the action is over. And this Alcibiades is no longer the timid and tongue-tied political neophyte of the dialogues that bear his name but the city's most famous and controversial figure. The *Symposium* takes place on the eve of the Sicilian Expedition and thus at the time of Alcibiades' greatest triumph as an Athenian statesman. Indeed, his overwhelming oratorical victory over Nicias in persuading the assembly to pursue westward imperial expansion may be the most significant rhetorical feat in recorded Athenian history. Our interpretation of the two *Alcibiades* dialogues suggests that the mature Alcibiades may owe at least some of his skill in political affairs to Socratic education. But perhaps for just that reason, Plato's presentation of Alcibiades includes no mention of his political accomplishments. It gives one pause to reflect that if Alcibiades were known to us only through the works of Plato, it would be hard to know whether he had ever achieved anything of note in Athenian politics.

The lack of explicit emphasis on Alcibiades' political career notwithstanding, however, the task of connecting the dots across the chronological gap left by Plato's portraits is much more daunting here than it was in the *Second Alcibiades*. The time that has elapsed since then is no matter of mere months but rather some fifteen years. The depictions of Alcibiades to be compared differ not in subtle details, but leave us searching for the least similarities between the character we have been studying so far and the drunken, boisterous figure whose entrance signals the beginning of the end of the *Symposium*. And most important, whereas the *Second Alcibiades* made only implicit reference to the Socratic conversations that preceded it, Alcibiades' speech in the *Symposium* explicitly recounts many details of his association with Socrates, few if any of which appear to refer to the scenes portrayed elsewhere by Plato. The effect of this is to suggest that the *Alcibiades* and *Second Alcibiades* were only the beginning of an eventful relationship, the most dramatic moments of which Plato passes over in silence as he whisks us ahead fifteen years from Alcibiades' youth to his final glorious days as the preeminent leader of Athens. To witness the spectacle of the ostentatious Alcibiades striding, or rather stumbling, into Agathon's house is to recognize that we cannot begin to say how the serious young man from fifteen years before has turned into this self-absorbed hedonist before we have first attempted to understand who this new man is.

Even before that, however, we must gain an understanding of Alcibiades' role in the *Symposium*. In one sense, his presence is more out of place in the dialogue than anyone else's. Alcibiades' entrance interrupts the orderly and urbane series of eulogies of *eros* delivered by the guests and threatens to turn a civilized evening into a drunken chaos (213e7–214b2). His strange speech about Socrates might seem, from this perspective, an unwelcome disruption that distracts from our primary thematic interest in following the action of the *Symposium*. Certain elements of the dialogue, however, suggest that many considered Alcibiades' speech , together with Socrates', the most important of the evening. The presence of these elements is made possible by the fact that unlike the *Alcibiades* and its sequel, the *Symposium* is narrated, not performed. The depictions of Alcibiades' and Socrates' early encounters bore no framing dialogue or narration through which Plato might more explicitly link those conversations to the later historical events that his readers surely had in mind, namely, the disastrous end to the Sicilian Expedition, brought about by Alcibiades' alleged participation in the profanation of the Eleusinian mysteries and desecration of the Herms and Socrates' condemnation by the city of Athens. But the *Symposium* conveys through its framing dialogue and nested settings that it pertains to the connection between Alcibiades' spectacular failure as an Athenian leader and the alleged corruption for which Socrates was blamed and killed. It is even suggested that the relevance of the *Symposium* to the matter of Alcibiades' Socratic corruption was the primary source of interest in the events of that evening among contemporary Athenians.

The dialogue begins with Apollodorus responding to the unspecified inquiries of some nameless companions. He reports that he is particularly well prepared to satisfy their request since just two days before he had narrated the very story he will now proceed to tell. At that time, Plato's brother Glaucon had sought out Apollodorus to learn from a more reliable source about "the erotic speeches" that were made at Agathon's party, at which "Socrates, Alcibiades, and the others" were present (172a1–b3). We are thus given the impression that Athens is at present abuzz with the telling and retelling of more and less precise versions of this story; Glaucon had heard reports but was quite eager to have a firsthand account (172b3–9), and was especially interested in what was said by Socrates and Alcibiades. But, as Apollodorus had superciliously pointed out to Glaucon at the time, Apollodorus's was itself only a secondhand account: the party took place long before Apollodorus had become a Socratic devotee (172c5–173a3, 173c2–d3, cf. *Memorabilia* 3.11.17). It seems it has been years since Glaucon has had any intimate acquaintance with the Socratic circle; Adeimantus, by contrast, appears to have remained somewhat closer to Plato and the others (*Apology of Socrates* 33d–34a). What explains Glaucon's sudden interest in and the apparent spike in general demand for the details of Socrates' and Alcibiades' speeches at Agathon's victory party some fifteen years ago? The answer begins to emerge in light of another chronological hint: it has been well over three years, Apollodorus says, since Agathon left Athens. This puts the framing dialogue as late as a year, no more than a few years, before Socrates' trial.[1] As the allegations against Socrates accumulate and public suspicion of him builds to a fever pitch, Athenians are eagerly inquiring, speaking, and hearing about the riveting and scandalous speeches made by Socrates and Alcibiades at Agathon's party years ago.

Those within the semifictional world of Plato's dialogues who are seeking the details of Socrates' alleged corruption of Alcibiades would have had at least two reasons to turn with interest to the tale of Agathon's party. One, the subject of our own investigation, is the drunken Alcibiades' unforgettable encomium and accusation of Socrates, describing the erotic character of their relationship—illuminated in turn by the speech that preceded it, Socrates' account of philosophic *eros* as presented by Diotima. The other is suggested by the chronological setting of the banquet mentioned above: the year is 416 BC,[2] just before the ill-fated Sicilian Expedition and thus also just before Alcibiades' alleged crimes of impiety, to which events the *Symposium* is full of references. Besides Alcibiades, two others symposiasts were implicated in the crimes of 416: Phaedrus in the profanation of the mysteries and Eryximachus in the mutilation of the Herms.[3] Allowing for some characteristic looseness in the Platonic chronology, we can at least entertain the suggestion that the drunken chaos that marks the end of the evening's erotic speeches rolled on into the Athenian night and resulted in the infamous acts of sacrilege.[4] And while the action of the *Symposium* could never be mistaken for the mock initiations in which Alcibiades, Phaedrus, Charmides, and others were said to have partaken, both Socrates and Alcibiades strikingly if playfully suggest in their speeches that they are divulging esoteric secrets to noninitiates (209e5–210a4, 218b5–7).[5]

The *Symposium* thus points from a number of directions to the question of Socrates' involvement in Alcibiades' becoming what he is known to have been. This is not to say that the *Symposium* necessarily answers that question better than the *Alcibiades* and the *Second Alcibiades*. But the conversations of those dialogues were private; there was no chain of reporters and narrators through whom they could become famous—at least, not *within* the world of the Platonic dialogues. The *Symposium* account is only presented as the more famous (or infamous) meeting of Socrates and Alcibiades, not necessarily the more revealing. And yet it is in this final scene of the *Symposium* that Alcibiades likens the proceedings to a courtroom prosecution before a jury in which he is to accuse Socrates of *hubris* (215b7–8, 219c3–d2). Plato thus gives us the impression that Alcibiades' speech is meant to contain the evidence we must weigh in considering Socrates' culpability for his student's actions and character.[6] The *Apology of Socrates*, it is to be remembered, does not include the prosecution's speech.

Here, then, is the last leg of the journey through Plato's presentation of Socrates and Alcibiades: the latter's wine-soaked retrospective on their complex relationship, an account tinged equally with loving admiration and bitter regret, a strange hybrid of encomium and indictment. Our goal, as always, is to seek in the details of this account some understanding of the way in which Socratic education nourished or stifled, corrected or corrupted, guided or transformed Alcibiades' political ambition. But while every aspect of the setting and tone of this final scene leads us to suspect that our questions will now be answered, we must recognize from the outset that the strangeness of this presentation—a drunken rant recounted thirdhand more than a decade after the fact, provocatively juxtaposed with a series of philosophic speeches about love at the climax of which Socrates had given his most moving and memorable depiction of philosophy—calls the true purpose or meaning of the speech into question. In fact, it will be my contention that the *Symposium* tells us much less about Socrates' corruption of Alcibiades than do the two dialogues we have already considered. But it is only because of our reading of those dialogues that we are prepared to recognize the hidden emptiness of the speech in the *Symposium,* and it is only by considering what we learn from the *Symposium* that the importance of what is further to be sought from the *Alcibiades* dialogues can be duly appreciated.

## The Purpose and Truthfulness of Alcibiades' Speech

The immediate impact of Alcibiades' arrival on the action of the *Symposium* is the preempting of Aristophanes' response to Socrates' speech (212c6–d4). In that speech, Socrates had referred to Aristophanes' myth, in which love is described as a longing for one's kindred "other half," by reporting Diotima's judgment that "a certain *logos* is spoken that those who seek their half are those who love; but my *logos* says that love is for neither a half nor a whole unless it should happen, comrade, to be good, since human beings are willing to cut off their own feet and hands if their own seem to them to be bad" (205d10–e5). Alcibiades' part in the *Symposium* thus takes the place of a discussion about whether *eros* is primarily a love of one's own or a love of the good. But this could mean either that Alcibiades prevents that debate from taking place or that Plato means for us to learn something about the disagreement between Socrates and Aristophanes by considering the case of Alcibiades as it is presented here.[7]

Alcibiades had at first come to wreathe Agathon as the "wisest and most beautiful" with fillets "from [his] own head" (212e6–7). His congratulations indicate a kind of acknowledgment that Agathon has joined him among the uppermost cultural elite. These two men, renowned for their beauty and in the prime of their adult lives, stand at the dizzying height of their fame, basking in the intoxicating adulation of their fellow Athenians.[8] The similar esteem in which the two are held by the Athenians is represented by the party's identical reactions to Alcibiades' entrance and to Agathon's speech (*pantas anathorubuēsai* at 198a1–2 and 213a3). Thus, Alcibiades appears to be erotically attracted to Agathon as a kindred spirit in the manner of Aristophanes' half-men (cf. 222d2–3). Their embrace (213b2–3) recalls the manly lovers whose *eros* is accorded the highest praise in the Aristophanean myth (cf. 191a6–7, 192a5, b5). But after having perceived Socrates, Alcibiades removes some of the fillets he had given Agathon and wreathes Socrates too, saying "I will wreathe also this amazing head of his lest he censure me because I wreathed you but not him, who is victorious over all human beings in speeches, and not only the day before yesterday as you did, but always" (213e1–5). Alcibiades thus shows himself so far to be divided with respect to the elided debate between Socrates and Aristophanes. His acknowledgment of Socrates' superiority over Agathon is partial—both men, after all, are wreathed—and appears to be given somewhat begrudgingly or half-mockingly. Nonetheless, Alcibiades clearly indicates that Socrates has laid a claim to his affection that rivals Agathon's, and Socrates has himself indicated that Alcibiades is disposed toward him as a madly jealous lover (213c6–d6).

The notion that Alcibiades is a lover of Socrates must strike at least some of those present as comical. Alcibiades had wreathed Agathon for being the "wisest and most beautiful"; there is no doubt about the category in which Socrates gave the poet a run for his money.[9] But we know from the *Alcibiades*, and will have further confirmation by the end of this speech, that Alcibiades' love for Socrates is not simply a joke. Alcibiades proclaimed his budding love for Socrates at the conclusion of their first conversation, brimming with the hope that Socrates could provide him with the education in virtue or self-knowledge that would allow him to fulfill his noblest political ambitions. We may be tempted, following this reflection, to assume that Alcibiades' love for Socrates is able to rival his love of Agathon on account of the promise of political success and happiness obtained through justice, piety, and prudence by means of which Socrates was able to seduce him.

But that assumption does not align as well with some other indications, which remind us of the long, opaque interval separating the *Alcibiades* dialogues from the *Symposium*. For example, the claim that Socrates is to be preferred over Agathon because he is always victorious over all human beings in speeches reflects an element of Alcibiades' love that was not yet present in their first conversation. It leaves ambiguous whether Alcibiades means that Socrates possesses and never deviates from the eternal truth (cf. *Gorgias* 481d1–482b1), or rather that he has an unmatched rhetorical ability, perhaps based on his skill at making the weaker speech the stronger.[10] Indeed, the latter possibility most accords with the suggestion that the competition between Socrates the wise and Agathon the beautiful reflects that between love of the good as emphasized by Socrates and love of one's own as emphasized by Aristophanes. For Socrates' initial seduction of Alcibiades was based on Alcibiades' love of the noble and of the Athenians. After all, the theme of Alcibiades' speech will be precisely the Socratic siren's song that nearly tore him away from the life and love of politics, from the upper crust of the city's *kaloi kagathoi*, and from the pantheon of Athenian statesmanship. That is, the speech confirms that Socrates had more success showing Alcibiades what was crucially missing from political life than Plato ever suggested in his portrayal of their conversations.

Thus, we must seek evidence in Alcibiades' speech of what he learned from Socrates in the time following their earliest conversations and of how he came to see and to love him. But we must also be prepared for the possibility that, drunk as he is, Alcibiades may not be entirely forthright. The truthfulness of his speech is a recurring theme of the speech itself;[11] doth Alcibiades protest too much? One might note that Socrates himself seems to affirm the truth of the speech by remaining silent despite Alcibiades' frequent appeals to Socrates for correction. But one might equally counter that evidence with Alcibiades' first accusation of Socrates: in reference to Socrates' claims that Alcibiades jealously forbids him from associating with any other beautiful youths, Alcibiades replies, "Has Socrates convinced you of what he just said? Or do you know that everything is the opposite of what he said?" (214c8–d2). Does Alcibiades actually expect the man whom he has accused of being an inveterate liar to endorse the whole truth and nothing but the truth if it should be reported? Or will Alcibiades' report, by omission, falsification, or both, distort the truth about Socrates in a manner tolerable to the latter?[12]

In evaluating the truthfulness of Alcibiades' speech, it is important to consider the only time Socrates ever does express disapproval—albeit before the speech itself has begun. The moment in question immediately follows Alcibiades' above quoted accusation that Socrates is a liar, itself a response to Eryximachus's request that he praise Eros in his turn. Alcibiades explains how "everything is the opposite" of what Socrates said by continuing, "If I praise anyone, whether a god or another human being, while [Socrates] is present, he will not keep his hands away from me" (214d2–4, cf. 213d3–4). Socrates immediately shoots back, "Won't you speak well?" (*ouk euphēmeis*), a phrase that implies Alcibiades is blaspheming and that is therefore often translated with the more urgent and imperative "Hush!" But perhaps the literal translation—especially given the emphasis on *euphēmia* in the *Second Alcibiades*—reveals the Socratic outburst as a request for Alcibiades to speak more prudently in what follows, especially as concerns the gods.[13] It is unclear from Alcibiades' immediate response, however, whether he intends to grant this request: "By Poseidon! Don't speak against these things, since I could praise not one other person while you are present." Then, when Eryximachus suggests that he praise Socrates, Alcibiades asks the crowd, "Shall I attack and take vengeance on him in front of you?"[14] Socrates appears to express some concern at this, asking whether Alcibiades will praise him in order to provoke laughter, but Alcibiades insists his intention is to tell the truth (214d6–e6). And as soon as he begins his speech, he emphasizes that although Socrates may suppose that Alcibiades is trying to provoke laughter, he is in fact speaking for the sake of the truth (215a5–6). We are left without a clear sense of Alcibiades' intention with respect to Socrates' only censure.

Socrates' objection followed directly upon Alcibiades' claims that (a) he has lied about the character of his relationship to Alcibiades and (b) he would actively oppose Alcibiades' attempt to praise any god or human being above himself. We might consider that the former claim invites those it impresses to potentially far-reaching speculation. What else might Socrates have been lying about—especially if one takes literally (and admittedly out of context) the claim that "everything is the opposite of what Socrates said"? Could this mean that Socrates does not consider Eros to be "a great daimon" and that philosophy does not really allow a human being to become immortal insofar as that is possible—or more simply, that Socrates never learned about *eros* from any "Diotima of Mantinea"?[15] At any rate, it would seem to raise some questions as to whether Diotima's had been a complete account of the effects of "correct pederasty" (211b5–6). The latter of the claims to which Socrates may be objecting would seem to suggest that Socrates attempted to persuade Alcibiades not only that his own wisdom was superior to that of all other human beings but even that the gods did not deserve more praise than Socrates himself. And yet Alcibiades' oath by Poseidon is not a clear concession to Socrates' wish that he speak more piously. Though it is a reference to a traditional Greek god, it is an unusual and powerful oath that hardly bespeaks pious reverence.[16] In fact, Alcibiades' swearing by Poseidon puts us in mind of the disastrous naval expedition he is about to lead: it reminds us, in other words, of his insufficient care to avoid gaining a public reputation for *hubris*. If nothing else, we are confronted with a difficult question that generally surrounds Alcibiades' political career in Athens: was he a shrewd public speaker and demagogue or an unapologetic narcissist who was undone by his refusal to maintain a pious facade or to humble himself, if only ironically?

The question of whether he will be forthcoming in his speech is made most perplexing by Alcibiades' suggestion that a praise of Socrates, if performed in public, would amount to an attack on him for the sake of revenge. He is aware that whatever makes Socrates most worthy of praise cannot unproblematically be discussed in public. The singular example of a successful, truthful, accusatory, public praise of Socrates—all the more relevant because Alcibiades will quote from it!—is Aristophanes' *Clouds*. The discussion of whether Alcibiades' speech will be for the sake of provoking laughter—which indeed recalls the preamble Aristophanes gave to his own speech (189b4–7)—suggests that its laughable elements may serve as a disguise for the more serious and delicate truth.[17] At the close of Alcibiades' speech, Socrates will praise him:

> You seem to me to be sober, Alcibiades. For [otherwise] you would never have attempted, by so cleverly enclosing yourself all around, to hide that for the sake of which you said all these things, and you put it at the end as though you were making a sidenote, as though it were not for the sake of this that you said everything, [namely] the pitting against each other of me and Agathon, since you suppose that I must love no one else but you, and that Agathon must be loved by no one else but you. But you have not escaped notice; rather, this satyr and Silenus play has been discovered.[18] (222c3–d4)

A satyr play is a comedy. Socrates here plays the part Alcibiades had assigned him (215a5–6), claiming to have taken his speech for a comedy. But that which Socrates claims to identify as the hidden meaning of the speech—Alcibiades' jealous love—was indeed the comedic element recognized by all (222c1–3). If, then, the comedic and obvious theme of Alcibiades' speech is his jealous love, then what is the serious and hidden meaning within it? Socrates helps Alcibiades deflect attention away from this hidden core of the speech by confusing it with its laughable exterior. But Alcibiades has already explained what would in fact be the non- or subcomedic subject of his speech: the true praise of Socrates.[19] In general, Socrates' praise of Alcibiades' speech is a helpful reminder that we should not underestimate the artfulness of this masterful orator at the height of his powers.[20]

One more intriguing suggestion about the forthrightness of Alcibiades' speech can be inferred from his implicit comparison of Socrates to Odysseus. In the midst of his speech, Alcibiades quotes a Homeric line: "'What sort of thing this mighty man did and suffered' . . . is worth hearing" (220c2–3). The line appears twice in Book Four of the *Odyssey*; Helen and Menelaus each use it to introduce their respective tales about Odysseus (4.242, 271). In Helen's story, Odysseus enters Troy disguised as a beggar. Helen recognizes him and, once he has explained his plan to her, agrees to keep his secret (4.240–264). Menelaus, in turn, tells the story of the Trojan horse. As the horse sat in the city, Helen walked around it imitating the wives of the soldiers within in an attempt to make the Achaeans give themselves away.[21] The soldiers within wished to call back, but Odysseus kept them in check, even putting his hand over the warrior Anticlus's mouth to muffle his cries (4.265–289).[22] Each story portrays Odysseus at the height of his brilliant deceitfulness. Moreover, each story recalls Odysseus's success in getting others to keep his secrets with him. Will Alcibiades reveal Socrates' disguise?[23]

## Alcibiades' Images and the Power of the Socratic Speeches

The opening of Alcibiades' speech straightaway heightens our expectation that he intends to reveal some Socratic secret. Having explained that he will attempt to praise Socrates "through images," Alcibiades first makes his famous comparison of Socrates to "these silenuses sitting in the Herm-sculptors' shops,[24] which the craftsmen make holding pipes or a flute, and which when split open are seen to have sculptures of gods inside" (215a7–b3). We thus begin to see that Alcibiades may not simply be under Socratic compulsion to praise Socrates above all gods and men; Alcibiades in fact has come to see Socrates *as a god* or at least somehow as an "image" or "sculpture" of a god. What could have made Alcibiades come to such a conclusion? He goes on to say that Socrates is also like the satyr Marsyas, and not just in form "but also with respect to the other things. . . . You are hubristic, aren't you? For if you should disagree, I will produce witnesses" (215b3–8). Alcibiades implies that Socrates is on trial; the charge, it appears, is *hubris*.[25] This scenario cannot help but put us in mind of Socrates' actual trial in which he faced a charge of "not believing in the gods in which the city believes, and introducing other, novel *daimonia*" (Diogenes Laertius, 2.5.40). One might well imagine on the basis of this connection that Alcibiades, both in saying that Socrates has something divine in him and in accusing him of *hubris*, has in mind Socrates' famous daimonic voice. Alcibiades is certainly familiar with it: it was effectively the first thing Socrates mentioned in their first conversation (*Alcibiades* 103a4–6).[26] It therefore comes as a surprise that Alcibiades never mentions Socrates' *daimonion*.

Then again, Socrates' *daimonion*, as his opening in the *Alcibiades* suggests, was very much a part of his public presentation: that is, it would not seem to fit Alcibiades' picture of a Socratic divinity that lies hidden beneath the well-known surface. What, then, does Alcibiades mean by that image, and what does he intend by the accusation of *hubris*? It may be helpful here to recall the story of Marsyas. In Greek myth, the hubristic Marsyas dared to challenge Apollo in a musical contest. When he lost, Apollo flayed him alive and hung his hide up in a cave.[27] Here again we are reminded of the *Apology of Socrates* and Socrates' Delphic mission to refute Apollo or Apollo's purported oracular decree that no one is wiser than Socrates (21a6–7, 22a6–8). Alcibiades' image agrees with the account in the *Apology*: Socrates, like Marsyas, lost the contest with Apollo. But in Socrates' case, that means confirmation that no one—and we are tempted to ask whether this includes even the gods—has any greater wisdom than Socrates' "human wisdom" (23a7). This is indeed an enigmatic matter. How much of it does Alcibiades grasp? We must not forget that the project Socrates describes at the end of his life as a kind of rivalry with Apollo is connected to Socrates' association with Alcibiades in their first conversation, when Socrates interprets and coopts the Delphic inscription "know thyself." The disingenuousness of his interpretation there is followed by his distortion of poetic and prophetic verses in the *Second Alcibiades*, and Alcibiades has by now begun to make it clear that he is at least aware of Socrates' willingness to be disingenuous. The question remains, however, as to how much Alcibiades has really understood about the particular matter of Socrates' antioracular quest for self-knowledge through the examination of virtue in the souls of the young. His reference to Marsyas, like most of his speech, is suggestive but hopelessly inconclusive.

Some indication would seem to be given, however, as Alcibiades elaborates upon the similarity between Socrates and Marsyas. He refers to Marsyas' songs as the only ones that "whether a good flutist or a paltry flute-girl plays them, make one possessed and make clear those who are in need of the gods and of initiation rites, because [the songs] are divine" (215c3–6, cf. *Minos* 318b). The only difference between Socrates and Marsyas, says Alcibiades, is that Socrates does with mere speeches what the other does with instruments; Socrates' speeches, like Marsyas's songs, are learned and recited, sometimes by poor speakers but always to great effect—at least among those "in need of the gods and of initiation rites" (215c6–d6). It should perhaps come as no surprise that there are people recounting Socratic speeches, since the *Symposium* itself provides the examples of Aristodemus and Apollodorus. But we must note here that precision, as Alcibiades now describes it, is of no importance to the effect of these speeches. It would seem there is a kind of Socratic "gist" that can be conveyed even by someone who mistakes the details. This peculiarity of Alcibiades' account goes together with the fact that he never once speaks of being persuaded by Socrates. Instead, Alcibiades speaks of becoming possessed (215d5–6); of his heart leaping and his being brought to tears (215e1–2); of becoming vexed at the slavishness of his own soul and coming to think that his life is not worth living (*mē biōton* 215e6–216a2, cf. *Apology of Socrates* 38a5–6); of being compelled to agree that he is deficient and careless (216a4–6); of being made to feel ashamed, which he is before no one else (216b1–2); and of being powerless to deny that he must do whatever Socrates orders (216b3–4).

Alcibiades describes what sounds like a powerful religious experience: the divine Socratic speeches move him to tears and make him feel the need for gods out of a sense of the shameful paltriness of his ordinary life and business. But the lack of any mention of argument or of being convinced, or indeed of any indication that the speeches are philosophic, goes together with Alcibiades' studied silence about their content. We can gain some insight into that matter, however, by juxtaposing Alcibiades' descriptions of his reaction to Socrates with what we have seen ourselves in the *Alcibiades.* We can begin by noting that the experience he describes at times recalls the perplexity and shame he feels in his first conversation with Socrates (*Alcibiades* 108e5–109a4, 116e2–4, 127d6–8) and at other times the enthusiasm he evinced for Socrates' exaltation of virtue (124b7-9, 135d7-e5). The divine experience described by Alcibiades appears to refer to a combination of the characteristic *aporia* into which Socrates famously leads his interlocutors and the characteristic reaction on the part of listeners to his discussions concerning virtue.[28] This suggestion can help us understand the relevance of the striking political notes Alcibiades adds to his description: he comments upon the vast superiority of the Socratic speeches to those of Pericles and says that he ceases to obey Socrates when he has been "overcome by the honor of the many" (*Symposium* 215e4–5, 216b4–5). The shame Alcibiades claims that Socrates made him feel sounds like the shame he felt when Socrates chastised him for wanting to be no greater than Meidias the quail-striker and demagogic flatterer (*Alcibiades* 120a9–c2).[29] It is the shame born of abandoning the hard work of self-improvement and the development of virtue, a course Socrates persuasively insisted was necessary for Alcibiades to become as worthy of honor as he supposed himself to be, in favor of easy political victories and meaningless honor.

But if we consider further the implications of Alcibiades' retrospective claims in the *Symposium*, we find that they tell us more than we could have known from the earlier dialogues alone. In comparing Socrates' speeches to the Sirens' song, Alcibiades for the first time reveals his awareness of what the true Socratic alternative would have entailed: "Shutting my ears by force, I left fleeing as from the Sirens, in order that I might not grow old sitting idle (*kathēmenos*) by this man's side" (216a6–8). His comparison of Socrates to the Sirens is indicative both of his acknowledgment of Socrates' wisdom and of the character of Alcibiades' erotic attraction to him.[30] But the elaboration of the analogy leaves no doubt about the character of the Socratic alternative Alcibiades was leaving behind. It was not another kind of active political life, more virtuous, more tyrannical, or otherwise. It was an inactive life from the point of view of politics. The shame Alcibiades describes, therefore, is not just the shame of lapsing in his pursuit of virtue but the shame that comes from pursuing the political life despite having become convinced that full-hearted democratic statesmanship, even that of Pericles, rests upon thoughtless assumptions about the good and the noble. We understood in the *Alcibiades* that Socrates was presenting him with an ultimatum: he must choose between the honor of those whose ignorance and imprudence Socrates painfully exposes and the indefinite suspension of that pursuit for the sake of Socratic education.[31] At that time, it seemed that Alcibiades had failed to grasp fully the gravity of the decision he was asked to make. We learn now that at some point he came to understand it more fully.[32]

Here, then, is the torment to which Socratic education has exposed Alcibiades. He has been unable to tear himself away from political life and the seductive honor it promises, and yet he has never been able to forget Socrates' powerful critique. Once he saw the Socratic critique of the many and of the desire to be adored by them, no human being besides Socrates himself appeared worthy of any consideration (cf. *Alcibiades* 105d7–e5), a fact already made visible in the *Second Alcibiades* by his respect for Socrates as one of the "few" prudent human beings. Alcibiades therefore says he would often wish to see Socrates gone from among human beings so that he could cease to be reminded of "the things to which [he] had agreed,"[33] but he also knew that that the Socratic arguments would not be any less true if that should happen (216c1–3). It is just one more masterful Platonic touch that when Alcibiades enters the party, he is unable to see Socrates because his wreaths obstruct his vision (213a5–7).

Alcibiades' abstraction from the content of the Socratic speeches obscures the fact that Socrates' effect was achieved in part by a powerful process of teaching and persuading—a fact that is more likely to escape the notice of a reader unfamiliar with the *Alcibiades* dialogues. We have seen, in those dialogues as well as from hints in the *Symposium*, that this teaching pertained to political life. But the religious elements of the experience Alcibiades now describes still need to be considered. He says that hearing Socrates' speeches makes his "heart jump much more than the Corybants."[34] Just as Alcibiades says that Socrates' speeches move him much more than Pericles' speeches did, he also suggests that the Socratic speeches are more spiritually powerful than traditional Greek religious festivals. Indeed, the comment about the Corybantic festival dancers brings out a strangeness in the claim that Socrates' speeches alone "make clear those who are in need of the gods and of initiation rites." Toward what initiation rites do the Socratic speeches point? To what gods? Alcibiades has quietly suggested that Socrates' speeches make certain hearers aware that the traditional Greek religious practices are insufficient; they discover that they are in need of, or rather lacking (*deomenous*), gods and initiation rites. Alcibiades came to wish to be initiated into the *Socratic* mysteries. As we already have already suggested, he came to see Socrates as a god.

Alcibiades sees Socrates as a singular combatant in two distinct but related contests of great import to Alcibiades himself. Socrates is in competition with the city for Alcibiades' devotion: we have recognized the similarity between this contest and the elided debate between Socrates and Aristophanes—love of the good versus love of one's own—and he is in some kind of competition with the gods. The passages we have been considering are reminiscent of Alcibiades' own turn to prayer as portrayed in the *Second Alcibiades* and of the conclusion of that dialogue in which Alcibiades' crowns Socrates with the wreath he had brought for the god (150c3–d6). Perhaps, then, the need for the gods described in this speech is the need that arises on account of a Socratic examination of the relation of the good to the noble (cf. *Alcibiades* 114d11ff with *Symposium* 204d2–e7). But the moral and religious crisis of the *Second Alcibiades* is now fifteen years in the past. What was the result of Alcibiades' renewed pledge to follow Socrates at the end of that conversation? To what conclusions about the existence, morality, and character of the gods did Socratic reflection finally lead him?

## The Bedroom Scene as Mock Philosophic Mystery

Given the charge of impiety that Socrates would eventually face, the repeated suggestion that he came to replace the gods in Alcibiades' esteem is as damning an accusation of Socratic *hubris* as one might reasonably expect. Alcibiades' accusation of *hubris* against Socrates is therefore a tantalizing suggestion that we will be treated to an account of Socrates' secret and impious, or at least heterodox, teaching about the gods. But we have already noted an oddity in the fact that Socrates' *daimonion*, a central feature of his self-presentation as somehow uncanny (cf. *Apology of Socrates* 31c4ff), is absent from Alcibiades' presentation. There is now another surprising turn in Alcibiades' accusation: the charge of *hubris* focuses not on Socrates' disposition with respect to the gods but to his utter indifference to Alcibiades' youthful attempt to seduce him. The *hubris* of which Alcibiades accuses Socrates is a manifestation of his moderation, but moderation and *hubris* are opposites (see, e.g., Xenophon, *Memorabilia* 1.2.19).

Alcibiades' failure to explain the deeper meaning of Socrates' *hubris* is easily forgotten on account of the salacious story that replaces it. The entire presentation of this vignette seems designed to leave the listener or reader who sensed that something scandalous was to be disclosed with the impression that the speech did not disappoint. Alcibiades begins by telling his audience, "Know well that not one of you knows this man; but I will reveal him, since I have indeed begun [to do so]" (216c7–d1), and he later explains the motivation for his attempted seduction thus: "I don't know if anyone has seen the statues within him when he is serious and has been opened up; but I had seen them once, and they seemed to me to be so divine, golden, altogether beautiful, and amazing, that whatever Socrates should command must be done" (216e5–217a2). The implication of this, soon to become explicit, is that Alcibiades, presuming Socrates to be a lover (*Alcibiades* 103a1–4, 131c5–e5), was willing to give him what lovers want (*Symposium* 184d3–185a5) in order "to hear everything he knew" (217a4–5). Then, having described his many failed attempts to seduce Socrates—by spending time alone with him, wrestling naked with him, and inviting him to dinner (217a6–e1)—Alcibiades interrupts his narration to mark the importance of what will follow. What he has recounted so far, he says, he would have told anyone, but since he is drunk and since it would be "unjust to hide Socrates' magnificently overweening deed, having entered into praise [of him],"[35] he will go on (217e1–6). More important, Alcibiades looks around at the "Phaedruses, Agathons, Eryximachuses, Pausaniases, Aristodemuses, and Aristophaneses—and what needs to be said about Socrates and the others?" all of whom "have taken part in the madness and Bacchic frenzy of philosophy"— and so decides they are fit to hear what follows. "But the servants, and if anyone else should be uninitiated and boorish, 'close very great doors over your ears'" (218a7–b7).

With this quotation of an Orphic hymn, and with the only explicit acknowledgment he ever gives that Socrates' business is philosophy, Alcibiades suggests that he will now divulge a terrible secret.[36] His slapdash attempt to keep the purported secret from the noninitiates seems to display a total carelessness about the matter, which is all the more striking in light of the fact that in the actual Athenian trials in which Alcibiades was accused of having performed mock initiation rites in private homes, uninitiated household slaves were brought in as witnesses (Andocides, *On the Mysteries* 11–12, 17–18). But Alcibiades' suspenseful digression is all the more tantalizing because he suggests the mysteries to be divulged are those pertaining to the cult of *philosophy*. Thus, we are led to expect that we will at long last be made privy to the deep secret that lies beneath the satirical surface of Socrates' superficial presentation. What follows, however, falls hopelessly short of that expectation. It is a magnificent trick of Alcibiadean rhetoric that this most disappointing portion of the speech should become the most famous and should give the impression, as I have suggested, that it contains the secret, juicy details of Alcibiades' and Socrates' relationship. The reader is apt to forget there was another, much more interesting, and much more important feature of that relationship about which we seem to hear nothing at all: Socrates' alleged *corruption* of Alcibiades. Perhaps it is Plato's own ironic joke that he has his Alcibiades perform precisely a mock philosophic initiation ritual, just as the Eleusinian rites he was said to have performed in private were something like "a joke in poor taste."[37]

Alcibiades' introduction to his disclosure of the mysteries—the only portion of his entire speech in which he mentions philosophy—deserves careful attention.

> The experience of being bitten by a viper is also mine. For they say, presumably, that one who has experienced this is not willing to say what sort of thing it is except to those who have been bitten, on the grounds they are the only ones who will recognize and be forgiving if he had dared to do and say everything because of the pain. So I, having

> been bitten by a more painful thing and in the most painful of the places someone could be bitten—for I, having been struck and bitten in the heart, or the soul, or whatever name one must give it, by the speeches of philosophy, which take hold more savagely than a she-viper whenever they grab a young and not ill-natured soul, and make it do and say anything whatsoever—and seeing now Phaedruses, Agathons, Eryximachuses, Pausaniases, Aristodemuses, and Aristophaneses—and what needs to be said about Socrates and the others? For you all have taken part in the madness and Bacchic frenzy of philosophy—because of this, you all will hear; for you will forgive the things then done and the things now said. (217e6–218b7)

With this cascade of drunken anacolutha, Alcibiades impressionistically describes his experience with philosophy. The experience was characterized by overwhelming pain—though Alcibiades has trouble describing the location of the pain because he is unsure whether to refer to his bodiless "soul" rather than to his physical "heart." Alcibiades has come to be unsure about the status of the soul, or about whether there is anything in him other than his physical body. Thus, at the very moment in which Alcibiades is describing his painful experience with philosophy, he gives one of the precious few clues as to what the substance of his philosophizing involved. We see that the question or dilemma that arose from his having been "bitten" by Socrates was not limited to the strictly political but extended to the deepest question of Socratic philosophy: what is a human being (*Alcibiades* 129d9, cf. *Theaetetus* 174a4–b7)? Perhaps this was indicated already in the *Second Alcibiades*, when Alcibiades intimated that the function of his soul was primarily to make beneficial use of the goods he acquired (*Second Alcibiades* 141c1–5)—recalling his discussion of the soul with Socrates in their first conversation (*Alcibiades* 129d11)—although the question he points to here suggests he has gone still further since then. In any case, Plato again gives us reason to suspect that Alcibiades, whether with Socrates' help or on his own, remembered, reconsidered, and made progress in answering the questions Socrates left half-buried or misunderstood in their early discussions.

It is also necessary to clarify the clear sense this passage gives to Alcibiades' seeming implication that he will be divulging esoteric secrets. It is only because he supposes that those present know what it is like to be driven mad by an obsession with philosophy that he is willing to tell them how far he went and how far he was willing to go in his pursuit of Socratic wisdom.[38] People who had never been struck by the need for philosophy would not understand and would think Alcibiades' actions shameful: we are reminded of Pausanias's remarks about the deeds dared by lovers in pursuit of their beloveds, which would "reap the greatest reproaches leveled against philosophy" if done for any other reason (183a1–2). But other than the barely discernible reference to considerations about the nature of the soul, Alcibiades continues to be exasperatingly silent about the Socratic questions or arguments that brought about his unshakable, intoxicating, torturously painful experience.[39]

Of course, the recognition that Alcibiades' love story distracts its audience from more important matters that had been alluded to—and here, Apollodorus's listeners past and present should be remembered—must not stop us from interpreting the important details he does relate. The connection between Socrates' *hubris* and his moderation is especially worthy of note. Alcibiades says that beneath the surface of Socrates' constant irony and playfulness, his attention to the beautiful young and claims of ignorance, Socrates teems with a moderation so great that he looks down in contempt upon beauty, wealth, and other things human beings honor (216d2–e5). His *hubris*, as it manifested itself toward Alcibiades, sprang from his incomparable self-sufficiency, from his apparent lack of any need for anything Alcibiades could offer: he rebuffs Alcibiades' advance in just the same way that Alcibiades' had rebuffed those of his own lovers (*Alcibiades* 103b4–104a4). This self-sufficiency is surely an important part of the sense in which Alcibiades came to see him as a god and therefore has a connection to the deeper sense of Socratic *hubris*.[40]

We can also take note of Socrates' response to Alcibiades' proposal as the two of them lay alone in bed. Quoting Homer, Socrates suggests that Alcibiades is attempting to acquire "gold in exchange for bronze" by offering to trade his physical beauty (which occupies the lowest rung on Diotima's so-called "ladder of love") for the "truth of beautiful things" (which sounds like the uppermost rung; cf. 210e2–212a7). But Socrates advises him to "examine better, lest it escape your notice that I am nothing" (218d6–219a4, cf. *Alcibiades* 130c2). Thus Socrates suggests that his wisdom—which Alcibiades believes he has glimpsed and recognized as divine, just as Socrates strongly insinuated to the other symposiasts that he obtained some divine wisdom from Diotima—may not in fact be the highest and most perfect expression of that for which the erotic soul longs. Is the beauty of philosophy, then, a mirage? Is Socrates' wisdom not beautiful but ugly? Or must we insist that, like Eros, it is in the middle (201e10–11)? Perhaps it is the wisdom of the Silenus after all.[41]

However much or little of this is implied in Alcibiades' recounting of the bedroom scene, the most crucial fact about it remains unchanged: this memorably scandalous—or rather, this memorably chaste tale—appears crafted for the sake of being remembered so that a graver matter will be forgotten. The painfulness of Alcibiades' exposure to philosophy was not his rejection by Socrates, since it was precisely this painful bite that led him to bid for Socratic wisdom with his overwhelming physical beauty. We are yet left wondering as to the content of Alcibiades' Socratic education, or corruption, or both.[42]

In the transition from this portion of Alcibiades' speech to the next, however, we are prompted to reconsider certain details with greater scrutiny. Alcibiades reveals that the whole series of encounters he has just narrated occurred before he and Socrates left on campaign to Potidaea (219e5–6). For the first time, we are invited to piece Alcibiades' *Symposium* retrospective together with the two Platonic dialogues we have already studied, the first of which certainly, the second apparently, took place before Potidaea. But the attempt to build a coherent timeline is quickly frustrated. Alcibiades says that it was only after he had been powerfully moved by a desire to obtain Socratic wisdom that he devised the plan to obtain it by means of his youthful beauty and that he then for the first time arranged to be alone with Socrates by sending his attendant away (216e5–217b1). Alcibiades says he expected Socrates to converse with him as a lover with a beloved, but instead he conversed just "as had been his wont" (*eiōthei*) and left after they had spent the day together (217b3–7).

Now in the *Alcibiades*, the two men are alone (118a5), but Socrates says he has hitherto never spoken to Alcibiades (103a1–4, 106a2–3). It is true that Socrates presents himself as a lover only to engage Alcibiades in a series of unerotic but characteristically Socratic dialectical exchanges. But the *Symposium* account makes it seem as though Alcibiades had had such conversations with Socrates before, had come to know his habitual mode of discourse, had gained a revelatory glimpse of the true Socrates beneath the ironic facade, and had then sent his handler away in the hope of sparking a more intimate and romantic conversation. Likewise, it is true that Alcibiades says early in the conversation that he had been on the point of inquiring as to what Socrates' business is (104c7–d5, cf. *Symposium* 217c4–6), but the dialogue as a whole clearly contains his first real exposure to Socratic thought: his initial wonder at Socrates' strangeness (106a2–3) must not be confused with the erotic attraction he is beginning to feel by the end of their conversation (135e1–5).

The *Symposium* thus suggests that Alcibiades' first private conversation with Socrates followed a number of nonprivate ones in which Alcibiades became deeply intrigued by Socratic wisdom, whereas the *Alcibiades* suggests that their very first conversation was private and that Alcibiades was intrigued by Socrates but still quite unsure of what sort of thing he might have to say. There can be no doubt as to which of these accounts Plato presents as more authoritative. The *Alcibiades* is a performed dialogue: the question of its historical accuracy notwithstanding—it is, after all, no real question—the speeches within it issue from the only infallible authority in the world of Plato's dialogues. The speech in the *Symposium* is delivered by a drunken Alcibiades, who insists suspiciously often upon his truthfulness, as remembered by Apollodorus, who heard it from Aristodemus and had its details corrected by Socrates, whose motives in the matter are unknown. In short, there is something fishy about Alcibiades' account of the origins of his relationship with Socrates. He leaves out crucial details we learned from the *Alcibiades*, for example, that Socrates followed him day and night for years during his childhood and adolescence (106e8–9) and that Socrates presented himself as a conventional pederastic lover. And to repeat the crucial fact, the *Symposium* speech makes not a single mention of the central refutation of the *Alcibiades* or any refutation like it.

On the whole, then, Alcibiades' account goes some way toward protecting Socrates by leaving the audience unaware that Socrates carefully selected Alcibiades as a pupil on the basis of his tremendous political hopes. No one could know on the basis of this speech what Alcibiades was led to believe about Socrates' unique ability to help him fulfill his grandest ambitions. If anything, Socrates is presented as reluctant. Alcibiades must convince him over time to join him for a dinner date, and even then he excuses himself and leaves promptly after dining. It is not likewise explained why or in what manner Socrates accepted the subsequent invitation (217c6–d6). Having recognized this odd feature of Alcibiades' testimony, we can finally turn to one of its most curious and striking details: the claim that Socrates would often wrestle naked with Alcibiades while no one else was present (217c2–3). Of course, the fact that these intimate encounters did nothing to further Alcibiades' designs strengthens the impression Alcibiades means to give of Socrates' total indifference to his looks (but cf. 213c3–5 and *Charmides* 155c5–e2). But in light of everything else Alcibiades will say about Socrates' moderation, the mention of these wrestling matches adds almost nothing; and besides, there is something strange about the picture of the short, paunchy, middle-aged Socrates wrestling with the tall and strapping Alcibiades in the bloom of youth (cf.

213d4–6). Given the looseness we have discovered in Alcibiades' narrative, we might wonder whether the wrestling bears some other, allegorical significance. Certainly, "stripping" is a Socratic metaphor for the exposure and examination of what lies beneath mere appearance, just as Socrates tells Alcibiades he must see the *demos* "stripped" (*Alcibiades* 132a5–6, cf. *Charmides* 154d1–e8).[43]

Immediately after suggesting that Alcibiades must see the *demos* stripped, Socrates tells him that he will have to train (*gumnasai*, 132b1) and from there goes on to describe the acquisition of self-knowledge by means of the soul's seeking its reflection in another soul just as an eye may find its reflection in the pupil of another eye. The wrestling matches and the "Delphic" quest for self-knowledge refer to the same activity. But whereas Alcibiades' speech for the most part makes Socrates appear less forward or aggressive than Plato shows him elsewhere to have been, in this one respect the *Symposium* account reveals the harshness of Socratic education in a way that Socrates himself decided not to (cf. 114e10–115a1). For as much as Alcibiades must have manhandled Socrates when they actually wrestled, Socrates' advantage in their dialectical sparring was much greater still. And yet the image of the *Alcibiades*, of two souls conversing and contemplating each other directly, is also to be remembered here. For Alcibiades stresses that both he and Socrates were naked; Alcibiades' opinions were exposed to Socrates' painful dialectical and elenctic maneuvers, but this also gave him the opportunity to reflect and to reflect upon the Socratic wisdom that lay behind and guided his relentless questioning. It is a feature of the eye-to-eye image we had not adequately considered before that it implies Socrates' exposure of himself.[44]

How much Alcibiades came to understand from this exposure can only be guessed at by considering the appeal he makes to Socrates just before his final humiliation. What is it that Alcibiades still so desperately wants, *after* having seen the "divine and golden" statues within Socrates, after conversing and wrestling with him alone? "You seem to me to have become my only worthy lover, and you appear to me to shrink from reminding me [of this]. I am disposed thus: I believe it to be very mindless not to gratify you in this and in anything else you might need from either my wealth or my friends" (218c7–d1). Socrates, that is, has succeeded completely where all of Alcibiades' other lovers had failed (*Alcibiades* 103a1–c6, 105e2–5, 131c5–e5). "For nothing is more important (*presbuteron*) to me than becoming as good as possible, and in this I suppose that there is no more authoritative accomplice for me than you. Indeed, I would be much more ashamed before the prudent if I did not gratify such a man [as you], than I would be ashamed before the many and imprudent if I did" (218d1–5). Alcibiades believes his seduction to have been successful when Socrates finally replies, "In the time to come, we will do upon deliberation what appears best to the two of us in these and other matters" (219a8–b4). Alcibiades appears to want Socrates as a friend, lover, teacher, and above all, adviser (cf. *Alcibiades* 119b1). Their conversations have persuaded him that it is shameful to gratify the many since they are imprudent—an opinion much in evidence in the *Second Alcibiades*. But since the pursuit of honor from the many has been up this point his raison d'être, he is in need of further guidance regarding what he ought to pursue instead (cf. *Cleitophon* 408b6–409c1).

By the time of the *Second Alcibiades*, it seems Alcibiades has become disappointed with the lack of guidance Socrates has given him. He has become confused and sullen in his attempt to provide that guidance for himself, especially because of the difficulty involved in determining what must be said and done about the gods. We seem compelled to conclude therefore that the *Second Alcibiades* is set after the bedroom scene described in the *Symposium* since that scene presents Alcibiades at the height of his early hopefulness for what Socrates could provide. By the time of the *Symposium*, Alcibiades has come to understand that Socrates has nothing more to offer as a replacement for the political life than a continuation of their habitual discussions (hence his comparison of Socrates to the sirens). This means Alcibiades became substantially more clear-sighted about Socrates' presentation of philosophy as the alternative to political life *after* the *Second Alcibiades*. As the conclusion of that dialogue suggests, Alcibiades would indeed go on to learn more from Socrates thereafter.

But that fact is not mentioned in the *Symposium*. Without the *Alcibiades* and *Second Alcibiades*, we would be left with the impression that the relationship between Socrates and Alcibiades reached its painfully awkward but decisive turning point when Socrates made clear once and for all that he was not a lover of Alcibiades in the ordinary sense. The very climax of this deceptive tale, however, is its most deceptive element. There is no doubt that Alcibiades, who derived much of his sense of worth from his youthful beauty (217a5–6, 219c5, *Alcibiades* 104a2–4), was stung by Socrates' indifference to his sexual advance and humiliated at having thus misunderstood Socrates' intention. But Socrates' abstinence, his refusal to accept Alcibiades' "bronze," is not the guarantee it appears to be that he gave nothing in return.[45]

Yet for all that this famous scene seems to conceal more than it reveals about Socrates' and Alcibiades' relationship, it may be as important a moment as any other in the *Symposium* for reflecting upon the fate of Alcibiades' political ambition. Alcibiades may never have made a closer approach to *philosophic* ambition than he did in this scene as he recounts it. It is clear that Alcibiades had by the time of his attempted seduction come to see the *demos* "stripped." He was no longer concerned to win their honor. Instead, he wanted to conduct himself in a way that Socrates would praise, for the honor of the wise is infinitely more valuable in truth than the honor of the foolish. This (anti)climax of Alcibiades' speech is also the moment at which Socrates achieves the victory over Alcibiades he predicted at the outset of the *Alcibiades*, that he would come to be honored by Alcibiades as Alcibiades wished to be honored by the Athenians. The powerful desire for honor, or *philotimia*, that characterizes Alcibiades' political ambition was the source of Socrates' greatest hope that he would be able to steer that ambition toward philosophy.

But it should also be clear that the promise of honor alone, or even the attainment of honor, can never quite be counted upon to hold political ambition in its place. When Socrates proved unwilling or unable to teach Alcibiades what he wanted to learn,[46] Alcibiades fell back into the orbit of the *demos*, seduced anew by the promise of honor won in the assembly. Now he has won as much of that honor as any statesman could hope to win, and yet he is still tortured by his awareness of the Socratic critique. Like pleasure, honor naturally makes a powerful, almost visceral claim to be among the greatest goods. Like pleasure, honor can be made to seem shallow by comparison to wisdom. And as with pleasure, the desire for honor is never simply conquered once and for all. Alcibiades' political ambition may have wavered, even dramatically, once he saw the Socratic critique of the *demos*, but it was not toppled.

## Is Soldier Socrates Still the Silenic Satyr?

Alcibiades now appears to turn from his praise of Socrates' moderation to a praise of his courage by telling stories of Socrates on campaign, and the portrayal of Socrates as uncanny and divine now takes center stage. This is the only Platonic portrayal of Socrates away from the city of Athens, and yet Socrates' behavior here is characterized by its total similarity to his ordinary manner. He marches barefoot and in his normal cloak despite the much colder winters (220a6–c1, cf. *Clouds* 363); he walks with his characteristic confidence even in the face of the greatest dangers (221b1–4, cf. *Clouds* 362); he stands transfixed in thought for hours on end, just as he often does in Athens (220c3–d5, cf. 175b6–c3). Indeed, Alcibiades begins to make it seem as though Socrates is completely unaffected by any physical circumstances: he is unbothered by long stretches spent without food and drink, and wine has no effect on him at all (219e8–a6).[47] His daylong meditation, which he seems finally to dedicate to the sun, even makes it seem as though Socrates lives only incidentally within a body for which he sometimes has no use at all: one almost imagines that during this period Socrates' soul has ascended to the heavens so as to contemplate the ideas.[48]

It is in relating the story of Socrates' eerily calm retreat at the battle of Delium that Alcibiades notes the accuracy of Aristophanes' depiction of Socrates in the *Clouds*. According to Alcibiades, Socrates' utterly confident demeanor struck fear into the pursuers, who preferred to run down and slay those who had taken flight in panic (221b1–c1). In the *Clouds*, it is the Clouds themselves—goddesses worshipped by the Socratics in lieu of the traditional gods (245–252)—who speak the line Alcibiades quotes to describe Socrates' confidence. The Clouds say they hearken to Socrates "because [he] swagger[s] in these streets and cast[s] his eyes about" (392). In short, these visible, emphatically natural, Socratic replacements for the gods reserve their highest praise for the outrageously impious, brazenly outspoken Socrates; the theme of the play, insofar as the theme is marked by its title, is Socrates' heterodoxy or impiety (*Apology of Socrates* 18b1–d2, 19b3–c6). In giving his assent to the Aristophanic depiction, Alcibiades potentially says much more than that Socrates walks with a swagger. For one thing, he says the swagger is unchanged even in the face of death. While the fear of death sends other Athenians into headlong flight, Socrates, apparently unfazed, strikes fear into the hearts of the terrorizers themselves, "it being clear to everyone and from very far away that if someone will lay a hand on this man (*andros*), he will defend himself very mightily" (221b5–6). Socrates' fearlessness seems even to grant him a kind of invulnerability; his apparent indifference to death causes one to wonder whether he could be killed at all. But Alcibiades compels us to suppose that this imperturbable fearlessness is somehow a result of Socrates' wisdom, as is the rest of his indifference to any matters concerning his body. This strange, uncanny, divine man has apparently seen and learned something from his examinations of the things aloft and under the earth that give him such tremendous power, but as always, Alcibiades neglects to mention just what that something is.

There is one matter in this section in which Socrates is portrayed as being less than totally detached. After he saves the wounded Alcibiades and his armor at Potidaea—an act of superlative courage and nobility (cf. *Alcibiades* 115a1–116b1)—he is not indifferent about the matter of the prize of honor that Alcibiades wishes for him to receive but emphatically insists that the prize be given to Alcibiades instead of himself (220d5). This may be the only time in Alcibiades' speech that Socrates appears to show any eagerness for anything: if he were truly indifferent to political honors, he need not even have actively accepted it; he could simply have acquiesced to its being conferred. Instead, Socrates is concerned that this conferral of public honor upon him not take place. For all of Socrates' apparent detachment, it seems here he has at least a modicum of concern for how he appears. And indeed, throughout Alcibiades' accounts of Socrates on campaign, he is always making a show of his endurance (220c8–d3, a1–5, b7–c1). It bears repeating that this is the section in which Alcibiades, in reference to Socrates' deeds, quotes Helen and Menelaus in their accounts of Odysseus's great and deceitful plots, which they helped him conceal. Plato's Alcibiades is responsible in this same section for lending to Socrates a divine aura that would inspire the awe and wonder of readers for centuries.

Alcibiades has presented Socrates more or less as a god. The remarks he turns to following his account of the campaigns are therefore quite surprising. He seems to build toward the climax of his speech thus: "So someone could praise Socrates for many other wondrous things; but while one could easily say such things of some other pursuits and concerning someone else as well, that Socrates is similar to no one among human beings, neither among the ancients nor among those who live now, *this* is altogether worthy of wonder. For someone could liken Brasidas and others to such as Achilles was, and in turn Nestor and Antenor to such as Pericles" (221c2–8). This is indeed high praise for both Pericles and Brasidas, though we might note the faintest hint of a dubious spartaphilia in the fact that the higher praise goes to the Spartan. In any case, we now expect Socrates to receive the highest praise; but what higher praise could possibly be given at this point? Alcibiades is comparing contemporary figures to Homeric heroes, but he has already said that Socrates is incomparable to *any* human being. It seems we must expect that Alcibiades will finally say what he has all but said already, that Socrates is more akin to a god than to a mortal. But instead, Alcibiades suddenly reminds us of the image he has already made of Socrates: "The likes of this human being, with respect to his strangeness," says Alcibiades, could only be likened "to the silenuses and the satyrs, both [Socrates] himself and his speeches" (221d1–6).

This is a jarring reminder because Alcibiades had by now left far behind the suggestion that Socrates' divine beauty was deep and hidden. In the seduction story, Socrates' comical lust and ignorance proved to be merely the disguise for his unconquerable, even hubristic, moderation. But in the campaign stories, the wondrous magnificence of Socrates' strangeness has been plain for all to see: he has surpassed all of his fellow soldiers in endurance and courage, and on the battlefield his uncanny strength was not only perceivable without having "opened up" his silenic guise but was even visible to enemy soldiers who stood "very far away." Now, all of a sudden, we are reminded that Socrates is not what he seems: he cloaks his true nature. Yet the cloak of Socrates the soldier was apparently one of divine self-sufficiency. What lay beneath *that* disguise? Was it perhaps the hubristic satyr, of whom Alcibiades also reminds us here? For Socrates seems to be no satyr on the battlefield. Suddenly Socrates begins to seem less like a wooden silenus and more like a Russian nesting doll!

But just as we are reminded that Socrates is not all divine contemplation but is also hubristic like a satyr, and in particular like the satyr Marsyas (whom Alcibiades does not mention again); that he is therefore in some kind of competition with Apollo; and that he has indeed come hubristically to replace the gods in the mind of Alcibiades who just now only barely stopped short of comparing Socrates to Zeus or Apollo—just as we are reminded of all this, Alcibiades shifts the target of the silenus metaphor so that it applies as well to Socrates' speeches as to Socrates himself. This, says Alcibiades, he had left out at the beginning, but now he points out that Socrates' speeches seem laughable to the "inexperienced and thoughtless" for the way they always refer to "asses, pack-asses, smiths, shoemakers, and tanners." But like the silenuses, Socrates' speeches can be opened up, and within them, one finds "first, that they alone among speeches have mind within them; and second, that they are most divine and have the greatest statues of virtue in them, and they stretch over the greatest expanse, or rather over everything which it is fitting to examine for one who intends to be beautiful and good (*kalōi kagathōi*)" (222a1–6). Recall that Alcibiades' first account of Socrates' speeches indicated that they were more beautiful by far than Pericles' orations and that they brought him to tears. Now Alcibiades suggests that they appear at first to be paltry and comical "like some hide of a hubristic satyr" and must be opened up and entered. *Hubris* and divine virtue: which is the surface and which is the secret core?

Some questions might remain about what is implied by this final account of the Socratic speeches. Socrates had statues of gods within him; the speeches contain the greatest statues of virtue. When Alcibiades saw the images inside Socrates, he believed he had struck upon a "lucky find" or "gift of Hermes" (217a2). We know what happened to the statues of *this* god.[49] And what of the statues of virtue to be found within Socrates' speeches? What did Alcibiades come to think of them? He gives us to understand that he "examined" them, as one who intended to be beautiful and good. This closing remark is the only suggestion in Alcibiades' speech that his association with Socrates involved an examination of virtue or indeed of the noble and good. But anyone familiar with the *Alcibiades* knows this was indeed the substance of their first conversation, and Alcibiades has told us that Socrates "often" put his soul into distress with his speeches (215e7). It is to that dialogue, then, that we are directed by Alcibiades' studied silence on the substance of anything he may have learned from Socrates. We are otherwise limited to these speculations on the basis of his closing remarks concerning Socrates' speeches, which actually offer the most pious and virtuous portrayal of Socrates yet. Alcibiades effectively ends on a high note.

The speech has an important coda. Alcibiades' warning that Socrates will do to Agathon what he did to Alcibiades, Charmides, and Euthydemus provokes laughter from the banqueters, who infer that Alcibiades is still jealously in love with Socrates (222a7–c3). Socrates then pays Alcibiades the compliment discussed above: on the basis of the laughter engendered by Alcibiades' transparently erotic motives, Socrates refers to Alcibidaes' speech as a "satyr and silenus play," a very unusual phrase (222d3–4). Socrates appears to be crediting Alcibiades with having composed a speech with layers. It will likely be objected, however, that Alcibiades is much more simple-minded and simply drunk than I have suggested, and that if his speech reflects or intimates some deep truths about Socratic philosophy, it is only thanks to Plato, who has Alcibiades say more than Alcibiades understands.[50] But there is a question yet worth asking: how much of Socratic philosophy *did* Alcibiades understand? It is helpful to recall how much more Xenophon is willing to show a young Alcibiades who has very quickly picked up some key Socratic lessons. In Xenophon's brief vignette, Alcibiades handily refutes Pericles concerning the weighty Socratic question "What is law?" (*Memorabilia* 1.2.40–46, cf. 14–16). Moreover, consider how much the relatively dull Euthydemus, cited by Alcibiades as another of Socrates' victims, picks up in Book Four of the *Memorabilia*. And this is to say nothing of Charmides. Students in the Socratic circle learned to critique virtue and the law; Alcibiades learned this too, but he never says so in his speech. He praises Socrates for his wisdom, moderation, and courage but never once says that Socrates is just or pious. Alcibiades, in trying Socrates on the charge of *hubris*, must be aware that he has refrained from attributing justice or piety to him.

If Alcibiades was able to make a silenus of his speech, he owes much of this ability to Socrates. A theme of Aristophanes' *Clouds* not yet mentioned is that the Socrates there is famous for turning his students—including Pheidippides, who bears some resemblance to Alcibiades—into powerful rhetoricians.[51] Alcibiades is, after all, the orator who convinced the Athenians to set sail on the Sicilian Expedition and is, as has already been noted, at the height of his rhetorical powers at the time of the *Symposium*. The dialogue famously ends with Socrates speaking to the only two people still awake at the end of the night, Agathon and Aristophanes, and "compelling them to agree that it belongs to the same man to know how to make comedy and tragedy, and that one who is a tragedian by art is also a comedian" (223d3–6). Socrates' speeches provoked both laughter in the "inexperienced and thoughtless" and tears in those who were shown to be in need of the gods. Socrates and his speeches seem to blend comedy and tragedy. Alcibiades displays a similar ability. He succeeds at making his speech, which shares no less of a tragic theme than *hubris*, the object of laughter.

But for however much Alcibiades may have learned from Socrates, it is important to emphasize that Socrates really did wound his pride. Socrates' rejection of Alcibiades' advances must have been difficult to take. Still more important is the way Socrates made Alcibiades' other beloved, the Athenian *demos*, appear to be ugly in comparison to Socrates himself (*Alcibiades* 131e10–132b5). At the core of Socrates' failure to turn Alcibiades fully toward philosophy is the fact that Alcibiades could not ultimately tear himself away from the city and political life, even though he had become convinced of philosophy's superiority and the worthlessness of the opinion of the many (216b3–5, 218d3–5). It is this tortured existence against which Alcibiades tries to warn Agathon. Socratic wisdom was insufficient to loosen the hold of the Athenians on the Athenian Alcibiades' soul, and so in this respect, we can perhaps say that Aristophanes won the contest with Socrates. The question remains as to whether Alcibiades' failure to free himself completely was the result of a failure to understand the depths of Socrates' wisdom.

# CONCLUSION

Plato's portrayal of the relationship between Socrates and Alcibiades fails to provide unequivocal answers to many of the more pressing questions it raises. Alcibiades' speech in the *Symposium* is a testament to the influence Socrates exerted on the aspiring statesman, but it is surprisingly difficult to give a full or satisfactory description of that influence on the basis of Plato's presentation throughout the dialogues. Plato sends mixed messages about the character of the education Alcibiades received, and since he makes no explicit reference to the details of Alcibiades' infamous political career, we are left to speculate as to whether and how his exposure to Socratic education may have been responsible for his notorious decisions and deeds. If we juxtapose the shocking introductory speeches in the *Alcibiades*—wherein Alcibiades is led to believe that Socrates can help him achieve universal tyranny—and the parallel passage in the *Second Alcibiades*—wherein Alcibiades openly affirms that possession of such tyranny must be counted among the greatest goods—we are left with the strong impression that Socrates somehow turned Alcibiades into an aspiring tyrant. But the concluding sections of both dialogues convey a very different message. Socrates ends each conversation with powerful exhortations to justice and piety, harshly condemning tyranny in the first case and deterring Alcibiades from his questionable prayer in the second.

Further consideration of the available evidence suggests that the theme of tyranny is something of a red herring in Plato's treatment of the corruption of Alcibiades. The histories of Thucydides and Xenophon do not portray an Alcibiades who tried to supplant the Athenian democracy by becoming a tyrant. It is true that Thucydides reports the Athenians' suspicion that Alcibiades had tyrannical designs, but Thucydides himself never endorses that suspicion (vi.15.4). It is also true that Alcibiades was responsible for, if not directly involved in, a failed oligarchic coup at Athens. But Thucydides tells us that these machinations were for Alcibiades only a means of being recalled and indicates that Alcibiades might just as well have supported democracy if doing so would have suited his purposes (viii.47–48, viii.63.4). In fact, when the Athenian soldiers at Samos clamor for Alcibiades to lead them in an attack on the Piraeus—effectively handing him an opportunity to seize Athens for himself—he resolutely refuses to take such action as would ruin the city, a decision that earns him high praise from Thucydides (viii.86). The regime that takes shape in the aftermath of this decision and that finally recalls Alcibiades after years of exile is the one Thucydides singles out as the best to rule Athens in his lifetime (viii.97.2). From all this we can say that while Alcibiades was certainly not devoted to democracy and even came to deplore its follies (vi.89.6), the evidence of his seeking tyranny is vanishingly thin.[1] Hence, regarding the charge that Socrates made Alcibiades aspire to tyranny, the exonerating evidence in Plato's presentation outweighs the incriminating evidence once one recognizes that the historical facts accord better with the former than the latter. If Plato's readers become convinced that the question of corruption comes down to the question of tyranny, they may well be left with the impression that Alcibiades' tyrannical streak—even if it was first exacerbated by Socrates' rhetoric—would have been worse had it not been for Socrates' mitigating efforts as portrayed at the end of each *Alcibiades* dialogue.

The same readers, however, may therefore neglect to ask whether Alcibiades' corruption might have consisted in something other than the endorsement of tyranny. Having been assured that there is no fire behind the smoke, they will not think to ask whether Plato has made use of a smoke screen. What about the possibility, hinted at throughout the *Symposium*, that Socrates corrupted Alcibiades' religious belief? Education to impiety was a crucial part of the corruption charge on which Socrates was convicted. And what of the challenging questions surrounding the relationship of the noble to the good that are raised in the *Alcibiades*' central refutation? Does Alcibiades ever take these questions any further? The retrospective he offers in the *Symposium* simply does not answer these questions. Plato appears to leave insolubly unclear the matter of how far Alcibiades' thinking ultimately progressed on these core Socratic questions.

But even if this crucial matter must remain unresolved, we can still provide some answers to the questions that brought us to the study of Alcibiades in the first place. How should we characterize Plato's portrait of powerful political ambition, and what lessons ought we to learn from it? What does this portrait teach us about the role of the love of the noble in political ambition and about the broader but related matter of whether political life always or necessarily contains the seeds of political ambition? And what conclusions can we draw regarding Socrates' intention in his attempt to educate Alcibiades and thus regarding the character and meaning of Socratic corruption?

## What Is Political Ambition?

The phenomenon of political ambition, by its psychological complexity, defies a simplistic or formulaic definition. But the difficulties in clarifying the Platonic understanding of political ambition are exacerbated by the fact that there is no explicit thematic treatment of *philotimia* or any other word that might be translated as *ambition* in the discussions between Socrates and Alcibiades. In order to piece together Plato's account, we must review the drives and desires characteristic of the Platonic Alcibiades that appear to fuel his political ambition. I will here consider individually and in relation to one another Alcibiades' desires for renown, power, honor, being a benefactor, and the greatest goods.

### *Desire for Renown*

Both of Socrates' characterizations of Alcibiades' ambition—in the opening speeches of their first conversation and in the discussion of his intended prayer in the sequel—emphasize the allure of fame. In the first, Socrates says that Alcibiades would choose not to live "if [he] could not fill all human beings, so to speak, with [his] name and [his] power" (105b7–c4). In the second, the best version of the god's offer is that "immediately, *everyone will perceive* that Alcibiades, son of Kleinias, is tyrant" (141b3–5; emphasis added). Each of these characterizations appears at the apex of Socrates' series of escalating descriptions of divine offers, all but the last of which (in each case) he suggests would fail to satisfy Alcibiades' political ambition. It is only in the final and most complete sketches of Alcibiades' fulfillment that Socrates introduces the universal recognition of Alcibiades' status as a component. But Socrates' most straightforward statement of the magnitude and importance of Alcibiades' desire for renown comes when he says of Alcibiades' "becoming famous [lit. becoming a name] among Greeks and barbarians" that the youth seems "to desire (*eran*) this as no one else desires anything else" (124b3–6). Perhaps this is an exaggeration, but it nonetheless singles out the fervent desire for fame as the defining characteristic of Alcibiades' political ambition.

Indeed, "desire" is not a strong enough translation to capture the Greek *eran*. Alcibiades is said to *love* renown, to long for it with the passionate yearning of *eros*. It is one of the few mentions of *eros* in the *Alcibiades* dialogues, their relative silence concerning this important theme standing in sharp contrast with the dialogue that Plato chose as the dramatic setting for Alcibiades' final appearance. It is elsewhere in the *Symposium* that Plato's Socrates provides some explanation of the erotic desire for fame—or rather, Socrates relates Diotima's explanation: "If you wished to look into ambition (*philotimia*) among human beings, you would be amazed at their irrationality concerning the things about which I have been speaking—unless you were to keep in mind and think about how terribly they are affected by desire (*erōti*) to become a name 'and set up for themselves glory for all time.' . . . I suppose that it is on account of deathless virtue and such glorious fame that all do all things, and inasmuch as they are better, so much the more do they do so. For they desire (*erōsin*) deathlessness" (208c2–6, d7–e1). Thus Plato invites us to explore the suggestion that the desire to escape or transcend the problem of human mortality is a fundamental if partly subterranean drive underlying the desire for glory or renown. The examples of past heroes, remembered in poetry and enshrined in marble and bronze, are constant reminders that one's life can be extended beyond that of one's body in the awe and memory of posterity. Taken literally, the idiom, "to desire to become a name," used both by Socrates in reference to Alcibiades and by Diotima here, suggests a hope for a transformation into something that can live on indefinitely in the minds of others.

But Diotima also stresses that the prospect of immortal glory is that for the sake of which the ambitious, "even more than for the sake of their children, are all prepared to risk dangers, to spend money, to undertake any toils, and to die" (208c6–d2). This is difficult to square with the *Second Alcibiades*, in which Alcibiades makes it clear that he would not give up his life or soul (*psychē*) for the sake of the universal acknowledgment of his tyrannical supremacy, for this would deprive him of the use of the great good he would ostensibly be obtaining. Moreover, Socrates' speech there about the dangers and toils of tyranny, generalship, and even child rearing appear to echo Alcibiades' own concerns—concerns that have evidently arisen in the time that has elapsed since the *Alcibiades*. But Diotima's suggestion is that the willingness to take risks and to die is crucial evidence that glory is sought for the sake of deathlessness.

The change in Alcibiades' outlook from the first conversation to the second—brought about, as I have argued, by Socrates' critique of courage as noble devotion—puts a question to Diotima's account of the love of renown. Must it always be tied to a desire for immortality? Socrates' image of universal tyranny in the *Alcibiades* refers to "all human beings," leaving open the possibility that future generations are to be included. But in the sequel, there is emphasis on the present: "Immediately" they will "perceive" that Alcibiades is tyrant, a formulation that does not so clearly encompass posterity. Alcibiades' desire to be known appears to have been detached somewhat from his desire to be forever remembered. The importance of being "perceived" to be tyrant, therefore, appears not to be the same as his earlier erotic desire to "become a name" among Greeks and barbarians. But in that case, what is the desire to be perceived really about? This question will have to be kept in mind as we continue our review of Alcibiades' political ambition. But if Diotima's account is called into question by Alcibiades' turn in the *Second Alcibiades*, her emphasis on virtue nonetheless remains relevant. Diotima specifies "deathless virtue" as the link to immortality sought by the ambitious lovers of renown, later citing the examples of Lycurgus and Solon (209d3–e3). As we have seen, Alcibiades remains consistently committed to obtaining his renown for *virtuous* leadership, even if that should require pursuing the paradoxical end of virtuous tyranny.

## *Love of Power*

Socrates' first mention of Alcibiades' desire for renown describes his need "to fill all human beings with [his] name *and [his] power*" (emphasis added). The word for "power" (*dunamis*) and its cognates appear eleven times in Socrates' opening speeches of the *Alcibiades*, and there are some reasons to think that the love of power is a feature of Alcibiades' ambition that is separate and separable from his desire for renown. One might argue that Alcibiades' devotion to Socrates ebbs and flows not according to how much fame he believes he can achieve with Socrates' help but how much power he can win over his competitors. It is the claim that Alcibiades cannot obtain "the power [he] desires" without Socrates that initially piques Alcibiades' interest (105e4–5), and it is Alcibiades' renewed confidence that he will achieve superiority over his fellow citizens in the assembly that causes him to turn away from Socrates' proposed education (see *periesomai*, 119b5–c1). Only Socrates' reminder of the power of the foreign kings restores Alcibiades' concern to improve himself. Socrates' persistent appeal to Alcibiades' need to obtain political power is an indication that Socrates himself believes the desire for power to be the strongest, or at least the most manipulable, component of the youth's political ambition.

Some indication of what makes power attractive to Alcibiades is provided in those same opening speeches of the *Alcibiades*. Socrates describes, for example, Alcibiades' belief in the "power that belongs to [him] on account of Pericles . . . who has the power (*dunatai*) to do what he wants not only in the city, but in all of Greece and among the many and great races of barbarians" (104b4–8); and he later speaks of Alcibiades' hope that once he has proved his great worth to the Athenians, "there will be nothing [he does] not have the power (*dunēsesthai*) to do" (104e1–2). Socrates thus describes tyranny without using the name: a kind of perfect freedom, a lack of impediments to the execution of one's will obtained by establishing one's superiority over others, imagined here as belonging to Pericles and being within the grasp of Alcibiades. It is therefore all the more important that when Socrates finally does mention tyranny by name, it is to suggest that the pursuit of it is slavish and that only virtue befits the truly free (135b3–c11).

An objection must be considered here: is it not likely that power for Alcibiades is only a means to his true goal of universal renown, as opposed to an end in itself? After all, it is not clear from his temporary satisfaction with his natural advantages in the assembly whether his goal is simply to prove his superiority or to be known for having done so, and even the "royal tale" that reclaims his dedication to Socratic education concludes, as we have seen, by suggesting that Alcibiades' greatest passion is directed toward "becoming a name among Greeks and barbarians" (124b5–6). One might therefore argue that Socrates is ultimately manipulating Alcibiades' desire for renown and that any desire for power is only intermediate. Moreover, the suggestion that ambition seeks power as a means to reputation may be corroborated by Xenophon's characterization of Alcibiades' and Critias's ambition in the *Memorabilia*: "The pair of them came to be by nature the most ambitious (*philotimotatō*) of all the Athenians, wishing all things to be done through them and that they become the greatest names (*onomastotatō*). They knew that Socrates was living most self-sufficiently on the least money, being the most continent with respect to all pleasures, and making use in speeches of all those who conversed with him however he wished" (i.2.14).[2] We may interpret this passage as suggesting that Alcibiades wished to learn Socrates' power of disposing of other human beings through speeches as a means to the fame that was the true object of his political ambition. This same power is a major theme in Alcibiades' retrospective account in the *Symposium*. Having said of Marsyas that "he bewitched human beings through instruments by the power (*dunamei*) of his mouth," Alcibiades tells Socrates, "you differ from him only this much: that you do the same thing without instruments, by means of bare speeches" (215c1–2, c6–d1). Plato's Alcibiades thus corroborates Xenophon's suggestion that Alcibiades came to be deeply impressed by what Socrates was able to do to others through speech. And indeed, the *Alcibiades* reveals again and again that the most obvious way in which Socrates could actually help Alcibiades become a more successful politician is by remedying his lack of appreciation and aptitude for political rhetoric.

That Alcibiades desires power as a good in its own right, and not only as a means to renown (or other political goods), is clarified by considering how much the relationship between him and Socrates was itself a struggle for power. Socrates says in the *Alcibiades* that he hopes to come to have the greatest power (*dunhsesthai*) over Alcibiades by proving his worth to him, just as Alcibiades hopes to gain the greatest power in the city by proving his worth before the assembly (105d7–e5). In the *Symposium*, we learn that Socrates succeeded. Alcibiades came to consider Socrates his only worthy lover (218c7–8) and offered to reward him for this as he presumed his other suitors had wished to be rewarded (cf. *Alcibiades* 103b4 ff). But just as Alcibiades' power over his lovers was made manifest by their inability to offer him anything he could not provide for himself, Socrates' power over Alcibiades was maintained through the latter's continually unsatisfied erotic desire for Socratic wisdom. According to Alcibiades' account, it was the fact that Socrates always maintained this power over him that drove him mad. Although Socrates drew Alcibiades in by provoking the concern that his greatest political rivals would be unconquerable without a Socratic education, it was Socrates himself who proved the most unconquerable, the one man Alcibiades could never succeed in overpowering. This struggle is likely the true meaning of the wrestling matches to which Alcibiades refers (*Symposium* 217b7–c3). And although we have seen that Alcibiades is all too reticent regarding just what it was that made him feel such a desperate need to obtain Socrates' wisdom, he vividly describes the shame he felt at his inability to conquer Socrates.

Thus we see that Socrates did draw Alcibiades in by playing on his desire for power, and we are helpfully reminded that he did succeed in blunting Alcibiades' desire for renown. What is unexpected and bizarre is that the Socratic success in channeling Alcibiades' desire for power toward philosophy took the form of making Alcibiades feel he needed to conquer Socrates as a lover. But it is at any rate fair to say that the desire for power, the need to feel oneself superior to all others so that nothing one desires can be held out of reach on account of someone else's superior strength, forms an independent part of Alcibiades' ambition, which Socrates frustrates and thereby manipulates to tremendous effect. Unlike the desire for renown, however, the desire for power has proven separable from Alcibiades' political ambition since Socrates was able to harness it to Alcibiades' short-lived philosophic ambition. It is interesting to note that every appearance of a cognate of *dunamis* that refers to Alcibiades in the *Second Alcibiades* expresses some doubt about his ability to pursue Socrates' education successfully (140a3, 145a5, 150e4).

## *Love of Honor*

We still have yet to resolve the difficulty we encountered in considering Alcibiades' love of renown. Diotima's account of the love of renown encounters a stumbling block in the *Second Alcibiades*, where it seems that Alcibiades' desire to be known no longer refers so clearly to a desire to be posthumously (and eternally) remembered. If Alcibiades is at this point no longer motivated by a desire for renown as Diotima describes it, we must consider whether he is driven especially by *philotimia* in the literal sense, that is, the love of honor. In describing what made him unable to continue pursuing a Socratic education in the *Symposium*, Alcibiades does not cite fame as such, nor does he make any mention of immortality. Rather, he says that he was unable to resist the honor of the many (216b4–5).

In the opening of the *Alcibiades*, Socrates says that Alcibiades believes he will "prove to the Athenians that [he is] worthy of being honored as neither Pericles nor anyone else who has ever come to be" (105b2–3). The honor desired by Alcibiades is, here and elsewhere, described in somewhat different terms than the universal power and fame Socrates identifies as Alcibiades' ultimate goal in the same passage. Whereas the desire to "fill all human beings with your name and your power" clearly transcends the particular place and time inhabited by his contemporaries in Athens, Alcibiades' love of honor is always connected to the *demos*, to an experience that Alcibiades can and will taste for himself and by which he will come to be enthralled. Since the desire for honor can be more immediately satisfied, it is not susceptible to the same Socratic critiques that undermine Alcibiades' "Diotiman" love of fame.

Perhaps the desire to be perceived as a tyrant described in the *Second Alcibiades* is more about honor than it is about renown.

Unlike the desires for fame and power, each of which is in its own way affected by Socratic education, Alcibiades' love of honor appears to remain largely unchanged and even to play a decisive role in weakening Alcibiades' devotion to Socrates as a teacher. This is not to say that Socrates did not attempt to have an effect on Alcibiades' love of honor. Indeed, for a time it even appeared that he was succeeding. In the bedroom scene recounted in the *Symposium*, Alcibiades tells Socrates that he would "feel much more ashamed before prudent men for not gratifying such a man [as Socrates] than [he would] before the many and imprudent for gratifying him" (218d3–5). This lack of concern for what the many think appears to be the high-water mark of the Platonic Alcibiades' attempt to make himself "as beautiful as possible" by looking upon the Athenian people "stripped" so as to avoid being "corrupted by becoming a lover of the *demos* (*dēmerastēs*)."[3] The strides he takes in this direction are the result of Socrates' subversive critique of the *demos*, which begins with his suggestion that the many are poor teachers of justice in the *Alcibiades* and which has clearly taken hold by the time of the *Second Alcibiades*. As we have seen, however, Alcibiades ultimately relapses into his addiction to the applause of the many, represented by the fillets he wears on his head when he stumbles into the *Symposium*. Even after having been persuaded that the *demos* is imprudent, Alcibiades cannot resist vying for its honor.

It is Athens that wins the battle for Alcibiades' devotion, realizing the fear Socrates expresses at the end of each of the two *Alcibiades* dialogues. This competition between Socrates and the city reveals the complex interplay of love and honor that contributed some of the intensity to the struggle for power between Socrates and Alcibiades discussed above. To begin with, Alcibiades is a lover of the *demos*, and Socrates suggests he will win Alcibiades over just as Alcibiades wishes to win over the Athenians. But Socrates also suggests that these roles will be reversed (*Alcibiades* 135d7–e3, *Second Alcibiades* 151c1–2), and Alcibiades himself later confirms it was indeed he that became the lover of Socrates (*Symposium* 222a7–b4). The pattern appears to be as follows. The lover pleads his worthiness to his beloved and, if successful, is repaid with honor. But if the lover refuses the honor, as Socrates does to Alcibiades and Alcibiades does for a time to the Athenians, then pursued becomes pursuer and the roles are reversed. Socrates' refusal to be overcome by Alcibiades provokes the latter's sense of powerlessness as described above. But

Alcibiades allows himself to be overcome by the Athenians, accepting their love and their honor. The love of honor is not unlike a love of being loved. And there is a sweetness and reassurance in being loved—also a certain power—that Alcibiades finally finds preferable to the cold, clear, and lonely life of Socratic philosophy.

To reiterate, however, the fact that there is power in being honored does not mean the related loves of honor and power are the same. Crucially, Alcibiades' desire to be honored and loved by the Athenians imposed a certain constraint on the means he would be willing to use to win power and renown.[4] It is no coincidence that Alcibiades' closest approach to tyranny, in the *Second Alcibiades*, aligns with the nadir of his sense of reverence for the Athenian *demos*. For as long as honor from the Athenians is seen as the most desirable end, the means to that end must be honorable; the more bare power is conceived as the goal, the weaker is that crucial constraint.

### *Desire to Be a Benefactor*

Even during this darkest period, however, Alcibiades maintains an abiding goodwill toward the Athenians. Perhaps, then, his desire to win honor in the assembly persists in some degree despite his newfound disdain for the *demos*. But it may be more precise to say that what remains strong in Alcibiades is the desire to benefit his fellow citizens. Indeed, this desire may in turn be an important motivator of the desire for honor since honor can partly be understood as gratitude for, and therefore confirmation of, benefit conferred.[5] That the desire to do good for Athens is a powerful and independent factor in Alcibiades' political ambition, however, is clearest from the final refutation of the *Alcibiades*, in which Alcibiades describes his vision for an Athens where hatred and factional strife have been replaced by a kind of fellow feeling akin to familial love. Alcibiades dreams of delivering a perfect and complete good to the Athenian people, at least in part as an end in itself rather than instrumentally for his own sake.

We learn most about this desire by considering the preceding refutation in the same dialogue, in which Socrates examines Alcibiades' attachment to courage. Alcibiades' desire to help his friends is put to the test, the good of providing that help being weighed against the harm of suffering death and wounds. The desire to help his friends is revealed in this passage as a powerful love of the noble, which is then examined. It is the nobility of courage, according to Alcibiades, that makes it a good on a par with life itself, and one without which it is not worth being alive (115b1–d7). This assessment of courage given by Alcibiades allows Socrates to refute his previous claim that the just and the advantageous are sometimes incompatible (113d1–8). The desire to be a benefactor, when examined as a love of the noble, thus proved to be at least as influential in shaping Alcibiades' political ambition as any hardheaded imperial realism or selfish lust for power and fame. It was only by considering the flaw in Socrates' refutation that we were able to uncover the problem in Alcibiades' opinion of the noble. By treating courage as if its nobility could simply be divorced from death and wounds, Socrates badly distorts the very idea of the noble. To the extent that the noble may require death and wounds for oneself, Alcibiades' initial assessment of its relationship to the advantageous could have received a fuller defense than he was able to provide in the face of Socrates' sophistry.

I have suggested that in the time following his first conversation with Socrates, Alcibiades had some opportunity to reflect on the inadequacy of the Socratic claim that the just or noble is always advantageous, and Alcibiades' attachment to nobility has been partially weakened by the time of the *Second Alcibiades*. But Alcibiades' pious outburst in that dialogue reveals the shallowness of his newly professed cynicism (143d2). Socrates' mention of matricide triggers a kind of pious fear in Alcibiades that suggests the gods may punish the mere thought of transgressing certain laws for the sake of personal gain. Despite the fact that Alcibiades appears to have been paralyzed by the Socratic critique of noble sacrifice, he continues to believe there are some essential constraints on what may be done in the pursuit of his own good. Throughout his relationship with Socrates, and even at his closest approach to tyranny, Alcibiades appears to maintain the belief that benefiting those he holds dear—or at least doing them no harm—is a crucial component of the good he is striving to obtain.[6] Alcibiades' attachment to the noble, his belief that one must sometimes restrict one's own pursuit of the good on the basis of a consideration of the good of others, proves to be an extremely resilient feature of his political ambition.

## *Desire for the Greatest Goods*

Alcibiades' desire to obtain the greatest goods for himself is not so much a separate feature of his political ambition as a way to understand the whole of it. Every good we have considered thus far—fame, power, honor, and the noble—is surely in Alcibiades' mind a candidate for the *summum bonum*. The disposition to view this tangled set of ends as representing or containing the highest end of human striving, combined with a confidence in one's ability to obtain them, *is* political ambition. Socrates' opening strategy in the *Alcibiades* is predicated on the hope that a critical examination of these ends will reveal them all to be lacking or flawed and that thereafter Alcibiades' extraordinary and restless longing to achieve the greatest good for himself will be required to seek its proper object through Socratic inquiry. That this hope is disappointed is evident not just from Alcibiades' rejection of the Socratic education midway through the *Alcibiades* but also from Alcibiades' unflinching assertion in the sequel that he, indeed that anyone, would count universal tyranny to be among the greatest goods (141b7–8).

It is difficult to say how close Alcibiades came to desiring a thorough and challenging examination of the goodness of political life. In the bedroom scene recounted in the *Symposium*, Alcibiades claims to think it most venerable that he should come to be as good as possible (*hōs beltiston*, 218d1–2), and he appears willing to turn away from politics and toward Socrates in order to do so. Furthermore, it is in the *Symposium* that Alcibiades finally acknowledges his awareness that philosophy is the characteristic Socratic activity and that a life with Socrates is a life away from politics (218a2–7, 216a6–8). Both *Alcibiades* dialogues conclude with an Alcibiades made more eager to join Socrates in the examination of some important question, and yet in both cases, Alcibiades continues to assume that the end for the sake of which that examination must be undertaken is his own political success. It may well be that nothing in Alcibiades is more resistant to change under the pressure of Socratic education than the simple belief that political rule is, or is a means to, the greatest good. Socrates is unable to turn Alcibiades' extraordinary political ambition into a lasting philosophic ambition.

## Political Ambition and Political Life

One of our motivating questions concerned the role of political ambition in political life more broadly.[7] Is it possible for a regime to suppress political ambition or to redirect it toward nonpolitical ends? Or are there some features of political ambition, such as the love of the noble, that are both ineradicably human and inherently political? To the extent that we thought this question might be illuminated by our study of Alcibiades, it was to be by way of considering the malleability of his ambition. Having laid out the major components of that ambition, let us now consider more synoptically how that ambition changed over time as a result of Socrates' influence.

The most noticeable change to Alcibiades' political ambition concerns his view of the Athenian *demos* arising from confrontation with his own previous confusion. In his first conversation with Socrates, we learn that Alcibiades seeks honor from the many as acknowledgment of the singularly beneficial advice he intends to give them—or at least, he agrees to this interpretation of his ambition once it has been suggested by Socrates (106c4–d1). Alcibiades' belief that he is worthy of more honor than anyone else (105a7–b3) therefore implies, whether or not it had occurred to him previously, that no one but him would be able to give this same advice. But this means he understands the *demos* to be at once unable to identify its own best course of action and yet able unfailingly to recognize and honor the adviser who points it out to them.[8]

It seems that Alcibiades is forced to resolve this dilemma in one of two ways. He may determine that the Athenians are after all able to confer honor correctly on whoever can give the best advice. In that case, however, Alcibiades must admit that he is not quite so worthy of honor as he had believed since it is unclear that the *demos* would need him to suggest advice it can itself recognize as best. Alternatively, he may conclude that the Athenians are truly ignorant of what the city ought to do and thus truly in need of him—in which case, however, they cannot be counted upon to recognize his great worthiness and to honor him accordingly. A deceptive or flattering orator might easily lead the people astray, and Alcibiades' own, worthy counsel could be mistaken for dangerous or harmful advice. The *Second Alcibiades* leaves no doubt that Alcibiades finds his way to the latter conclusion, allowing him to maintain his high estimation of his own worth at the cost of his confidence that the *demos* will recognize it, and we have seen that the *Symposium* directs us toward the suggestion that he came at some point to see honor won from the imprudent many as worthless.

What most calls for careful reflection, however, is the fact that Alcibiades eventually returns to his desire for honor from the many. Especially if the goodness of honor is seen in its being an affirmation of one's own worth, we might expect that the whole appeal of honor would evaporate once it had been shown that those who are affirming one's worth are ill suited to evaluate it. But as we have seen, Alcibiades was left without a viable alternative to replace the Athenians' honor as the object of his desire. Socrates' great though temporary success was to make Alcibiades consider honor and love from Socrates himself to be the only good worth striving for on account of his great prudence or wisdom. But Socrates refused to grant this honor and love to Alcibiades as cheaply as the many, that is, on the basis of his beauty, charm, family, and other natural gifts. We noted that Socrates' own counsel to Alcibiades in the *Symposium* calls into question whether he thought that he had anything to offer Alcibiades to replace the goods the youth had been seeking in political life (219a1–2). According to Socrates' own speech in the *Symposium*, what should replace fame, power, and honor from the *demos* as the object of Alcibiades' longing is the eternal Beautiful or Noble itself, grasped through philosophy (210c6–211b5). But everything about Alcibiades' appearance in the *Symposium*—his merrily drunken emergence in the likeness of Dionysus, his embrace of Agathon, and his jealous vying with Socrates for the tragedian's affection—reminds us that his *eros* continues to be directed toward the common, finite, and familiar objects that Diotima insists are pursued in vain.

It is tempting to suggest that the persistence of Alcibiades' attraction to political honors is due to his love of the noble, his unabated desire to be the benefactor of the Athenians. But it must be said that while his basic goodwill toward his city remains, his pursuit of the noble has undergone some marked changes along the lines suggested by the refutation concerning courage in the *Alcibiades*. By the *Second Alcibiades*, he seems unwilling to entertain political pursuits that implicitly rely on any notion of happiness enjoyed after death: in the *Symposium*, he does not even know whether to refer to his soul or to his physical "heart" (218a3–4). Certainly, the most infamous decisions of Alcibiades' career (in the aftermaths of the mutilation of the Herms and the fiasco at Notium) highlight his willingness to put his own good, and in particular his own life, ahead of the good of the Athenians or of the nobility of serving them. These are the deeds of an Alcibiades whose ability to immerse himself in the pursuit of political goods, as he himself suggests, has been ruined by a Socratic critique. Without Socrates' peculiar *eros* for wisdom, Alcibiades cannot follow him in the philosophic life, but neither can he unlearn what he has learned to see in the *demos*. He claims to need to run from Socrates with his ears covered so as not to be overwhelmed by the force of Socrates' critique (*Symposium* 216a6–8). It is fitting, then, that he arrives at the party surrounded by hedonistic distraction, complete with the music of flute girls to drown out the sound of the Socratic *logos*.[9] Alcibiades will still derive satisfaction from conquering and outwitting his political and military rivals for the benefit of the city he loves—but we must recall both how willing he is in Thucydides' portrayal to apply his efforts and abilities for the benefit of Athens' rivals and the fact that Xenophon ends his narration of Alcibiades' career with an inconspicuous retreat to private life.

What do we learn from all of this about the place of political ambition in political life? It seems at first that Socrates' attempt to redirect Alcibiades' ambition away from politics by educating him would be a perfect lens through which to consider how Plato might assess the project of someone like Hobbes or Locke, who wishes to suppress political ambition or to channel it into more innocuous pursuits. But the more one considers the comparison between Socrates' education of Alcibiades and the modern political project of enlightenment, the more one sees how poor the analogy really is. Socrates may be trying to educate Alcibiades, but the purpose of this education remains strikingly unclear. Who is to say that he might not have succeeded in tempering Alcibiades' ambition had his primary aim been to make of Alcibiades a constructive and moderate contributor to the order and prosperity of the city? What we can say about Plato's presentation of extraordinary ambition is that almost no component of it is unsusceptible to weakening through Socratic critique, including the love of the noble. But *Socratic* critique may not at all be what would constitute the most prudent course of cultural and political reform. All of this must remain rather abstract and speculative, however, until we can say with somewhat greater clarity what Socrates' aim may actually have been and in what sense his education can rightly be called a corruption.

## The Meaning of Socratic Corruption

The most striking and troubling feature of the *Alcibiades* dialogues is the impression that Alcibiades was led to desire tyranny (*Second Alcibiades* 140e10–141b8) on account of Socrates' critique of the Athenians and their leaders, including Pericles (*Alcibiades* 110e2–3, 118a8–e2), as well as his apparent endorsement of the Persian kings as models (105c4–d4, 122b8–c4). From this perspective, the corruption charge against Socrates looks rather well founded: Socrates' critique of democratic honor unmoored Alcibiades' political ambition from the need for Athenian approval. But we have already seen that this impression is in need of correction since the charge that Socrates made Alcibiades into a seeker of tyrannical rule is ill supported by historical fact. What is the evidence that does suggest that Alcibiades' Socratic education may have had deleterious effects for him and for Athens? The allegations of Alcibiades' participation in the crimes of impiety of 416 BC are telling, but they are, after all, only allegations. Less ambiguous are the details recorded in the histories of Thucydides and Xenophon, already alluded to, but worth laying out with more clarity: (1) Alcibiades refused to return to Athens to stand trial out of (justified) fear of summary execution; (2) Alcibiades helped Sparta recover while the Athenians were in Sicily; (3) Alcibiades precipitated the oligarchic coup of 411 BC in an attempt to secure his safe return to Athens; and (4) Alcibiades deserted from the Athenian military when the city lost patience with his generalship following the defeat at the battle of Notium.

These events all suggest that the mature Alcibiades was keenly aware of the possible disjunction between his own good and the demands or legal requirements of the city. In particular, it is clear that Alcibiades came to fear the wrath of a proud *demos*, whipped up by pious fear, and not to share in the Athenians' beliefs about whom or what must be revered and obeyed. The real danger in Socrates' critique of democratic imprudence, then, is not the possibility of Alcibiades developing a will to oppress or dominate the Athenians. It is rather that having come to see the source of democratic law as deeply flawed, he may seek to subvert, transcend, or dispose of the law for the sake of his ends, include as they may the glory of Athens. Of course, this in itself may not constitute corruption, especially from the genuine Socratic point of view, even if it means a willingness to improve the lot of the Athenians in opposition to their mistaken judgment of what is best. Rather, the question of Alcibiades' political corruption hangs on whether he in fact possesses in every case the prudence the Athenians lack.

The need for Alcibiades to obtain this prudence is an important theme of the *Second Alcibiades*. When Socrates questions the goodness of tyranny or generalship on account of the risks they entail, Alcibiades' response suggests he is aware of the need for political prudence in navigating such dangerous waters (143a6–b5). Above all, we noted that Alcibiades does not propose courage as the virtue needed in facing the dangers of political and military rule. Political prudence, with emphasis on the need for rhetoric, is the best replacement for courage, putting well-informed calculation in the place of belief in the ennobling and protective aura of courageous devotion (and in the place of the hope that Alcibiades had been willing to put in prayer). To whatever extent Alcibiades attempted to lead the Athenians without being in possession of the "science of the best" Socrates describes, he was potentially exposing the city to danger—but no more than any other public speaker who equally lacked that science. If Alcibiades' corruption consisted in his willingness to guide the

Athenians without perfect prudence, he was hardly more corrupt than its other great leaders, especially if the "science of the best" is in principle unattainable.

But it is also worth stressing that Socrates responds to the *aporia* concerning the riskiness of political life with advice from a wise *anēr*, or "man" in the sense that is associated with the virtue of manliness or courage (*andreia*) (143b6–c3). And the Socratic prodding that, in turn, follows the mention of this *anēr sophōteros* focuses precisely on the pious fears that continue to bar Alcibiades from the full challenge of philosophy. Political prudence, then, is only part of what Socrates holds out to Alcibiades. He also points the way to philosophic courage, and the line of questioning that would need to be taken up in order to allay most fully the pious fears that have brought Alcibiades to the altar. How much of this lesson Alcibiades learned in the months and years that followed is difficult to know, but the extent to which he failed in this respect may represent the true measure of his corruption. The portrait in the *Symposium* might have shed some further light on the matter had Alcibiades not been so completely silent on the effect of his Socratic education on his understanding of moral, religious, and political affairs.

Still, we may learn enough about Alcibiades himself from the *Symposium* to say more about his later political missteps than that he lacked a Socratic "science of the best." In particular, one element of Alcibiades' appearance in the *Symposium* accords rather well with Thucydides' most important suggestion about his corruption. Thucydides says that the Athenians feared Alcibiades' "lawlessness with respect to his own body" and that this helped form their suspicion that he had tyrannical designs.[10] Perhaps Alcibiades' entrance in the *Symposium* is Plato's attempt to help us interpret Thucydides' enigmatic claim. There, Alcibiades' apparent hedonism (which is of a sort that recalls Thucydides' formulation) disrupts the plan of moderate drinking and ordered speeches that had been agreed upon by consensus following a reasonable deliberation (176a1ff). Thus, Alcibiades' immoderate and indecent bodily habits resulted in his tyrannical subversion and usurpation of the symposiasts' constitutional order. This episode could likewise be counted as an example of the "undemocratic (*ou dēmotikēn*) lawlessness of his way of life" (Thucydides vi.28.2).

How do we interpret this suggestive Platonic vignette? Alcibiades' tyrannical streak, such as it is, is expressed by his lack of concern for what the others take seriously. Part of this speaks to an exaggerated sense Alcibiades has of his own importance, which formed part of the reason that Socrates was attracted to him in the first place. It is therefore a facet of his nature that preceded his Socratic education. What is unsettling, given the emphasis Socrates had put on the need for prudence, is Alcibiades' refusal to accommodate the others' desire for order and moderation or even, at first, to recognize it. He seems unaware of the uncomfortable imposition his audacity puts on the reserved and cautious. Eryximachus, objecting to Alcibiades' regime of forced wine guzzling, asks, "Do we thus neither say nor sing anything over the cup, but crudely drink like the thirsty?" (214b1–2). A doctor and student of natural science, Eryximachus is not particularly pious (see Chapter 4, 149–50), but he is attached to the civility of forms and even of religious tradition, such as singing songs to the gods (cf. 175a3). Alcibiades' transgression here is minimal, but it reflects a carelessness of the complex Athenian disposition toward the hubristic, the lawless, and the impious. The ambivalence of the Athenians in these matters is characteristic of their behavior during the war with Sparta.[11]

This is not to deny what was suggested above, that Alcibiades recognized the dangerousness of an Athenian *demos* animated by pious fear.[12] His willingness to flee once the ire of the assembly had been aroused speaks to Alcibiades' political prudence and thus may reflect some lessons learned after the *Second Alcibiades*.[13] But the political lesson Alcibiades never fully learned concerns a theme that has arisen in every Platonic depiction of him: the need for rhetoric in democratic statesmanship. To be sure, Alcibiades became an able speaker, debater, and, to take a suggestion from Xenophon's *Memorabilia*, Socratic refuter, and his rhetorical abilities are on display in the *Symposium*. Alcibiades was clever, and his willingness to be deceitful—as, for example, in the affair of the Spartan emissaries in the Peace of Nicias—furthered his political career.[14] But he was deficient in being unwilling to dissemble with respect to his own worth.[15] His speech endorsing the Sicilian Expedition in Thucydides famously begins, "It is proper for me more than for others, O Athenians, to rule" (vi.15.1). The speech was wildly successful, but in part because it forced any dissenters into silence and thence to conspiracy (vi.24.4, vi.28.2). Alcibiades' pride was such that he refused to conceal his tremendous sense of superiority over the Athenians or to present a public image of himself as more traditional, more pious, more concerned for ordinary decency and moderation than he was or had come to be.

Without taking up a more elaborate study of Thucydides than is appropriate here, however, we are forced to leave open the possibility that even Alcibiades' public haughtiness and unapologetic self-importance were part of a calculated plan to govern Athens as effectively as possible. The opening of the *Alcibiades*, after all, suggests that Socrates at first understood the power of Alcibiades' natural boastfulness better than Alcibiades himself (103b2–104a2, 105d8–e5, cf. *Symposium* 219e5–221c1). In the course of that conversation, Socrates suggests to Alcibiades that were he to be captain of a ship, "it would be necessary for [him] to surpass [his fellow sailors] by so much that they did not deem themselves worthy to compete against him, but, having been looked down upon, would fight with [him] against the enemy" (119d9–e2). Moreover, the rehabilitation of Alcibiades' belief in the possibility of effective democratic statesmanship in the *Second Alcibiades* does nothing to defuse his newfound contempt for the ignorance or imprudence of the *demos*. It does just the opposite: Socrates encourages Alcibiades to think of the orator in the assembly as the "mind" that is in control of the actions of the entire, otherwise mindless city (144e3–145a2, 146c11–13). But if Alcibiades' prideful rhetoric was calculated to win the total obedience of the Athenians, should we infer that he *did* learn the necessary Socratic lessons concerning democratic rhetoric? Once again we must admit that the *Symposium* leaves us in the dark, with no way of knowing just how clear-sighted Alcibiades ultimately became. Perhaps the Athenian backlash against him should be seen as the realization of an unfortunate possibility that had to be risked in pursuit of Periclean (or greater) leadership—a risk that could be mitigated by the use of political prudence but never eliminated. Or perhaps Alcibiades' recklessness and unwillingness to humble himself before the proud Athenians were uncorrected flaws of character for which both Alcibiades and Athens paid dearly.

Whatever Alcibiades' rhetorical strategy as an Athenian statesman was, it must be reiterated that the whole Platonic drama of Socrates and Alcibiades—including the summary of their relationship given in the *Republic*[16]—suggests that Alcibiades' pursuit of a political career was a second-best outcome from Socrates' perspective. Socrates' statement that "it is a beautiful sign that the knowers know whenever they are able to produce another knower" (*Alcibiades* 118d6–8) suggests that he seeks confirmation of his supposed wisdom in the considered agreement of an Alcibiades made wise. The procedure whereby Socrates might still hope to confirm his wisdom, even without leading Alcibiades to philosophy, is cryptically sketched in Socrates' purported elaboration of the Delphic inscription "know thyself." Socrates' image of the eye seeking its own reflection in another eye, which he says is a metaphor for the attempt to obtain knowledge of the self, suggests that Alcibiades' careful attention to

Socrates will provide Socrates with an invaluable opportunity to study himself. But the specific questions Socrates has in mind to investigate are not made clear in the same works in which he is carrying out the investigation. Plato does not show everything at once. We know only that Socrates had an eye toward what is "divine" within the human being, especially thought (133c4–6, cf. *Second Alcibiades* 143d2), and that this appears to be related to the question "What ever is a human being?" (*Alcibiades* 129e9).

# NOTES

## Introduction

1. Plato, *Alcibiades* 104a1–c6. See also Ellis 1989 (1–9), and de Romilly 1995 (17–34).

2. Thucydides, vi.8–26.

3. Aristophanes sums up Athens's opinion of Alcibiades perfectly: "She longs for him, she hates him, she wants to have him" (*Frogs* 1425). For an illuminating account of the Athenians' paradoxical disposition toward Alcibiades and other Athenian elites, see Gribble 1999 (1–69).

4. Thucydides, vi.15. The claim that the "lawlessness" of Alcibiades' private life, especially with respect "to his own body," led to the Athenians' suspicion of him is a typically Thucydidean puzzle: what does lawlessness with respect to one's body mean, and how did it arouse the Athenians' suspicion of Alcibiades with regard to his political ambitions? Cf. Gribble 1999 (69–89).

5. Thucydides, vi.27–28. For a thorough consideration of the possible culprits of the mutilation of the Herms and a defense of Alcibiades' probable innocence, see Ellis 1989 (58–62).

6. Thucydides, vi.53, 61, 88–92, viii.12–17; De Romilly 1995 (125–42).

7. Thucydides, viii.45, 47–49, 81–82; Xenophon, *Hellenica* i.4.11–18, 5.16–17; Ellis 1989 (69–93); De Romilly 1995 (143–83, 191–220); Kagan 1987 (112–16).

8. Thucydides vi.92.2–4. The passage is discussed thoroughly by Pusey 1940 (216ff). See also Forde 1989 (106–15), Faulkner 2007 (68–69), and Verdegem 2010 (261–64).

9. For a study of Thucydides' Alcibiades meant as a prelude to a study of Plato's, see Faulkner 2007 (59ff).

10. Lutz 1998 suggests that "after Socrates himself, [Alcibiades] may be the most significant character in all of Plato's writings" (111).

11. De Jouvenel 1963 (14).

12. Socrates seems to caution, at different times in the *Alcibiades* alone, that Alcibiades lacks the practical knowledge needed to govern well; that he will fail as a general if he does not first examine his opinions concerning justice; that he can only defeat his true political enemies if he takes the trouble to become wise; that his vision of the prosperous city is incoherent; that he is doomed to a life of error until he gains an understanding of the relationship between the noble and the good; that he will be corrupted by his love for the *demos*; that he cannot rule himself or others well without obtaining self-knowledge or moderation; and that the pursuit of tyranny will lead him and Athens into misery and destruction.

13. Lutz 1998 provides a good example of how this sort of conclusion can be drawn from a study of the Platonic Alcibiades (146–47).

14. Grote 1867 deftly traces the passage of the Platonic corpus from Athens to Alexandria, and thus almost from Plato to Aristophanes, arguing that no corruption of the manuscripts could

have taken place in the time between Plato's death and the arrangement into trilogies (272–87). Grote surely overstates the certainty of his thesis. But he presents a historically compelling argument that is rarely addressed by modern scholars, who tend to dismiss his defense of the entire traditional canon, as did Harward 1932, "as an eccentricity on the part of a man whose judgment was generally sound" (61). See Irwin 2008 for a recent account of the corpus's early history (64–68).

15. For a recent and thorough bibliography of the debates surrounding the authenticity of the *Alcibiades*, see Jirsa 2009, who ultimately finds the arguments against authenticity decisively lacking. Renaud and Tarrant 2015 provide a thorough and even-handed survey of the most important substantive arguments, ultimately declining (judiciously, to my mind) to pronounce a final verdict regarding authenticity (260–69). Other important and relatively recent works include Smith 2004 (against authenticity), Denyer 2001 (for), Pradeau and Marboeuf 1999 (for), and Gribble 1999 (260–61) (against). Among the many other treatments worth considering, I mention as particularly important Schleiermacher 1836 (against), Grote 1867 (for; includes a helpful albeit adversarial survey of the important nineteenth-century German scholars), De Strycker 1942 (against), Bluck 1953 (against), Friedlander 1964 (for), Annas 1985 (for), and Pangle 1987 (for). Of these, Schleiermacher, Grote, Friedlander, and Pangle also refer, directly or indirectly, to the *Second Alcibiades*, which is generally less well regarded and therefore less studied. On this dialogue, see also Johnson 2003 (for), Howland 1990 (for), and Taylor 1926 (against). For statistical stylometry, the definitive works are still Ledger 1989 (for both) and Brandwood 1990 (against both), although a more recent study, focusing on (and athetizing) the *Alcibiades* in particular, was done by Johnson and Tarrant 2012 . The critique of stylometric analysis (in the broad sense) by Howland 1991 is exquisite.

16. See Tigerstedt 1974 (14-21).

17. For a fuller picture of Platonic studies in late nineteenth-century Germany, see Lamm 2000 (218–20) and 2005 (92–97). Tigerstedt 1974 carefully traces the history of scholarly rejection of neo-Platonism, leading up to "The New Situation" in eighteenth-century Germany (63). Note his emphasis on the pre-Schleiermacher examples of interpreters who rejected traditional interpretations of Plato, especially Montaigne, Serranus, Brucker, Tiedemann, and Tennemann. For a more general history of "criticism" and of the importance of "the historical spirit" to *Kritik* in German Romanticism, see Wellek 1981 (300–302).

18. At stake in the debates surrounding this question was a matter of great importance, not to be overlooked: was Platonic philosophy a uniquely Greek phenomenon, or did it grasp some permanent and universal truth? The Kantian Tennemann, convinced that Plato had something like a Kantian philosophic system but unable to discover it in the dialogues, was left to suppose that the full elaboration of it formed the content of the famous *agrapha dogmata* (Lamm 2000, 230–31; Tigerstedt 1974, 65). The obvious deficiencies of Tennemann's work served as a partial spur to Schleiermacher, who denied the existence of a Platonic system and of Platonic esotericism (except in a sense; see his 1836 "Introduction," 18).

19. See Diogenes Laertius iii.62, 37, and Asclepius's commentary on *Metaphysics* 991b3; cf. Denyer 2001 (14).

20. A version of what Heidegger would later call the "hermeneutic circle." See Leitch 2010 (521–22).

21. See Schleiermacher's concise assessment of the philological and interpretive challenge in the general "Introduction" to his translation of Plato (27–30).

22. Actually, Schleiermacher 1998 goes on to concede to his prominent rivals Wolf and Ast

that a third and distinct "grammatical" element must also be included, so that finally, "The complete solution of this three-fold task is only possible in an approximate manner when they are linked together, during a philologically developed era, and when the task is carried out by exemplary philologists" (4). An apparently similar problem is described by Schleiermacher's treatment of the inseparability of "doctrinal" and "philological" criticism (160–66).

23. Arnaldo Momigliano has put the point well in discussing a different set of historical puzzles: "The most dangerous type of researcher in any historical field is the man who, because he is intelligent enough to ask a good question, believes that he is good enough to give a satisfactory answer" (1987, 5).

24. Or rather this mistake having been once made by an influential authority, we may find ourselves in the shadow of an interpretive tradition made imposing by the scores of academics who were able to make careers of variations on the original mistake. Thus, in "the middle of the nineteenth century, especially in Germany, the 'athetizing' of Platonic dialogues became a fashionable amusement for scholars" that still wields tremendous influence on the standard view of Platonic philosophy (Taylor 1926, 11). We find ourselves needing to throw off the yoke of a tradition that began with an attempt to throw off the yoke of tradition. Sadly, we likely cannot continue in this spirit for long before the magnitude of the philosophic tasks we face vastly exceeds our abilities. One needs, at least to begin, the comforting support of authority or tradition, and evidence from which to derive confidence in one's ability to escape that need is hard to find.

25. It may be said of Schleiermacher that his work is characterized by its falling into *both* of these traps. Cf. Lamm 2000 (209).

26. Howland 1990 (64).

27. That there are striking differences along these lines is noted at length by Smith 2004, who concludes on that basis that the *Alcibiades* is probably spurious (unless a coherent interpretation, such as will be attempted here, can be provided).

28. Gill 1990 presents a good survey of such interpretations (with emphasis on Nussbaum's), in the course of his own attempt to disentangle the "nature, and the cogency, of Platonic thinking about love" from the "modern assumptions about the role of individuality in personal relationships."

29. Especially Socrates', as, e.g., in Nussbaum 1986 and Gagarin 1977. Bury 1909, citing the critical edition of Arnold Hug, agrees that the "speech of Alcibiades is related to that of Socrates 'as Praxis to Theory'" (Introduction vi.3.a).

30. See Bury 1909 (Introduciton ii.A). Shorey 1933 goes even further: "In spite of the . . . calumnies which the supposed discipleship of Alcibiades drew down upon [Socrates, Alcibiades is] portrayed as his familiar [friend] in the *Symposium*, and the intoxicated Alcibiades there pronounces upon him an encomium which is Plato's most memorable expression of his own admiration and love" (7).

31. Gagarin's even-handed and illuminating analysis of Socratic *hubris* might be summed up by reference to Socratic irony (cf. 24 with *Nicomachean Ethics* 1108a20–23, 1124b27–30), albeit not by Gagarin himself (33). For his incisive critique of interpretations that fail to take Alcibiades' accusations seriously, see 22–23, 32–34. Among those who ignore the *Alcibiades* dialogues, Gagarin stands out for his taking seriously the possibility that "Plato presents Socrates as a failure in certain respects."

32. Note that authors who accept either or both of the *Alcibiades* dialogues as authentic tend more toward the conclusion that Alcibiades' speech reveals the morally questionable character

of Socrates' effect on him. See Nichols 2007 (503) and Bloom 2001 (166), as well as the discussion of Lutz 1998 and Newell 2000 below (19–20).

33. For example, Denyer 2001 takes Socrates' "tricky" argument that the just is advantageous to be intended merely to "intensify Alcibiades' confusion" so that he will become more humble—a strategy that pays off with the "fairly serious philosophizing" Alcibiades is able to do when Socrates presents "the superb argument" about body and soul toward the end of the dialogue (24, 10). He claims that Alcibiades is left "unmoved" by the argument that the Athenians are as ignorant about justice as he is (7). Guthrie 1971, also inclined to accept the authenticity of the *Alcibiades* (150 n.2), likewise considers the primary interest of the dialogue to lie roughly in its last third (150–54).

34. Lauriello 2010 notes Scott's failure to recognize Socratic pointers to theological questions (254–55, addenda 6, 8). His critique is helpful in understanding why Scott comes up short in determining Socrates' own motives. Scott, after inferring from Socrates' argument the conclusion that "all people must seek a superior in wisdom," is right to ask, "why would the superior person be interested in staking her or his chance at self-knowledge on a less worthy interlocutor? In any relationship, indeed in any dialogue, how will the less capable partner—presumably the one inferior in wisdom—facilitate the self-knowledge of the wiser person?" (97). He later suggests that Socrates performs a kind of *self*-examination through his refutations (107), but never clarifies what it is about himself that Socrates might still need to know. Cf. the attempt by Renaud and Tarrant 2015 to answer the same question (16–22).

35. This is by no means to say that all accounts that take their bearings from the *Alcibiades* and *Symposium* give attention to the political implications of Alcibiades' Socratic education. Abstraction from the political element, however, often leads to rather strange interpretations of Socrates' intentions. Consider the suggestion of Fagan 2013 that Socrates develops with Alcibiades a new form of pederasty in which the forceful exertion of intellectual superiority through "sophistry" replaces the end sought by the conventional pederast, i.e., the "expression of his domination" through "anal intercourse" (14–15, 17–18; compare Nussbaum's vastly subtler, more perceptive, and better-researched treatment of related thematic elements, 188–91, but cf. the persuasive rebuttal of Nails 2006, 194–96). Wohl 2012 is led to a similarly superficial account of Socrates' motives, seeing his *eros* as "structured by a fundamental narcissism" and as an attempt to see "himself as a god" (47).

36. See also Renaud and Tarrant 2015 (24).

37. Here, the interpretation of the *Alcibiades* and *Second Alcibiades* contained in Christopher Bruell's *On the Socratic Education* (1999) must be mentioned. Bruell's careful exposition of these dialogues is a challenging and invaluable guide to their most important questions and themes, and I note interpretive insights I owe to his work throughout the following chapters. He does not, of course, provide an interpretation of Alcibiades' speech in the *Symposium* and does not foreground the theme of political ambition. But more important, Bruell's way is less to provide answers than to provoke questions, and thus he graciously leaves room for a longer and less subtle treatment such as this.

38. For a Platonic reflection on a closely related matter, cf. *Second Letter* (310d–311e).

39. Xenophon, *Memorabilia* 1.2.12ff; cf. Forde 1987 (222–23, 239).

40. The difficulty we face concerning the term "political corruption" is similar to that noted at the outset regarding "political ambition." It seems more than coincidence that the most familiar meanings of both terms nowadays overlap considerably. The difference between ancient and modern conceptions of political corruption, with emphasis on the case of Socrates, has been

discussed insightfully by Saxonhouse 2004 (26–31). For the contemporary relevance of the issue of "corrupting youth" in particular, see Euben 1997 (3–31).

41. For a fuller discussion of the rationale behind Socrates' trial and execution, see Saxonhouse 2006 (100ff).

## Chapter 1

1. Lutz 1998 (113), Forde 1987 (222), Friedlander 1964 (231), and Renaud and Tarrant 2015 (6, n.8). Renaud and Tarrant have produced by far the most thorough study of ancient "neo-Platonist" thought on the *Alcibiades*.

2. For a different organization of the *Alcibiades*, see Blitz 1995 (339).

3. Cf. Blitz 1995 (340).

4. Cf. Aristotle, *Constitution of the Athenians* 42.

5. On how to translate *telos* at 105d3, compare the obtrusive translation of W. R. M. Lamb 1955 *ad loc.*—"Without me it is impossible for all those designs of yours to be crowned with achievement"—to Bruell's artful paraphrase—"Socrates astounds Alcibiades . . . by claiming that it will be impossible for [Alcibiades'] ambition to be fulfilled (*or brought to an end*) without his help" (1999, 21, my emphasis).

6. As Bruell 1999 points out, Alcibiades' *political* ambition is only the most recent, and not in all respects the most important, manifestation of his desire for what is best (21–22).

7. The logic of the refutation does not require that these premises come first. The effect of obtaining Alcibiades' agreement to them now rather than at the end of the refutation is to put them at a distance from the refutation's disorienting and potentially even painful final moment, in which Alcibiades will be faced with the conclusion that his ambitions are in danger of going unfulfilled on account of his ignorance. Here is an example, then, of the kind of rhetoric deftly employed in Socratic refutation. In Alcibiades' crucial moment of *aporia*, he will not think to lash out at the dubious premise concerning knowledge but will rather be focused on the theme Socrates wishes to emphasize, namely, justice. But Plato invites the reader to consider with more care what Alcibiades overlooks.

For a different take on the faultiness of the Socratic argument regarding ignorance as a prerequisite of knowledge, see Bruell 1999 (24).

8. Renaud and Tarrant 2015 suggest that the Greeks would have seen the art of divining as being rather more similar to the other arts here mentioned than it appears to the modern reader (37). But cf. the counsel of Poulydamas to Hector in the *Iliad* (12.200–229) as well as Chapter 3 (208n 46) below.

9. Cf. 115a1, 127e5–7. Also consider again *Republic* 495a1–b6 together with *Laws* 908b4–d7.

10. To be clear, Alcibiades' naïveté is striking given how cunning he will eventually become, but his belief about the character of Athenian political debate is not unusual per se. On the contrary, we can say that it is the typical view of the decent, civic-spirited Athenian who believes in the justice and prudence of Athenian democracy. See *Protagoras* 319a8–d7.

11. Faulkner 2007 notes this among other impressive features of Alcibiades' performance in this dialogue (88).

12. Gribble 1999 is so struck by the presentation of a "submissive and unintelligent" Alcibiades in this dialogue that he takes it as evidence against the dialogue's authenticity (261); Schleiermacher 1836 drew a similar conclusion (334–35) (but cf. Friedlander 1964, 232). The possibility that Alcibiades' unimpressive showing here is due to his not yet having associated with Socrates is dismissed by Gribble on account of his adoption of the popular misconception that the lively

and impressive Alcibiades of Plato's *Protagoras* is even younger. The most thorough attempt at providing dramatic dates for Plato's dialogues has been done by Nails 2002, who rightly puts the *Protagoras* and *Alcibiades* at about the same time, without certainty about which is earlier (309–10; cf. Bruell 1999, 48). But that Alcibiades is still quite unfamiliar with Socrates' "*pragma*" in the *Alcibiades* (and not in the *Protagoras*) seems undeniable (*Alcibiades* 104d3–5, *Protagoras* 336b–c). Bruell 1999 provokes the interesting observation that Alcibiades' slowness is especially evident in his inability to recognize the central importance of justice to his aspirations (35). See Chapter 3 (144–46) below.

13. For a reflection on how the *Gorgias* carries the discussion of rhetoric beyond what is alluded to in the *Alcibiades*, see Friedlander 1964 (239–41).

14. Blitz 1995 likewise notes Alcibiades' apparent lack of an appreciation for the power of rhetorical skill and suggests that the reference to music is related to "the place of rhythm, tone, and display in speaking before assemblies" (341–42). See also Bruell 1999 (31–32).

15. Or "clever," "tricky" (cf. *Apology of Socrates* 17b1). The word is *deinon*.

16. For a helpful reflection on the likely character of such a law as understood by Greeks at this time, see Denyer 2001 (115).

17. Cf. Forde 1987 (225) and Renaud and Tarrant 2015 (38–39).

18. Lutz 1998 emphasizes the character and purpose of the rules Alcibiades recognizes and wants obeyed but does not consider, with reference to this anecdote, the primary surface question: how does Alcibiades recognize injustice? (116).

19. Cf. *Republic* 358e3–359b5.

20. See also Forde 1987 (226).

21. Cf. Aristotle, *Metaphysics* 981a1–30.

22. Cf. *Iliad* 23.382-400.

23. Cf. *Iliad* 23.532ff.

24. Cf. *Apology of Socrates* 24c4–25c4.

25. Cf. 110e5–7 with *Republic* 487b1–c3 and *Hipparchus* 229e2–6. See also *Parmenides* 135c8–d6.

26. Bruell 1999 notes an exception at 110e4–6 (24).

27. It is not immediately clear whether this is the view of Bruell 1999 (26).

28. For discussions of Alcibiades' involvement in Melos, see Vickers 1999 and Benson 1928 (134–35).

29. Consider for example the Athenian purification of Delos (iii.104) and the oracular interpretation of the plague (ii.54) despite the weakening of piety it produced (iii.47.4, 52.3–4, 53.4).

30. The *Alcibiades* may indeed portray the moment when it dawns on Alcibiades that an education from sophists could be beneficial. See Chapter 1 (34) below.

31. In this respect, it can be helpful to compare Alcibiades with Glaucon. Glaucon, too, suspects that the unjust often succeed and attributes a closely related view to "the many" (*Republic* 358a4–6; see Bruell 1966, 4ff). But as much as Alcibiades shares with Glaucon the impression that the many are dismissive of justice, Glaucon's situation is considerably different on account of the marked effect the sophists have had upon his thinking (358c7–d3). That this makes for a significant difference in the nature of Socrates' relationship to each of these young men is evident in the differences not only between the *Alcibiades* and the *Republic* (see Chapter 2 (81–82, 84) below) but especially between the *Alcibiades* and the conversation between Socrates and the twenty-year-old Glaucon in the *Memorabilia* (iii.6). This chapter represents an important Xenophontic parallel to the *Alcibiades* from which we can see (among other things) a) what Socrates

might do if his *only* aim were to dissuade his interlocutor from entering politics (iii.6.1), and b) what an interlocutor is like who believes he has determined that war is fought for the sake of profit (iii.6.7). The differences between the two texts with respect to these two considerations are related. Cf. *Alcibiades* 109d6 with *Memorabilia* iii.6.12. See also Chapter 2 (203n25) below.

32. For a more elaborate interpretation of the reference to the *Phaedra*, see O'Connor 1999 (41–42).

33. But see Chapter 1 (203n31) above.

34. Lutz 1998 suggests that Alcibiades may have in mind his own father's death on the battlefield (116).

35. Lutz 1998 presents a related but distinct reflection: "Socrates conceals the good consequence that seems to come from shameful cowardice, namely, that through it one at least remains alive" (118). See also Faulkner 2007 (104–105).

36. Cf. Bruell 1999 (27–30).

37. Cf. *Theages* 127d3–128b8. Schleiermacher 1836 fails to notice Socrates' attempt to make himself out to be the only possible teacher of what Alcibiades needs to know (331).

38. Cf. *Protagoras* 319d8–320b8. Anyone who would place the dramatic date of the *Alcibiades* after that of the *Protagoras* must explain why Alcibiades cannot offer the same explanation of his failure to have learned from Pericles as Socrates gives in the *Protagoras*. See (144–46) below.

39. Lutz 1998 remarks that "Alcibiades is strikingly unperturbed by [the] revelation" that "he is not only confused but poorly educated" (118–19). He does not consider how great a shift this is from Alcibiades' state of mind moments earlier when he "curses vehemently, and exclaims that he does not know what he has been talking about" (118). Seeing the sudden change in Alcibiades' demeanor is crucial to understanding the importance of this moment in the dialogue.

40. Literally, it is a question of how one might "go up into the sky" (*anabēsēi eis ton ouranon*), but the voyage of Trygaeus in Aristophanes' *Peace* makes clear enough that the phrase can be taken as a reference to the home of the gods (102–103, 198–99, 821–23), as does the entire conceit of his *Birds* (177–93).

41. The word is *tekmērion*, which can mean *sign* or *evidence*, but also *proof* in a rigorous sense. I have refrained from using the translation *proof* on the grounds that it is likely too strong, but the possibility of this meaning should be kept in mind.

42. This is a central claim in the interpretation of Lutz 1998 (123–27, 141). Consider also Howland 1990: "Socrates' interest in Alcibiades is partly intelligible in light of the nature of the young man's eros. For Alcibiades' love of honor manifests, albeit incoherently, an underlying desire to regard his own worth in the light of standards which are prior to, more authoritative, and more universal than, those sanctioned and sustained by indigenous custom (*nomos*)" (79).

43. Alcibiades seems somehow to divine the scope of the task Socrates is pointing to (119b5–9); cf. "postpone . . . indefinitely," Bruell 1999 (19).

44. Gribble 1999 provides helpful explanation of *philotimia* in setting the political stage for his study of Alcibiades (11ff).

45. The word for *worthy* and its cognates appear fourteen times in the *Alcibiades*: 105b2, c5, e1, e3; 119c2, c7, d1, e1, e3, e5; 121d3; and 123b4, c6, d3.

46. As Lutz 1998 puts it, "Alcibiades will love the Athenian people because he hopes to share in their nobility and also because he hopes that by inducing them to share in this nobility he can achieve a kind of immortality" (146).

47. An argument Socrates could have made, especially had he gone down the road of examining advantage rather than justice at 113d ff, though as noted above, this would less clearly point

to Socrates as the only available teacher. Consider Xenophon *Memorabilia* iii.1 and iii.6 (cf. 200n31 above).

48. Gribble 1999, in a broader survey of Alcibiades' portrayal in ancient literature, agrees that Alcibiades saw no tension between the pursuit of his own goals and his civic-mindedness (58).

## Chapter 2

1. Renaud and Tarrant 2015 are helpful in pointing out that this same suggestion is central to the interpretation of Olympiodorus (54–55).

2. See Lutz 1998 (146).

3. See Chapter 1 (201u45) above.

4. On the contrast between this approach and that taken at the outset of the conversation, see Bruell 1999 (32–33).

5. Quail striking was a sport that pitted man against quail. The object was to force a quail out of a small circular area by flicking it on the head (see Denyer 2001 [168]). For a fuller account of what Socrates is trying to accomplish with the comparison to Meidias, see Forde 1987 (229).

6. Thus, Faulkner 2007 rightly calls the coming speech "a genially absurd proof from authority—from the alleged counsel of Spartan and Persian royalty to take trouble and seek wisdom" (87).

7. The Persians were not always masters of Asia. Cf. Herodotus i.95ff.

8. For example, the heredity of the Persian monarchy was broken in 522 BC (a fact known to Plato—see *Laws* 695c).

9. Cf. Herodotus i.136.2 and 138.1. In general, Plato seems to have been drawing from or responding to Herodotus's account of Persian customs (i.131–140) in composing Socrates' account of the Persian education.

10. The numbering is not in the original. I have numbered separately whatever Socrates separates with *kai*, except where he also uses *te* (numbers 3 and 5 in the first list, and number 1 in the second).

11. Hence, Faulkner 2007 claims that "the first *Alcibiades* supplies a picture of what would consume Alcibiades in the absence of either the grand politics to which he tends or the philosophic life of a Socrates: luxuriousness" (106). Cf. Lutz 1998 (120). Gribble 1999 considers Alcibiades' outrageously ostentatious display at the Olympics (Thucydides, vi.16.2) to have been one of the defining moments of his career (64).

12. Cf. Bruell 1999 (34–35).

13. Saxonhouse 1984, in discussing the image of Socrates as a siren, suggests that Alcibiades may have "done better to have left his ears uncovered, to have listened to the flute and the siren's call of the feminine Socrates" (13; see also 22–23, and cf. 106b6–7).

14. Forde 1987 interprets Socrates' conjured queens as part of this speech's overall (and successful) strategy of sparking an *erotic* desire in Alcibiades that had not been present in the first half of the dialogue or before (230ff). For another perspective on the importance of women in the *Alcibiades*, especially the Persian and Spartan queens, see Renaud and Tarrant 2015 (45–53).

15. See Chapter 1 (34) above, and Plutarch *Pericles* (6–8).

16. See Lutz 1998 (121). Also compare *Apology of Socrates* 20d5, Leibowitz 2010 (61–62).

17. Cf. Faulkner 2007 (105).

18. Cf. Xenophon *On Horsemanship* (xi–xii).

19. Cf. *Lysis* 207d5–e6.

20. Cf. *Symposium* 207c8–208b6.

21. Cf. *Meno* 71e1–73c5.

22. In particular, the regime of the *Republic* purports to do away, as much as possible, with distinctions between the work of men and women. See Saxonhouse 1986 (411–13).

23. For another take on the conflict this creates in Alcibiades' thinking, see Faulkner 2007 (103–104, 112–13).

24. Cf. Renaud and Tarrant 2015 (55–56).

25. This is not the only place in the *Alcibiades* in which Socrates withholds an insight or possible solution to a problem that he elaborates at great length elsewhere. Indeed, those who allege the spuriousness of the *Alcibiades* have sometimes done so on the grounds that the work is too much of an introductory textbook to Platonic-Socratic problems to have been the serious work of Plato himself. But that conclusion overlooks the possibility that in fact the *Alcibiades* is the dialogue in which Socrates *has no need* of the city in speech, the theory of recollection, the Ideas, and so on. Only in the *Alcibiades* is Socrates' interlocutor so unspoiled by Athenian intellectual life that he is unable and unconcerned to divert the conversation by means of sophisticated objections, which must then be countered by Socrates' rhetorical doctrines. The *Alcibiades* may seem to be a guided tour of the on-ramps to genuine discussions of Socratic problems, but in fact it portrays the uninterrupted flow of Socratic dialectics.

26. See Denyer 2001 (211–12) and Blitz 1995 (355). The reference to a "self itself" is taken by Bluck 1953 as evidence against the authenticity of the *Alcibiades* (46), but the argument is typically circular. Bluck must suppose he already knows which other dialogues are merely "pseudo-Platonic" in order to claim that one or another question of interest in the *Alcibiades* does not arise until sometime after Plato's death. But moreover, I see no reason to deny Plato the possibility of having addressed a question before it came to be *au courant*.

27. Obviously, such a conclusion, if reached, would have to be suspended for the sake of most every practical concern; cf. 111e4–6.

28. Alcibiades is not the only one to be fooled by Socrates in this way. See Denyer 2001 (7–9).

29. The two most authoritative manuscripts disagree here. One reads *tōi theōi* (to the god), while the other reads *tōi theiōi* (to the divine).

30. For two other suggestions as to why Socrates may want to draw in Alcibiades and impress him with his wisdom, see Lutz 1998 (115, 120).

31. According to the discussion of knowledge and error in the dialogue's central exhortation, this would mean that the moderate man not only has self-knowledge but, more important, has knowledge of what he does not know, that is, that he does not know it. In general, the considerations about self-knowledge and moderation given rather summarily by Socrates here are treated more thoroughly in the *Charmides*.

32. Faulkner finds this final appeal to Alcibiades "rather preachy" (105–6), but Gary Alan Scott 2000 (whose work has been astutely critiqued by Lauriello 2010; see Introduction above, 198n34) recognizes some important Socratic reflections contained in the passage (98). See also Forde 1987 (239) and Blitz 1995 (357).

## Chapter 3

1. Scholars who give the titles of the two dialogues as *Greater* and *Lesser Alcibiades* or *Alcibiades Major* and *Minor* do not cite their reason for doing so. It is true that Diogenes Laertius once refers to the "the greater *Alcibiades*" (*Alkibiadou tou meizonos*, III.62), but this seems to be a casual reference, as opposed to his citation of the title *Second Alcibiades* (*Alkibiadēs deuteros*) in

the context of his cataloguing the dual titles attested by Thrasylus (III.59). The latter convention, which I adopt, is also preferred by the editors of the Oxford and Loeb texts.

A few more words may be added about the authenticity of the dialogue since (recorded) doubts have existed for much longer than is true of most of the Thrasyllean canon. In Athenaeus's *Deipnosophistae*, the philosopher Pontianus notes (in the midst of a scathing attack on Plato) that the *Second Alcibiades* is thought by some to be the work of Xenophon (11.114). This is taken by some as indication of lost evidence of Xenophontic authorship (see Gribble 1999, 215). But the suggestion in Atheneus likely arises from the similarities between the discussion of prayer in the *Second Alcibiades* and the one found in *Memorabilia* i.3 (cf. Strauss 1998, 18–19). Moreover the *Second Alcibiades* could just as easily be said to echo the treatment of prayer in the *Laws* (687d–688d, 801a–b, 884a–888d, 907d–910d).

2. There are in fact two contradictory indications within the *Second Alcibiades* of its dramatic date, but the other is absurd: Socrates at one point mentions that Archelaus, tyrant of Macedon, has recently been killed (141d5–e3). But Archelaus ruled until 399 BC, the same year Socrates himself was killed and several years after Alcibiades had died. Interestingly, this is not the only instance of an anachronistic reference to Archelaus in Plato. A similar problem arises in the *Gorgias*; in both cases, Plato pairs the mention of Archelaus with an adaptation of the Homeric line "yesterday or the day before," by which Odysseus introduces his vivid recollection of events that had occurred nine years earlier (*Gorgias* 470d). Plato thus appears to acknowledge the anachronism of these references to Archelaus and, whatever the purpose of that anachronism may be in the *Second Alcibiades*, thus encourages us to take the other indication of the dialogue's dramatic date more seriously.

3. See *Charmides* 153a1b–6, Thucydides i.56–65, ii.58, 70.

4. Cf. Nails 2002 (311).

5. See Hoerber 1957.

6. Howland 1990 says, on the basis of this opening passage, that Alcibiades has come to exhibit "a dour aloofness: [he] will not meet Socrates' eyes or reveal to him his apparently weighty thoughts" (64) and, like Bruell 1999 (39), suggests that Alcibiades has failed to keep the promise he made at the end of the *Alcibiades* to follow Socrates attentively and to care for justice (135d9–10, e4–5). These are helpful interpretive suggestions, but they tend to obscure the great extent to which the *Second Alcibiades* tells the story of what Alcibiades has learned from Socrates since their first conversation. Whether or not my interpretation of the dialogue regarding this question is ultimately at odds with Bruell's or Howell's would likely be determined if we could know whether either of them would agree with the following statement of Faulkner 2007, which I believe captures the primary point of disjunction between his reading and mine: "Alcibiades probably hopes to obtain [from Socrates] arts of politics, especially arts of obtaining power. He never gets them" (85).

7. Prudence (*phronēsis*) is a key term in the *Second Alcibiades*. It may mean prudence in the sense of active or practical wisdom, the application of clear-sighted understanding to real deliberations and choices; but its root, *phro-*, refers broadly to thinking and thought, and the verbal form *phronein*, "to be prudent," can simply mean "to think," especially when it is not in explicit contrast to abstract or theoretical thinking (*noēsis*, *noein*, etc.).

Bruell 1999 helpfully points out that Socrates is "repeatedly pointing to . . . the possibility of someone's being (in different respects) both prudent and imprudent" (41), and goes on to indicate that many may be prudent with respect to the *means* for obtaining the goods they seek but not with respect to the selection of those goods. Socrates seems to "point to" this possibility by repeatedly asking Alcibiades to say who "the prudent and imprudent" people are. But are Bruell's parenthetical qualifier and its subsequent explication necessary? What of the possibility that prudence, insofar as it requires obedience to mysterious divine command, must be considered imprudent (in the same respect) from the point of view of any rational appraisal of those commands?

8. Perhaps he has been persuaded of the validity of this argument by Socrates' and Protagoras's agreement at 332a2–333a1.

9. Alcibiades thus acknowledges that as Socrates has suggested, he has come to see the city as full of madmen. But Howland 1990 seems to say that Socrates is provoking Alcibiades to accept a more "daring" condemnation of democracy here than he had already (69). This would seem to go together with Howland's failure to consider how much of the "gloomy atmosphere" of this dialogue is due to the uncomfortable stage to which *Socrates* has brought Alcibiades, but note his concluding mention of the unadorned Socrates' "experimental detachment" (87).

10. "Most euphemistic" translates *euphēmotatois*, the superlative of *euphēmos*, a word of some importance in the *Second Alcibiades*.

11. The example of ophthalmia, as well as the discussion of Oedipus, has been seen by some as a reference to the metaphor of an eye seeking its reflection in another eye in the *Alcibiades*. See Howland 1990 (65), Faulkner 2007 (107), and Sharpe 2012 (136–37). Given the importance of poetry and poets in this dialogue, it may be helpful to remember that Homer himself was said to have been blind, an attribute surely connected to his claims to divine inspiration (cf. Teiresias).

12. On the opposition between Socrates and Oedipus, see Faulkner 2007 (107). For a fuller account of the meaning of Socrates' reference to Oedipus in this dialogue, see Howland 1990 (71–74).

13. The fact of Alcibiades' flirtation with tyranny in this dialogue contributes to making it an indispensable part of Plato's presentation of him. The turbulence of his Socratic education would not be so fully evident from the *Alcibiades* and *Symposium* alone. Lutz 1998, for instance, felt compelled, by inclusion of the *Second Alcibiades* in his interpretation, to qualify his claim that Alcibiades' ambition fits Diotima's description of the erotic desire to be noble and good. It is in reflecting on the description of Alcibiades' desire for tyranny and his reaction to the coming Socratic speech that Faulkner 2007 notes, "The two *Alcibiades* . . . don't dwell on fame undying" (92).

14. As Bruell 1999 rightly notes, "We never hear in the course of the new conversation what he is intending to ask the god for, and it is perhaps impossible to figure this out with certainty" (39).

15. The passage in Homer uses "reckless wickedness" or "sinfulness" (*atasthaliaisin*). The suggestion of "imprudence" as an alternative is Socrates' own.

16. See *Odyssey* 1.35–43, and cf. Aeschylus, *Libation Bearers* 269ff.

17. That is, the conjunction in the phrase *turannos te kai eudaimōn* is somewhat ambiguous: are these two distinct ends or are they meant (by the beloved at least) to be somehow more intimately connected?

18. This is a major theme of Xenophon's *Hiero*. As for Archelaus in particular, Socrates says elsewhere that he is unable to know whether or not Archelaus is happy because he has not met him: the Athenian generals, as he stresses here, provide more readily available evidence (cf. *Gorgias* 470d5–e3 with *Second Alcibiades* 141e3–4; consider also *Apology of Socrates* 21b–22a).

19. It is along these lines that Bruell 1999 explains the most immediately puzzling feature of this speech: "This coupling of the high and rare with the common (if not low)—which appears

barely warranted by the consideration advanced in the context: that both rule and children entail great risks—becomes fully intelligible once one recalls the *Symposium*, where Socrates points to offspring and fame (if not exclusively political fame) as *the* ends aimed at by human eros, that is, by the fundamental longing of our nature prior to its having been educated or purified" (43). Cf. Howland 1990 (74–75).

20. Bruell 1999 suggests that "Alcibiades' confidence in Socrates as a teacher" has been declining since partway through their first conversation (37).

21. Of all the insights that Plato suggests Socrates shared with Alcibiades, this appears to have been the most consequential with respect to Alcibiades' political career. Twice, Alcibiades deserts the Athenians rather than risk facing the judgment of a rancorous *demos*: first at Catana, marking the end of his leadership in Sicily (Thucydides, vi.61.6), then after the battle of Notion, leaving Athens almost entirely without his guidance at Aegospotami (Xenophon, *Hellenica* i.4.16–17, ii.1.25–26). The Sicilian Expedition and the battle of Aegospotami were the two most significant Athenian military setbacks of the war. Thucydides makes it clear that Alcibiades was right about the Athenians in the first instance (Thucydides, vi.61.1–4 and vi.53–60 in context); the events following Arginusae appear to vindicate him in the latter as well (Xenophon, *Hellenica* i.7).

22. Perhaps one could say that Socrates refers only to the dangers and toils faced by the "siege" mounted by the sycophants in the city, and that he therefore leaves open the possibility that the dangers and toils on campaign *are* beneficial, mediately or in themselves. But even so, Alcibiades' failure to object is surprising in light of, for example, *Alcibiades* 107c4–d4.

23. It is interesting to note in light of Alcibiades' silence on courage here that immediately after his reply, Socrates conjures a hypothetical objector to the preceding exchange whom he refers to as "a man" (*anēr*): that is, he uses a word associated with the virtue of courage or manliness (*andreia*). See Conclusion (191) below.

24. The other six uses of words related to *kalos* are in the dialogue's closing pages: 148c3, e5–6, 150c8, 151a8, b9, c2. Words related to *dikaios* occur five times: 139d3, 147a8, 149e8, 150a7, 150b2.

25. For other interpretations that see Alcibiades' mood of somber concern as the result of his anxiety regarding the potentially immoral requirements of political life, see Faulkner 2007 (107), Howland 1990 (65, 75), and Bruell 1999 (42–44).

26. See Chapter 3 (206n23) above.

27. Both figures committed matricide. Orestes was commanded by Apollo to murder his mother, Clytemnestra, who had killed her husband and Orestes' father, Agamemnon, upon his return from Troy. Alcmaeon slew his mother Euriphyle in compliance with his father Amphilocus's dying request: Eriphyle, accepting a bribe from Polyneices, had persuaded her husband to join Polyneices' attack on Thebes, even though she knew that Amphilocus would die in the battle. Both men were thereafter tormented by the Furies.

28. Cf. Faulkner 2007, 101–2.

29. Interestingly, Homer never says explicitly that Orestes killed his mother, Clytemnestra. However, he does make it clear that she helped Aegisthus in the plot to kill Agamemnon (*Odyssey* 3.235 4.91–92, 11.404–439, 24.96–97). Moreover, at one point, it is said that after Orestes killed Aegisthus, he gave a funeral feast "for both his hateful mother and craven Aegisthus" (3.309–310). In Aeschylus's *Oresteia*, however, the matricide is not only explicit but thematic (*Libation Bearers*, 892–930).

30. Bruell 1999 seems to suggest that the discussion of murdering Pericles clarifies the

meaning of Socrates' initial question about matricide: the question had effectively been whether Alcibiades would be willing to kill his mother in order to become a tyrant (43–44). Cf. Faulkner 2007 (107) and Sharpe 2012 (138).

31. Faulkner 2007 thus notes an important feature of the *Second Alcibiades*: "When in that dialogue Alcibiades attacks ignorance, Socrates defends ignorance. . . . More knowledge may not be a good thing if it is an instrument of tyrannical ambition" (94).

32. See Howland 1990 (66).

33. Aristotle tells us that Homer's *Margites* is to comedy as his *Iliad* and *Odyssey* are to tragedy (*Poetics* 1448b38–49a2). The name Margites means something like "madman."

34. Accordingly, scholars debate the reasonableness of the Athenians' suspicion, reported by Thucydides, that Alcibiades' aimed at tyranny (vi.15.4). See Seager 1967 (16), Palmer 1982 (118), Faulkner 2007 (59, 77–78), and Forde 1989 (93).

35. The contrast between *ton agathon*, *ton esthlon*, and *ton kalon* is a conspicuously inexplicit theme of Socrates' interpretation of Simonides in the *Protagoras* (340aff). That passage as a whole bears comparison to the closing sections of the *Second Alcibiades*. Consider especially Socrates' characterizations of Sparta and his discussions of poetic interpretation.

36. Ammon was the most important Egyptian god, and his oracle in Libya was one of the most important in the Greek world. Socrates' mythical account in the *Phaedrus*, in which Ammon is skeptical of the benefit of the art of writing invented by Theuth, may be of interest here (274c–275b).

37. Herodotus claims that Ammon is merely the Egyptian name for Zeus (2.42.3–5). Plato, however, despite referring to Ammon on a number of occasions, never indicates that possibility but instead has Socrates claim that Ammon was originally the divine Egyptian king Thamus (*Phaedrus* 274d2–4).

38. Cf. *Alcibiades* 108c5–d2.

39. Cf. *Republic* 364c–365a, *Laws* 885b, 905cff. Consider also the description in Faulkner 2007 of the action of the *Second Alcibiades*: "Alcibiades is bent on evasion, this time of the evils he knows are likely to follow on what he seeks. Socrates shows that he should not think the gods will help him be evasive" (99–100).

40. See also Sharpe 2012: "Diomedes disregards the warning of the goddess. Instead, he becomes 'over-spirited' (*huperthumos*) and 'overweening' (*huperêphanos*), so that—as Alcibiades was soon to do in Athens—he 'rages furiously against immortal gods' and 'would even fight father Zeus' (*Iliad* 5.121ff.)" (145).

41. Howland 1990 notes that Socrates invited this mistake by identifying himself with Athena (83).

42. See Howland 1990: "Socrates' reference to Euripides' tragedy amounts to a prediction that he will fail to conquer Alcibiades' other lovers, and that this failure will raise up a sea of troubles for him" (66).

43. Cf. Bruell 1999 (41–42).

44. Socrates' classification of *megalopsuchia* as a type of imprudence has been cited as an indication that the *Second Alcibiades* was written, well after Plato's death, as an attack on the Cynics' view of *megalopsuchia* as a key philosophic virtue: Sharpe 2012 defends the dialogue ably against that argument (139–40).

45. Sharpe 2012 helpfully reminds us that "as Xenophon's *Hiero* attests, the tyrant's tragic unhappiness comes in no small measure from how the tyrant depends on the admiration of others he at the same time despises as beneath him. This is perhaps the deepest reason why, we

propose, the author of the *Alcibiades* II so boldly lists *megalopsuchia* as a species of ignorance or mindlessness" (144).

46. Consider especially Plutarch, *Nicias* 13.1–2. It is a special point of emphasis for Xenophon that Socratic political prudence includes the willingness and ability to provide interpretations of divine signs: *Memorabilia* i.1.2–6, *Apology of Socrates to the Jury* 12–13, *Hellenica* iii.3.4, *Education of Cyrus* i.6.2, *Anabasis* v.6.28–29, and compare *Anabasis* iii.2.9 with Plutarch, *On Socrates' Daimonion* 11. For the mature Alcibiades' understanding of the relationship between piety and prudence, consider *Hellenica* i.4.20.

47. Pace Zuckert 2009 (229–30), Renaud and Tarrant 2015 (19, 29), and others; see also Chapter 1 (199n12, 201n38) above.

48. This includes Alcibiades' masterful stroke in cutting short what would have certainly been a long-winded and self-indulgent digression from Hippias. Faulkner 2007 insightfully observes that this confrontation features the two characters for whom Plato named *two* dialogues—not obviously a mark of distinction "since Hippias is rather an ass"—and shows Alcibiades' "superior promise for certain Socratic purposes" (84).

49. Faulkner 2007 suggests that the *Protagoras* portrays an Alcibiades who has already been formed by a Socratic education that includes the *Second Alcibiades* (85, 90).

## Chapter 4

1. Agathon is thought to have left Athens in 407 BC (see Bury 1909, Intro. viii), but it is not clear what evidence for this date exists aside from Aelian's charming but hardly historically precise anecdote (*Varia Historia* 13.4). Still, the claim in Aristophanes' *Frogs*, produced in 405 BC, that Agathon has gone away to the "feast of the blessed" (86) is a good indication that he left Athens some time before then. See Bode 1859, 551–53. Nails 2006 claims that the framing dialogue is mere weeks before the trial (180).

2. For this date, cf. 173a5–7 with Athenaeus, *Deipnosophistae* 5.57.

3. Andocides, *On the Mysteries* 15, 35.

4. Cf. Nichols 2007 (516), Strauss 2003 (287), and Rosen 1967 (285).

5. See Strauss 2003 (14–16) and Scott and Welton 2008 (159–60). For the Orphic hymn quoted by Alcibiades, see Bernabé, *Poetae epici Graeci: Testimonia et fragmenta* OF1.

6. For an extensive review of scholarly opinions regarding Alcibiades' speech as accusation of Socratic corruption, see Sheffield 2001 (207 n.4).

7. On how to interpret Alcibiades' speech vis-à-vis Aristophanes' aborted rejoinder, see Lutz 1998 (130-31), Rosen 1967 (279), Nichols 2007 (511), and Strauss 2003 (255).

8. Cf. Rosen 1967 (308).

9. Cf. Xenophon, *Symposium* 4.19–20, 5.

10. See Xenophon, *Memorabilia* i.2.14–15, Plato *Republic* 340d1ff, 487a10–c5, *Protagoras* 335a4–8 with 338e3–5, and *Theages* 128c2–5 in light of 127e5–128a1.

11. Cf. Rosen 1967 (295 n.46).

12. Though he draws conclusions quite different from mine, Lutz 1998 helpfully shows the dubiousness of Socrates' endorsement: "Because Socrates does not interrupt Alcibiades' speech at any one point, it appears that Alcibiades says nothing false. Yet at the end Socrates says that he believes that Alcibiades has been only pretending to be intoxicated and that his whole speech has been a veiled attempt to make Socrates love him rather than the tragic poet Agathon (222c–d). Thus Socrates' failure to interrupt Alcibiades does not mean that Socrates agrees with Alcibiades' story" (138).

13. Plato's only other use of this formulation is also in the *Symposium*, at 201e10. Diotima uses it in response to Socrates' asking whether Eros, if he is indeed neither beautiful nor good, is rather ugly and bad. By contrast, the imperative *euphemei* (speak well!) appears eleven times in the Platonic corpus: *Hipparchus* 228b1; *Second Alcibiades* 143d2; *Protagoras* 330d7; *Gorgias* 469a2; *Republic* 329c, 509a; *Meno* 91c1; *Euthydemus* 301a7, 302c3; and *Laws* 329c, 509a.

14. This is the second time Alcibiades speaks of taking revenge on Socrates (cf. 213d8).

15. Lutz 1998 also considers the possibility that Alcibiades casts doubt on the Socratic/Diotiman teaching but suggests that Diotima may have been wrong rather than that Socrates may have lied (130).

16. Socrates is the only other Platonic character to swear by Poseidon (*Euthydemus* 301e1).

17. See *Clouds* 518–62. It may be a sign of a certain affinity between Aristophanes and Socrates that the latter, too, mixes the playful with the serious (*Apology of Socrates* 20d4–6; *Alcibiades* 124d1–2; Xenophon, *Symposium* 1.1, 4.28).

18. Sheffield 2001 takes Socrates' characterization of Alcibiades' speech here as the key to understanding "the tone of the speech and, in particular, its relationship to Socrates' speech" (195).

19. Cf. Rosen 1967 (292–93).

20. Alcibiades' initial disclaimer, that his speech may be out of order on account of the difficulty of giving an account of Socrates' strangeness (215a1–3), may indicate that he has learned some rhetorical tricks from Socrates. Cf. *Apology of Socrates* 17d7–c3.

21. Thus Helen, who double-crossed the Trojans by agreeing to protect Odysseus in the first story, now double-crosses Odysseus!

22. Cf. Nichols 2007 (512, n.26).

23. Cf. 174a3–d3.

24. The word for Herm-sculptor's shop, *hermoglupheion*, appears to be otherwise unattested in extant Greek literature. It is unclear whether a word like *agamaltoglupheion* or *andriantopoieion* could have served the same purpose here. But even if it was necessary in the context to refer to the shops of the herm-sculptors in particular, the word seems intended to put us in mind of the desecration of the Herms. See Nichols 2009, 83 n.97.

25. On accusations of Socratic *hubris* in Plato, see Gagarin 1977 (24 n.11).

26. Socrates' claim at *Theages* 129c8–d8 is particularly interesting in this context.

27. See *Republic* 399e; Xenophon, *Anabasis* 1.2.8; Herodotus 7.26.3.

28. For the former, see *Charmides* 169c3–d8, *Theaetetus* 149a7ff., *Meno* 79e7–80b7; for the latter, see *Cleitophon* 407a5–408c4, *Republic* 357a1ff.

29. Cf. Friedlander 1964 (243).

30. On Socrates as a siren, compare Saxonhouse 1992 (180–81).

31. Socrates was beginning to lay the same choice before Agathon earlier in the *Symposium* before Phaedrus interrupted (194a1–c10).

32. Lutz 1998 also notes that Alcibiades sees Socratic education as an indefinite retreat from politics but does not compare this characterization to the impression of Socratic education Alcibiades received in the *Alcibiades* (133).

33. The mention of Alcibiades' agreements is the closest he comes to acknowledging that he was not merely moved by compulsion or emotion but that he offered some reasoned assent. One might also consider the passing mention of Socrates' characteristic manner of conversing at 217b5–7; the word for conversing is *dialechtheis*, which is cognate to the important Socratic mode of inquiry, "dialectic."

34. The Corybants performed festival dances in celebration of certain gods and goddesses. See Nichols 2007 (509).

35. "Magnificently overweening" is Benardete's compromise in translating the difficult word, *huperēphanon* (in Bloom 2001). The word usually has a negative connotation of excessive pride. The *LSJ* s.v. cites this passage in noting that the connotation can be positive, though rarely, as in "magnificent" or "splendid." But given Alcibiades' confusing mixture of praise and blame, it is unclear which meaning is most appropriate here.

36. See 208n5 above. For another take on Alcibiades' lack of emphasis on philosophy in this speech, consider Lutz 1998 (145).

37. Ellis 1989 (61).

38. Incidentally, he may well be mistaken in this supposition: Socrates' speech was received with noticeable ambivalence by the present audience (cf. 212c6 and 198a1–2).

39. In this respect, the puzzle of Alcibiades' speech shares something with the puzzle of the Delphic Oracle story that is meant to explain Socrates' reputation for wisdom in the *Apology of Socrates*, namely, what made Chaerephon think Socrates was wise in the first place? See Leibowitz 2010 (64).

40. The most eloquent elaboration of the interpretive idea that Socrates' moderation is his *hubris* is in Nussbaum 1986, but is seen also in, e.g., Bury 1909, Rosen 1967, Gill 1990, Lutz 1998, and Fagan 2013.

41. See Nietzsche, *Birth of Tragedy* 3, *The Gay Science* 340, *Twilight of the Idols*, "The Problem of Socrates" 1, 12. Cf. Plutarch, *Consolatio ad Apollonium* 27.

42. Plato's artfulness here must, however, be acknowledged, for he makes it quite possible for a reader to get the impression that Alcibiades' speech does disclose the content of his Socratic education. Thus Dominic Scott 2000 states, "Alcibiades also tells about the content of these *logoi*: they are concerned with moral education" (30).

43. The word for stripping, *apodunai*, is not used here, but Socrates' and Alcibiades' nudity, which is crucial to the sense of the anecdote, is repeatedly emphasized by Alcibiades' use of the word *sungumnazein*, "to train naked together."

44. Faulkner 2007 says of the *Alcibiades*, "One sees a master wrestler trying his holds upon a powerful young athlete who contends for the world title passionately as if by nature, but who also learns from the superior technique of his victorious opponent" (94).

45. Lutz 1998 points out that Socrates' response to Alcibiades, though misunderstood (at the time) as ironic, should be taken as "congratulating Alcibiades on his determination to be as best as possible" (139).

46. Cf. *Cleitophon* 410b4–c6.

47. Alcibiades draws extra attention to the claim that Socrates is impervious to alcohol by noting that it is in evidence even as he speaks (cf. 176c). This feature of Alcibiades' portrait is, of course, particularly fitting in the context of Alcibiades' central claim that Socrates is not moved by *eros* as ordinary people are. Given that Alcibiades is implying throughout that Socrates' impressiveness is somehow the result of his philosophizing, it may be even more insightful to suggest that Socrates' inability to become drunk reflects his having ceased to experience the inspiration of Dionysus. But the two points are, of course, deeply related, as is suggested by Alcibiades' resemblance to Dionysus when he enters Agathon's house. On this resemblance, see Nichols 2009 (70) and Scott and Welton 2008 (154–55).

48. As described in the *Phaedrus*, "Only the mind (*dianoia*) of the philosopher is furnished with wings; for he always, by the power of memory, faces those things by facing which a god is

divine. A man who uses such memories correctly is always being initiated into perfect mysteries (*teleous aei teletas teloumenos*) and he alone becomes really perfect; but becoming separated from the things human beings take seriously and coming to be in relation to the divine, he is admonished by the many for being disturbed, but it escapes the notice of the many that he is inspired" (249c4–d3). Also compare Socrates' famous entrance in the *Clouds* 225–34.

49. Reeve 2006 has helpfully noted that the word for the "statues" (*agalmata*) that Alcibiades said he saw within Socrates is the same as the word for the statues that are famously carried behind the fire so as to cast shadows on the wall of the cave in Plato's *Republic* (125).

50. See, e.g., Nichols 2007 (512).

51. *Clouds* 94–98, 260, 655–59, 872–88, 1105–11, 1148–53. Cf. Xenophon, *Memorabilia* 1.2.14–15, 17, 27, 31, 39, 47; Plato, *Apology of Socrates* 19b–c, 23c–d, *Theages* 128b–c.

## Conclusion

1. See Chapter 3 (207n34) above.

2. Note the similarity between Socrates' ability to dispose of his interlocutors "however he wished" and the Periclean or tyrannical power, discussed above, that is the object of Alcibiades' desire.

3. Compare *aischunoimēn* at *Symposium* 218d4 with *kallistos* and *aischiōn* at *Alcibiades* 131d7 and 132a2, respectively.

4. Cf. Hobbes, *Leviathan* xi.6: "Desire of praise disposeth to laudable actions, such as please those whose judgment they value."

5. Cf. *Republic* 346e7–347a6.

6. See Bruell 1999 (43–45).

7. See Introduction (3–4) above.

8. See Bruell 1999 (19). Cf. also *Charmides* 169d3ff.

9. On the significance of the flute girls, cf. *Protagoras* 347b–348c.

10. See Introduction (195n4) above.

11. To cite only, as it were, bookend examples, see Thucydides i.8.1 and Xenophon, *Hellenica* ii.2.3.

12. See *Hellenica* i.4.8–21.

13. For the sake of comparison, consider the lessons Pericles learned from Anaxagoras: cf. *Alcibiades* 118c2–6 with Plutarch, *Pericles* 6–8. (See Chapter 1 (54) above.)

14. Cf. Xenophon, *Memorabilia* iii.1.6, Plutarch, *Alcibiades* 23.4.

15. See Chapter 2 (65) above. Cf. Aristotle, *Nicomachean Ethics* 1108a19–23.

16. See Introduction (17–18) above.

# WORKS CITED


Annas, Julia. 1985. "Self-Knowledge in Early Plato." In *Platonic Investigations*, edited by Dominic O'Meara, 111–38. Washington, DC: Catholic University of America Press.

Benson, E. F. 1928. *The Life of Alcibiades*. London: Ernest Benn.

Blitz, Mark. 1995. "Plato's *Alcibiades I*." *Interpretation* 22.3: 339–58.

Bloom, Allan. 2001. "The Ladder of Love." In *Plato's Symposium*, translated by Seth Benardete, 55–177. Chicago: University of Chicago Press.

Bluck, Richard S. 1953. "The Origin of the Greater Alcibiades." *Classical Quarterly* NS 3: 46–52.

Bode, Georg Heinrich. 1859. *Geschichte der Hellenischen Dichtkunst: Dritter Band*. Leipzig: Karl Franz Köhler.

Brandwood, Leonard. 1990. *The Chronology of Plato's Dialogues*. Cambridge: Cambridge University Press.

Bruell, Christopher. 1966. *Plato's Criticism of Conventionalism*. MA thesis, University of Chicago.

———. 1999. *On the Socratic Education: An Introduction to the Shorter Platonic Dialogues*. Lanham, MD: Rowman and Littlefield.

Bury, R. G. 1909. *The Symposium of Plato*. Cambridge: W. Heffer and Sons.

Denyer, Nicholas. 2001. *Alcibiades*. New York: Cambridge University Press.

Ellis, Walter. 1989. *Alcibiades*. Oxford: Oxford University Press.

Euben, J. Peter. 1997. *Corrupting Youth*. Princeton, NJ: Princeton University Press.

Fagan, Patricia. 2013. *Plato and Tradition: The Poetic and Cultural Context of Philosophy*. Evanston, IL: Northwestern University Press.

Faulkner, Robert K. 2007. *The Case for Greatness: Honorable Ambition and Its Critics*. New Haven: Yale University Press.

Forde, Steven. 1987. "On the *Alcibiades I*." In *The Roots of Political Philosophy: Ten Forgotten Socratic Dialogues*, edited by Thomas L. Pangle, 222–39. Ithaca, NY: Cornell University Press.

———. 1989. *The Ambition to Rule: Alcibiades and the Politics of Imperialism in Thucydides*. Ithaca, NY: Cornell University Press.

Friedlander, Paul. 1964. *Plato Vol. 2*. Translated by Hans Meyerhoff. New York: Bollingen Foundation.

Gagarin, Michael. 1977. "Socrates' Hybris and Alcibiades' Failure." *Phoenix* 31: 22–37.

Gill, Christopher. 1990. "Platonic Love and Individuality." In *Polis and Politics*, edited by Andros Loizou and Harry Lesser, 69–87. Aldershot, UK: Avebury.

Gribble, David. 1999. *Alcibiades and Athens: A Study of Literary Presentation*. Oxford: Clarendon.

Grote, George. 1867. *Plato and the Other Companions of Sokrates*. London: John Murray.

Guthrie, W. K. C. 1971. *Socrates*. New York: Cambridge University Press.

Harward, J. 1932. *The Platonic Epistles*. London: Cambridge University Press.

Hatzfeld, Jean. 1940. *Alcibiade*. Paris: Presses Universitaires de France.

Hoerber, R. G. 1957. "Thrasylus' Platonic Canon and the Double Titles." *Phronesis* 2.1: 10–20.

Howland, Jacob A. 1990. "Socrates and Alcibiades: Eros, Piety, and Politics." *Interpretation* 18.1: 63–90.

———. 1991. "Re-Reading Plato: The Problem of Platonic Chronology." *Phoenix* 45.3: 189–214.

Irwin, Terrence. 2008. "The Platonic Corpus." In *Oxford Handbook of Plato*, edited by G Fine, 63–87. Oxford: Oxford University Press.

Jirsa, Jakub. 2009. "Authenticity of the 'Alcibiades' I: Some Reflections." *Folia Philologica* 132.3/4: 225–44.

Johnson, David M. 2003. *Socrates and Alcibiades*. Newburyport, MA: Focus Philosophical Library.

Johnson, Marguerite, and Harold Tarrant, eds. 2012. *Alcibiades and the Socratic Lover-Educator*. London: Bristol Classical Press.

Jouvenel, Bertrand de. 1963. *The Pure Theory of Politics*. New Haven: Yale University Press.

Kagan, Donald. 1987. *The Fall of the Athenian Empire*. Ithaca, NY: Cornell University Press.

Lamb, W. R. M. 1955. *Plato, Volume 8*. Cambridge, MA: Harvard University Press.

Lamm, Julia A. 2000. "Schleiermacher as Plato Scholar." *Journal of Religion* 80.2: 206–39.

———. 2005. "The Art of Interpreting Plato." In *The Cambridge Companion to Friedrich Schleiermacher*, 91–108. Cambridge: Cambridge University Press.

Lauriello, Christopher L. 2010. "Political Science and the Irrational: Plato's *Alcibiades*." *Interpretation* 37.3: 237–57.

Ledger, Gerard R. 1989. *Re-counting Plato, A Computer Analysis of Plato's Style*. Oxford: Oxford University Press.

Leibowitz, David. 2010. *The Ironic Defense of Socrates*. Cambridge: Cambridge University Press.

Leitch, Vincent B., ed. 2010. *The Norton Anthology of Theory and Criticism, Second Edition*. New York: W.W. Norton.

Lutz, Mark J. *Socrates' Education to Virtue: Learning the Love of the Noble*. Albany: State University of New York, 1998.

Momigliano, Arnaldo. 1987. *On Pagans, Jews, and Christians*. Middletown, CT: Wesleyan University Press.

Nails, Debra. 2002. *The People of Plato: A Prosopography of Plato and Other Socratics*. Indianapolis: Hackett.

———. 2006. "Tragedy Off-Stage." In *Plato's Symposium: Issues in Interpretation and Reception*, edited by James Lesher, Debra Nails, and Frisbee Sheffield, 179–207. Cambridge, MA: Harvard University Press.

Newell, Waller R. *Ruling Passion: The Erotics of Statecraft in Platonic Political Philosophy*. Lanham, MD: Rowman and Littlefield, 2000.

Nichols, Mary P. 2007. "Philosophy and Empire: On Socrates and Alcibiades in Plato's 'Symposium.'" *Polity* 39.4: 502–21.

———. 2009. *Socrates on Friendship and Community: Reflections on Plato's Symposium, Phaedrus, and Lysis*. Cambridge: Cambridge University Press.

Nussbaum, Martha. 1986. *The Fragility of Goodness: Luck and Ethics in Greek Tragedy and Philosophy*. Cambridge: Cambridge University Press.

O'Connor, David K. 1999. "Socrates and Political Ambition: The Dangerous Game." *Proceedings of the Boston Area Colloquium in Ancient Philosophy* 14: 31–51.

Palmer, Michael. 1982. "Alcibiades and the Question of Tyranny in Thucydides." *Canadian Journal of Political Science* 15.1: 103–24.
Pangle, Thomas L. 1987. "Editor's Introduction." In *The Roots of Political Philosophy: Ten Forgotten Socratic Dialogues*, edited by Thomas Pangle, 1–20. Ithaca, NY: Cornell University Press.
Pradeau, Jean-François, ed.; Chantal Marbouef, trans. 1999. *Platon: Alcibiade*. Paris: Flammarion.
Pusey, Nathan Marsh. 1940. "Alcibiades and *to Philopoli*." *Harvard Studies in Classical Philology* 51: 215–31.
Renaud, François, and Harold Tarrant. 2015. *The Platonic Alcibiades I: The Dialogue and Its Ancient Reception*. Cambridge: Cambridge University Press.
Reeve, C. D. C. 2006. "A Study in Violets: Alcibiades in the *Symposium*." In *Plato's Symposium: Issues in Interpretation and Reception*, edited by James Lesher, Debra Nails, and Frisbee Sheffield, 124–46. Cambridge, MA: Harvard University Press.
Romilly, Jacqueline de. 1995. *Alcibiade*. Paris: Editions de Fallois.
Rosen, Stanley. 1967. *Plato's Symposium*. New Haven: Yale University Press.
Saxonhouse, Arlene. 1984. "Eros and the Female in Greek Political Thought: An Interpretation of Plato's *Symposium*." *Political Theory* 12.1: 5–27.
———. 1986. "From Tragedy to Hierarchy and Back Again: Women in Greek Political Thought." *American Political Science Review* 80.2: 403–18.
———. 1992. *Fear of Diversity: The Birth of Political Science in Ancient Greek Thought*. Chicago: University of Chicago Press.
———. 2004. "Corruption and Justice: The View from Ancient Athens." In *Private and Public Corruption*, edited by William C. Heffernan and John Kleinig, 25–51. Oxford: Rowman and Littlefield.
———. 2006. *Free Speech and Democracy in Ancient Athens*. Cambridge: University Press.
Schleiermacher, F. E. D. 1836. *Introductions to the Dialogues of Plato*, translated by William Dobson. Cambridge: Cambridge University Press.
———.1998. *Hermeneutics and Criticism*, translated by Andrew Bowie. Cambridge: Cambridge University Press.
Scott, Dominic. 2000. "Socrates and Alcibiades in the 'Symposium.'" *Hermathena* 168: 25–37.
Scott, Gary Alan. 2000. *Plato's Socrates as Educator*. Albany: SUNY Press.
Scott, Gary Alan, and William A. Welton. 2008. *Erotic Wisdom: Philosophy and Intermediacy in Plato's* Symposium. Albany: SUNY Press.
Seager, Robin. 1967. "Alcibiades and the Charge of Aiming at Tyranny." *Historia: Zeitschrift für Alte Geschichte* 16.1: 6–18.
Sharpe, Matthew. 2012. "Revaluing *Megalopsuchia*: Reflections on the *Alcibiades II*." In *Alcibiades and the Socratic Lover-Educator*, edited by Marguerite Johnson and Harold Tarrant. London: Bristol Classical Press.
Sheffield, Frisbee C. 2001. "Alcibiades' Speech: A Satyric Drama." *Greece and Rome* 48.2: 193–209.
Shorey, Paul. 1933. *What Plato Said*. Chicago: University of Chicago Press.
Smith, Nicholas D. 2004. "Did Plato Write the Alcibiades I?" *Apeiron* 37.2: 93–108.
Strauss, Leo. 1998. *Xenophon's Socrates*. South Bend, IN: St. Augustine's.
———. 2003. *On Plato's Symposium*. Edited by Seth Benardete. Chicago: University of Chicago Press.
Strycker, Emile de. 1942. "Platonica I: l'authenticité du Premier Alcibiade." *Les Études Classiques* 11: 116–51.

Taylor, A. E. 1926. *Plato: The Man and His Work*. London: Meuthen.
———. 1933. *Socrates*. New York: D. Appleton.
Tigerstedt, E. N. 1974. *The Decline and Fall of the Neoplatonic Interpretation of Plato*. Helsinki: Societas Scientarum Fennica.
Verdegem, Simon. 2010. *Plutarch's Life of Alcibiades: Story, Text and Moralism*. Leuven, Belgium: Leuven University Press.
Vickers, Michael. 1999. "Alcibiades and Melos: Thucydides 5.84–116." *Historia: Zeitschrift für Alte Geschichte* 48.3: 265–81.
Wellek, René. 1981. "Appendix." In *What Is Criticism?* edited by Paul Hernadi, 297–321. Bloomington: Indiana University Press.
Wohl, Victoria. 2012. "The Eye of the Beloved: *Opsis* and *Eros* in Socratic Pedagogy." In *Alcibiades and the Socratic Lover-Educator*, edited by Marguerite Johnson and Harold Tarrant. London: Bristol Classical Press.
Zuckert, Catherine H. 2009. *Plato's Philosophers: The Coherence of the Dialogues*. Chicago: University of Chicago Press.

# INDEX

# ACKNOWLEDGMENTS

It would be a fairly colossal understatement to say that this book would never have been possible without the guidance, wisdom, and support of Thomas Pangle, Lorraine Pangle, and Devin Stauffer. They read numerous drafts of my work, commented copiously upon them, talked endlessly with me about Socrates and Alcibiades, and honed my thinking at every turn. But more than that, these three challenged and invited me to live the life of the mind with more seriousness and more passion than I could ever have hoped to find. Among the ways in which they did this were their weekly reading groups, of which one in the fall of 2010 on the *Alcibiades* was what first gave me the idea to write this book. To them, as well as to my many other friends and colleagues in Austin, who discussed Plato with me for hours on end and pushed me to think ever more clearly, I owe more than I can repay.

Peter Ahrensdorf and Arlene Saxonhouse provided extremely valuable feedback on a late draft of this work, and the anonymous reviewers at the University of Pennsylvania Press provided insightful suggestions that led to a number of needed revisions. The encouragement and counsel I received from University of Pennsylvania Press editor Damon Linker was a welcome and appreciated source of support. I owe thanks as well to the Earhart Foundation and to the Government Department at the University of Texas at Austin for providing financial support necessary for my studies and writing.